THE COMPLETE MARTIAL ARTS STUDENT

The Master Guide to Basic and Advanced Classroom Strategies for Learning the Fighting Arts

•

Martina Sprague

SOUV... RESS

First published in the USA by Equilibrium Books,
A division of Wish Publishing.

First published in Great Britain in 2008 by Souvenir Press Ltd
43 Great Russell Street, London WC1B 3PD

ISBN 9780285638273

Printed and bound in Great Britain by
CPI Antony Rowe

This Book is Dedicated to Tony Martinez, Sr.
— Martial Artist, Teacher, Friend —

Table of Contents

Introduction

Many students have little knowledge of what to expect or how to increase retention, motivation and rate of learning when first signing up to study the martial arts. Thye are left in the hands of an instructor who is often a student himself, not a teacher by profession, and who has little or no knowledge of the learning process or the psychology of teaching. As a result, the instructor simply states the facts—this is the name of the technique and this is how it is done—without considering why the technique is done, what the concepts are behind it, and how to tailor it to fit a student's individual traits.

Learning the facts, or learning the mechanics of a technique, is the first stage of learning. But if you fail to go beyond rote memorization, you are unlikely to gain proficiency even in the simplest techniques. To understand this idea better, I like to use the analogy of the historian. The historian does not merely memorize battle dates and names of great generals. She studies with the intent of uncovering the underlying currents that shaped those events and, if possible, to learn from them. The same is true when learning the martial arts. Whether learning from a book or through hands-on experience, the underlying currents help you understand why a technique or concept is important. For example, a recent article about self-defense for the street stated, "No matter how scared you are, don't let your emotions show." The fact is, "Don't let your emotions show." While it is easy to agree with this statement, theoretical knowledge of the fact does not make you proficient at performing or understanding the technique. When confronted with death, just *how* do you learn not to let your emotions show?

As students of the martial arts, we often go to the training hall without considering exactly what we can do to further our own learning. The glory is in performing our art, not in pondering the learning process. The purpose of this book is to educate you about the science of learning, to instill confidence through familiarization with and recognition of a multitude of scenarios, and to give you the power to act when you encounter specific problems. This study is about making your education more profitable by showing you *why* rather than *what* to learn, and by providing specific details on how to work with your instructor and peers, even when your instructor and peers are uneducated about the learning process and cause you "problems." By looking at different situations from both the student's and the instructor's viewpoints, you will learn about the many difficulties the instructor faces. These insights will help you appreciate the instruction more and give you options for a mutually productive learning experience.

You will learn how to turn a mediocre training session into an advantage, where everything your instructor and peers say and do is used for your gain.

As you continue deeper into your training remember that, although it is your instructor's responsibility to help you progress in the martial arts, it is equally your responsibility to help your instructor pave the way for good learning to occur. I once overheard two ladies discussing how much fun it was returning to college years after graduating from high school. One lady said that she didn't understand why the youngsters didn't want to go to school, when you "just sit there and get spoon fed." But learning is a two-way street and often not as simple as taking in what is fed to you. Your instructor, no matter how talented, is only half of the learning process. Although you can't do much about your instructor's teaching methods, you do have considerable control over how you approach the lessons. This book will show you how to extract the information that your instructor and peers possess but don't necessarily know how to express. Next time you go to class, you can meet your instructor halfway and contribute the missing half that makes the learning process whole.

Student Tips for Accelerated Learning

You don't become a world champion simply because your instructor is a world champion. A good instructor can take you past her own level of skill, but she cannot increase your efforts, and it would be unfair of you to require this of her. If you fail to meet your instructor halfway, progress will be slow no matter how good your instructor is. Before you commence your studies, familiarize yourself with the following tips for accelerated learning.

BE AN ACTIVE LEARNER

Learning is an active process. There must be at least some activity in order for good learning to take place. Look for ways to extract as much information as possible from the lessons. For example, research the lesson beforehand and physically participate in every activity. Listening and observing are also active processes. You listen actively by taking notes and asking or answering questions. You could observe your peers practicing forms or sparring while you critique them silently. You increase your understanding of the material by explaining the techniques and concepts to yourself and others. When you become an active learner, you gain insights that may take others years to attain or articulate.

PARAPHRASE THE TECHNIQUES

When sparring or exploring techniques, you learn as much from what did not work as from what did work. For example, first do the technique the way it is intended. Then do the technique again, but explore a thing or two that could go wrong. Explain to yourself why the technique worked or why it didn't. For example, "It is easier taking my opponent down if I can catch him already off balance. If I allow my momentum to stop, the takedown is less effective and my opponent may overpower me. This happens because I fail to take advantage of the moment of surprise."

STUDY THE CONCEPTS

A concept can be thought of as the underlying current of a technique. Make an effort to study the concepts rather than just memorize the moves. In order to study the concepts, you must already have a good understanding of the mechanics of the technique. It makes little sense studying takedowns, for example, if you lack knowledge of what makes a person lose balance. When you leave class, explain to yourself what you learned. If you can only name the technique, you haven't learned much. Name something specific you learned *about* the technique and explain why it was important.

USE VISUALIZATION

Physical preparation and practice are essential to the martial arts student. But mental practice also helps catapult you to new heights. When you have experienced the battle mentally and it is time for actual practice, you will feel as though you have already been there. For example, visualizing all possible scenarios prior to a test or competition alleviates much of the stress associated with these events, because you have already conditioned yourself to behave appropriately when the stress appears. When you visualize the technique, belt test or competition, your body rises to the level needed to perform during the event. Of course, you must also be a realist. If you can't do the splits because you have a physical limitation in your hips, simply visualizing yourself doing the splits will not help you. Visualization exercises may be the most effective when used prior to or after training, rather than during training.

PRACTICE WITH INTENT

We emphasize practice and repetition in martial arts training. But physical practice without receiving corrections creates bad habits that are difficult to break. You must practice good technique, but you must also concern yourself with the specific details of movement. For example, if you beat the heavy bag for an hour, you develop stamina and reasonable power in your punches. But if you beat the heavy bag for an hour five days a week for 52 weeks, you don't improve 260 times (5 X 52 = 260). Challenge yourself with specific details. Is your goal to throw the spinning back kick smoothly within a hand combination? Then, how do you transition from hands to the spinning back kick? How do you adjust for distance? Can you think of more than one hand technique that provides you with a smooth transition?

Consider the length of your workouts. The compactness and details of the workout, not necessarily the length, determine its effectiveness. If you have little time available for practice, you must give your full effort in order to reap the greatest benefits. Set a timer for 20 minutes. If you waste time, you cannot accomplish everything you had planned to do. Setting a specific goal before starting a workout makes the workout more productive. The same is true in a group class. Although your instructor is in charge of the specific exercises you do, you can still assign yourself an objective within those exercises. For example, decide to do every technique half a beat faster than your peers. Or when sparring, include at least one kick for every punch combination. Good planning results in intense and economical training sessions.

PERFORM REALISTIC SELF-EVALUATIONS

You alleviate stress about your progress by doing realistic self-evaluations. For example, if you are stressed about an upcoming exam, compare yourself to the other students in your class. Chances are you will find you are at least as talented as your peers. If you come to class regularly, do your homework, and allow enough time to elapse between exams, you will most likely find that you have little reason to be nervous. It is easy to get the idea that you are alone.

Remember, your peers are going through the same emotions. Talk to others for emotional support. Surround yourself with the types of people you admire and wish to emulate.

COMPETE IN THE ARENA OR CLASSROOM

Experience makes you grow. The martial artist who pushes himself to be better than his peers or competitors will likely gain more insight into the art than the martial artist who accepts a mediocre routine. The intense experience of competition gives you insights that enable you to hold intellectual conversations about the art that you study. It is not necessary to perfect your techniques before you compete in an official arena. You can also compete within the training hall, either through open competition against other students, or through silent competition without the other students' knowledge. You do this by constantly comparing your own performance to the performances of your peers and by striving to become better than the best in your class. I have found silent competition to be a great motivator. But there must be other students who are better than you, so that you have something to strive toward.

PRACTICE YOUR STRENGTHS

The day prior to my intermediate-rank belt test in karate, I practiced the required forms. I had already been training for an hour, was getting tired, and failed to practice one particular form. Ironically, that was the one I stumbled on at the test, despite the fact that it was my favorite form and I had practiced a hundred times over the previous months.

Don't neglect training in the techniques you already know inside out. These are the techniques that often come back to bite you at a time when it matters. Practice every technique at least once, even if you think you already know it well. And, of course, strive to improve your weak areas, even if you don't enjoy it or you think you can wing it on test day.

BE REALISTIC ABOUT YOUR INSTRUCTOR

Instructors are individuals; they favor different techniques and emphasize different points of importance. An opinionated instructor is wrong only if he relies on outdated information or pure stubbornness. In order to benefit from these different insights, you must keep an open mind and avoid getting too attached to your instructor. Students want their instructor to be that all-knowing and powerful figure. But as time goes by, you will discover that your instructor has many flaws. If you have cultivated a vision that he is the person you admire and look up to, you may become severely disappointed when you learn that your instructor is human and can't live up to your ideals. Remember, your primary reason for going to the training hall is to learn the martial arts. Don't let your instructor's personal "faults" get in the way.

BE YOUR OWN BOSS

Be respectful toward your instructor, but don't give her too much power. Maintain autonomy regarding all issues that extend outside of the training hall. For example, many instructors require that children bring their report cards from school to martial arts class. If they fail to maintain at least a B average, they are ineligible to test for a higher rank in the martial arts. Some parents love this discipline, because it gives the child the motivation to study. But children have rights, too. Consider how you would feel if your martial arts instructor wanted to see your annual job evaluation before she allowed you to test for a higher rank. My opinion is that if parents want to impose these kinds of rules on their children, they have the right to do so. But the martial arts instructor should avoid it. Remember that your instructor does not own you physically, mentally or emotionally. Bowing or touching gloves prior to sparring is the kind of healthy respect you want to give your instructor and other students. When you understand the expectations regarding your relationship with your instructor, you can proceed with a good conscience and allow her to teach you the fighting arts.

Part One
Student Qualities

1

What You Must Understand

WHY YOU NEED AN INSTRUCTOR

Practice makes perfect, right? Or to extend the cliché, *perfect* practice makes perfect. Given sufficient time, most students will learn, whether they receive instruction or not. But it is difficult to learn the intricate details of an art or to correct your own mistakes this way. Martial arts training as your only means of perfection, no matter how perfect, can only take you to the limit of your knowledge and not beyond. Perfect practice, including the elimination of poor habits, is only a small part of the learning process.

Trying to learn without an instructor is like writing a book by copying the words of others. Humans are unique because of our ability to catalogue centuries of knowledge. Each new generation can quickly refer to the experiences of previous generations and avoid starting. There should never be a need to reinvent the wheel. You gain insight by taking what you already know and treading on new ground. Still, many martial arts students lack vision. We repeat, often verbatim, what others have taught us without considering where our journey might ultimately lead. We fail to question, experiment and research beyond the basics. We go through our paces until learning becomes the same mundane grind every day.

Although it is possible to become a martial artist by trial and error, it normally takes years to discover how to fine-tune our skill without a good student/instructor/peer group relationship. A skilled instructor alongside an eager and cooperative student can break the pattern of poor practice almost instantly. Still, many of us could write volumes about when and how the "martial spirit" has gone awry. We must deal not only with inflated egos and problem peers talking out of both sides of their mouths while emphasizing humbleness, but we must also learn from an instructor who has six red stripes on his black belt but who possesses less-than-admirable communication skills. This text assumes that your instructor is not fully educated about the learning process, and that you, the student, must use your knowledge and ingenuity in order to benefit from the experience.

The 56 learning scenarios scattered throughout the text, along with several examples of common situations that you might encounter in the training hall, will help you gain an edge by recognizing situations where learning can be improved. Use these scenarios to role-play with other students in order to trigger your critical-thinking skills and arm yourself for an upcoming situation. Let's jump in and test your behavioral knowledge by assuming that you are a lower-ranking student studying with an assistant under-belt (not yet a black belt) instructor. Read the question and choose your answer. You will see more of these scenarios throughout the text.

 SCENARIO 1

You are practicing the roundhouse kick when an assistant instructor tells you that your kick is so slow she "saw it coming three days ago." How should you respond?

1. Go home and practice more.

2. Throw 10 powerful roundhouse kicks on the heavy bag to show the assistant instructor that she is wrong.

3. Ignore it, because the instructor is just trying to intimidate you.

The fact that you spend time practicing the kick is commendable, but you must also receive some constructive feedback from your instructor. Try this:

1. Study the mechanics of the kick, breaking it down into segments. For example, start by bringing your knee up high and pivoting your hips. Extend your leg from the knee.

2. Tie segment one and two together, and segment three and four together. The idea is to make the kick flow without a stop in momentum, while maintaining balance and proper mechanics.

3. Tie all the segments together. Continue

practicing for about 10-minutes.

4. Ask your instructor to watch a few times and offer suggestions for improvement. Request that she talk to you about why a kick is faster and more powerful when proper mechanics are used.

5. Explore the strategic advantages of chambering your leg prior to kicking. Ask what can be gained by chambering the leg, and what happens if you don't.

6. Make a point to use the kick the way you have learned it at least three times in your next sparring session.

As a new student in the martial arts, you probably need constant reminders of the details that comprise your techniques. There is no guarantee that you will remember tomorrow a technique or concept you have learned today. The need to be reminded may be especially prevalent when you are introduced to new techniques that have not yet become habit through muscle memory.

Even advanced students need to be reminded of correct performance. For example, you may have a tendency to drop your guard dangerously low when getting tired in sparring, without being aware of doing so. When your instructor tells you, "Raise your guard!" try to comply without stopping the sparring session or making frustrating or critical remarks or gestures about your performance. Your need to hear the correction is a natural phenomenon and not a result of your laziness or inattentiveness, even if your instructor has to remind you to raise your guard every 10 seconds.

When I was flying sailplanes back in my

teens, one of my more effective instructors sat in the back seat and chanted, "Increase the bank, don't increase the bank, increase the bank," correcting minute mistakes before they grew. (The bank is the number of degrees the wings are tilted in a turn. Increasing the bank shortens the turn radius and speeds up the turn.) Another instructor would yell, "What the hell are you diving for?!" if I dipped the nose just a fraction of an inch. Or, "You're galloping like a horse!" when a student would bounce on landing. From a learning standpoint, I found the yelling and insults less effective and believe that this method leaves students ill at ease.

SCENARIO 2

Your instructor observes you in a sparring session and notices you are dropping your hands low. Which would be the most effective corrective action on the part of your instructor?

1. Tell you, "Raise your guard!"

2. Spar with you and hit you to show that it is dangerous to drop your guard.

3. Tell you, "Don't drop your guard!"

4. Ignore it, because this is just light contact.

Whether we learn better from positive or negative commands can be debated. Most psychologists and motivational speakers seem to argue in favor of the positive command, "Raise your guard!" rather than, "Don't drop your guard!" but I am not sure

I agree. We often jump to conclusions before we have analyzed the situation on our own. In fact, I have found that I learn just as well from either positive or negative commands. However, an argument in favor of the positive command is that it allows you to make the direct connection between the command and the action it is intended to bring about. For example, if your instructor says, "Don't drop your guard!" you must first visualize what you are *not* supposed to do (drop your guard), before you can visualize what you *are* supposed to do (raise your guard). If he says, "Raise your guard!" you can immediately visualize what raising your guard means, thus shortening the learning time. An argument in favor of a

If you get hit to the head a lot, but your instructor fails to give you feedback, how would you assess the situation?

combination of positive and negative commands is that it might prevent the command from going in one ear and out the other, as so often happens when we hear the same thing too many times. After your next sparring session, think about the commands your instructor gave you and make a point to eliminate those commands in your next sparring session. If your instructor didn't give you any commands at all, does it mean that your performance was perfect or that your instructor had an off-day and was inattentive? If your instructor failed to give you feedback on your performance, where did you feel you needed improvement? Remember to make *realistic* self-evaluations. Include at least one thing you did well and one thing that could stand improvement.

So, you see, good instruction speeds up the learning process and promotes insight by helping you relate one area of learning to another. The reason we need an instructor is because somebody must show us the right path. But learning to do a technique correctly should not be the limit of your knowledge. A more important goal may be to help your instructor advance you beyond your own and your instructor's perceived limits and onto new heights.

– INSTRUCTOR TIP –

Distinguish between the student who truly wants to learn but experiences difficulties, and the student who is simply inattentive. Some students get frustrated when they don't "get it" quickly enough. To help your student through periods of frustration, break the technique into smaller segments, or put aside that particular technique for now and focus on something different. Then take five minutes to review the technique with your student af-

ter class when he or she has had time to take a breath and relax.

– STUDENT TIP –

When your instructor corrects you but you fail to make the correction, it may be because you are nervous or inattentive. If you are inattentive, being "punished" with push-ups may actually help. Make a point to review any technique that resulted in push-ups before the start of the next class. If you don't understand why you were "punished," ask your instructor to clarify.

CHOOSING YOUR INSTRUCTOR

You see a sign that reads, "Classes Taught by World Champion Joe Schmoe." What signal does it send you regarding his instructional abilities?

Some say a that if you know how to teach but cannot perform, you are not a teacher. Others say that a world champion is not necessarily qualified to teach. I am sure you have heard the expression, "Those who can, do; those who can't, teach." I don't know where the exact truth lies, yet some of my best instructors have been proficient at the art but not anywhere near world-champion caliber. A great instructor does not need to be the world champion, but she does need to know the intricacies of the art or she will not have enough insight to teach the finer points. In contrast, an exceptionally skilled instructor may be more concerned with her own performance than with the progress of the students.

The instructor role may be the most important rank in the martial arts. A great instructor, world champion or not, is miles ahead of her nonteaching peers, because not only does she take an interest in the art, she also takes an interest in the *students* of the art. To demonstrate a point, I like to use the analogy of the doctor and the nurse, or of the airline pilot and the flight attendant. We are generally under the misconception that doctors are somehow "better" than nurses, and that pilots are "better" than flight attendants. Likewise, many martial artists (and nonmartial artists, for that matter) are under the misconception that the world champion is better than the nonchampion.

But just as the doctor's skill in the operating room does not automatically translate into skill in caring for the patient, the world champion's skill in the ring does not automatically translate into skill in teaching, or skill in caring for and relating to the students. A good instructor must know how to perform the art, and how to dissect, analyze and convey her findings to others.

But to really succeed, she must have people skills. I am not saying that the world champion can't be a great instructor; I am saying that she must first know what every other great instructor knows, namely how to teach. And, most importantly, she must have a true desire to teach. Choosing the wrong instructor could possibly place you years behind your potential for achievement. When choosing your instructor, make sure that you understand the importance of her position. Knowledge of how people learn and how to capitalize on your instructor's ideas will help you help your instructor teach a better lesson.

– INSTRUCTOR TIP –

Many schools require that students teach in order to advance to higher ranks. However, not everybody is suited to be an instructor. You may be a superb martial artist yet make a lousy instructor because you lack people skills or the patience to teach, or because you are disorganized or more concerned with your own progress than with the progress of your students. After a careful evaluation of your personality traits, your background and your goals, you may find that teaching is not for you. This is totally okay; you can be a good person and a good martial artist even if you choose not to teach. You will do yourself and the students a service by suggesting that the senior instructor choose somebody with a true interest in teaching.

– STUDENT TIP –

Be wary of those instructors who teach because of ulterior motives. When you interact with your instructor, pay attention to how focused he is on your progress. For example, when he suggests methods for improvement, does he remember that he has done so the next time you come to class, and does he check on your progress? If not, he may lack a true interest in your advancement as a martial artist.

WHAT YOUR INSTRUCTOR MEANS TO YOU

What is in a word? Is an instructor a coach, a mentor, a teacher, a trainer, or a facilitator? Each word has certain connotations, but I like to think of the person I am learning from as an *instructor*. What I am looking for is somebody who can take me from here to there. The instructor's mission is to make you physically and mentally strong, but it doesn't end there. His mission extends also to helping you achieve certain objectives within a certain time frame, and to bring forth understanding. The instructor's job includes answering questions and telling you about your errors, as well as taking an active role in helping you analyze your mistakes. True teaching differs from just sharing information. As somebody said, "A good instructor makes himself progressively less needed."

Instructors are sometimes too quick to view their own style as the only right one. They tend to forget that the martial arts are many and diversified. I had studied kickboxing extensively when I went to a traditional karate school to get some help with stretching. After working with me in private for five minutes, the instructor wanted to see my front kick. I had been taught to keep my guard high for protection in kickboxing, which is a full-contact sport with head strikes. The karate instructor told me to "pull" with my arm in order to increase the flexibility in my kick. But pulling with my arm also caused me to drop my guard. As a student in another school, I didn't want to argue with the instructor. However, it was unlikely that I would change years of habit building at the spur of the moment. In my view, the instructor should have prodded a little into my background, or I should have offered him the information prior to the start of the lesson.

When you seek an instructor, pay attention to whether she quizzes you on your background and acknowledges the validity of your prior experiences. If you want to bond and build a productive relationship with your instructor, you must understand that martial arts instructors are individuals. For

example, two instructors from the same school may favor different types of techniques, depending on their personal build, flexibility and background. In order to benefit from the teachings of different instructors, you must keep an open mind. However, you must also understand that it is seldom necessary to take your instructor's teachings as law. Here is some simple advice: Never say "no thanks" to information. Gratefully accept whatever is offered you. What you do with this information later is up to you.

Unfortunately, some instructors are opinionated to the point of being annoying. It is then your responsibility to decide whether or not you want to continue studying under this instructor. Being opinionated is not necessarily bad; it is bad only if the instructor relies on outdated information or pure stubbornness. Take some time to evaluate your instructor's background and determine whether her ideas have merit.

The best instructors are teaching for the benefit of the journey and not for some ulterior motive. In other words, they teach because they want to and not because they have to. I have taught people to fly airplanes for many years, and an educated guess is that 90 percent of all flight instructors teach only because it allows them to build time toward a higher rating. As soon as they have logged enough flight time, they stop teaching and start flying for the airlines. This lack of interest in teaching clearly shows. Few flight instructors take adequate time to prepare the student for the flight or to do a post-flight debriefing, because time spent on the ground does not add up in the instructor's logbook. The same problem happens in the martial arts. Many instructors teach only because it is a requirement for a higher rank. Yes, teaching is a great learning experience, and the person who does teach will often be better for it. But ultimately the instructor should look at how the student benefits. All teaching should be done with the student in mind, and should be geared primarily toward improving the student, not the instructor. In principle, this idea is similar to competition: Those who compete would love to reach world-champion caliber and are excited about the belts and trophies, but ultimately it is the competition itself that they enjoy. If you hunger for the right to call yourself a world champion but don't enjoy the journey of getting there, believe me, it will be a very long haul.

– INSTRUCTOR TIP –

A great instructor inspires the students to go beyond the instructor's limitations. Don't despair when your students leave your class-

Certificates, belts and trophies have little meaning unless accompanied by appropriate skill.

room and open their own schools. See it instead as a compliment to your abilities and the fulfillment of a mission.

– STUDENT TIP –

Never say "no thanks" to knowledge. Gratefully accept whatever instruction others offer you, even if it doesn't feel agreeable at the moment.

TEN STUDENT QUALITIES

Many people know theoretically the characteristics of a good student but are unable to become one. This may be especially true if you have been away from a formal learning environment for some time. You are experienced enough to know what it takes, but not experienced enough to apply your knowledge. Learning how to learn takes practice. You cannot become a great martial artist simply by reading a book, nor can you become a great student through theoretical knowledge alone.

Your skill increases when you practice your art consistently and with intent, when you make realistic self-evaluations, and when you consciously try to adopt the characteristics of a good student. A good student:

1. Has an inquisitive mind and has thought about his goals and the requirements to attain them;

2. Knows how to extract knowledge from the instructor's teachings;

3. Understands how the learning process functions and how to motivate himself and others;

4. Knows how to organize an effective

Book learning should complement your martial arts training; physical practice is still essential.

home-review of the lesson;

5. Shows a true interest in the learning process and is not in it just to satisfy a degree or other ulterior motive;

6. Has a good attitude and can use the knowledge of others without letting his ego get in the way;

7. Is honest, takes his position seriously, and employs a healthy mix of disciplined yet compassionate behavior;

8. Understands that no one size fits all and that learning must be tailored to his particular needs;

9. Is consistent in his behavior and excludes mood swings from the learning environment; and

10. Continuously seeks to improve himself

by keeping an open mind, yet strives to stay with the times and modifies outdated techniques and thinking patterns.

Let's talk about these attributes in greater detail.

The inquisitive mind

Many great martial artists don't know why a technique or principle works; only that it does work. This knowledge comes from experience and a personal feel, or talent. But if you want true ownership of your skills, you must have a clear understanding of the *why* along with the *how*. An inquisitive mind is a prerequisite for good learning to take place, but can sometimes cause friction between you and your instructor.

 SCENARIO 3

You are learning a defense technique against a wrist grab, which calls for breaking the grip before proceeding with a follow-up strike. You think that you see a more practical way to do this technique and tell the instructor, "If you hit your opponent *before* you try to break the grip, you can break the grip more easily." The instructor feels that you are challenging her authority and asks if you want to teach the class. What should you do?

1. Pretend that you didn't hear.

2. Challenge the instructor to grab your wrist before you can hit her.

3. Apologize and volunteer to do 10 push-ups in the back of the room.

4. Say, "No, but . . ." and give the instructor 10 reasons why her idea stinks.

5. Smile and say, "I'd love to!"

★★★★★

It is possible that your comment actually taught the instructor something about the martial arts. But although teaching might be a by-product of learning, you are not in it to set the instructor right. Hopefully the instructor knows why she teaches a technique a certain way. Hopefully, she has analyzed it and determined that this is, in fact, the best way to teach it. Exactly how to proceed may be debated, but I don't recommend that you challenge the instructor with a smart comment (even though she might have done that to you). Ask instead what you can learn from the situation.

1. Consider the positive elements of the way the technique is currently taught. This still leaves you with the option of exploring new avenues on your own.

2. Paraphrase both the good and the bad parts of the technique to yourself or others. Exploring both sides broadens your understanding and helps you remember the technique better. If you fail to elaborate, you have made no effort to go past your own or your instructor's limitations.

3. If you feel that elaboration causes friction between you and your instructor, you can do it at home with a friend, without your instructor's knowledge.

4. If your instructor says "good idea" or "bad idea" without discussing why, what can you do to gain further insight into the underlying reasons?

Remember that opinions vary greatly among instructors. If you ask your instructor a question, and then ask the same question of another instructor within the same training hall, you will likely get two different answers. When I was a new student in karate, one instructor told me to turn my hand with the knife edge toward the ceiling when doing the upward block; another instructor told me not to. Who was right? Some of this may be trivial, but if you are a new student concerned with learning "the right way," studying from two different instructors simultaneously may not be a good idea early in your training.

Sometimes you may wonder why a particular technique or concept is important. If you are especially interested in free sparring, for example, you might question why you have to learn forms. If your instructor simply tells you that it is a requirement for a higher rank, you may find the answer dissatisfying. The good student wants real answers that he can relate to. If your instructor can't tell you the true value of a technique, you might want to reevaluate the curriculum, your goals, and the importance of studying under this particular instructor.

We tend to idolize our instructor. But just how much should a martial arts instructor know? He is not likely to know it all, even with 20 years of experience under his belt. How much the instructor knows often depends on his diversification in the arts, and whether or not he has studied with the intent of extracting information. As a guideline, he should be able to answer most questions about techniques that are related to the particular art he is teaching, but he does not need to be able to answer every possible question. If you have problems getting an answer from your instructor, try to draw from the experiences of other students, especially those whose background gives them authority.

1. If a student works in law enforcement and you have a question about the particulars of a wrist-control hold, it may be a good idea to ask him to talk to you about it.

2. If a student works in the medical profession, she may be able to talk about how damaging or incapacitating a technique really is.

3. If a student has studied a grappling art before coming to your karate class, you may ask him to give some examples of ways to proceed after you have taken your adversary down.

There is seldom only one correct answer to your question. I am not implying that it is

The value of exercises such as forms practice should be stated.

okay for an instructor to be wishy-washy. Nothing is worse than an instructor, who is supposed to know the material, beating around the bush or never gettin to the point, or answering your question by listing 10 different variations until you think that just about anything will do. What I am saying is that just because somebody else would have explained the mateial differently doesn't mean that he is incorrect. How we view a technique or concept is often the result of our background and experiences. Absolute streamlining of the techniques, or zero tolerance, is not possible in a good learning environment.

 # SCENARIO 4

Your prior martial arts experiences leave you confused about the mechanics of a technique. You tell your instructor that when you were studying under sixth degree black belt Sensei Schmoe across the street, he told you that the technique should be done differently. Your instructor says, "It doesn't surprise me, since Sensei Schmoe got his rank through a mail-order company." What is your reply?

1. Really? I'd better stay away from him.

2. No, that's not true. I have known Sensei Schmoe since childhood.

3. I'm sorry, I shouldn't have asked.

4. Yeah, but . . .

★★★★★

The possibility exists that both your current

instructor and Sensei Schmoe are correct and are just expressing themselves differently or talking about different parts of the same technique. Remember the story about the blind men and the elephant? Whether it is "like a thick tree trunk" or "like a long snake" depends on which part you are talking about. This is why clear communication is so important, so that you and your instructor can operate on the same wavelength. The possibility also exists that you are misunderstanding either your current instructor or Sensei Schmoe. If you wholeheartedly believe that your instructor is the one who is wrong, you should avoid talking her down. It looks bad and may cost you her or the other students' respect for the rest of your career. It is better to consider the fact that many instructors come from different backgrounds and teach with different objectives in mind. While your instructor may be focusing on the traditional aspects and ethics of the martial arts, Sensei Schmoe may be focusing on the modern-day applications. Consider this statement by Miyamoto Musashi, perhaps the greatest Japanese swordsman of the 17th century: "The views of each school, and the logic of each path, are realized differently according to the individual person." (From the *Book of Five Rings*, translated by Thomas Cleary, Shambhala, 1993.) Here is a simple rule: When in doubt, define. Define down to the tiniest detail, if needed.

Extracting Knowledge from the Instructor's Teachings

When I was a new student in the martial arts, I was sparring with a more advanced student. My instructor kept telling me to "set him up." But my limited experience left me

Each student will block kicks in a slightly different way. Some may even choose to catch the kick instead of blocking it.

unable to recognize situations where a setup was appropriate. I wasn't even sure what exactly he meant by setting up, as I had no previous examples to draw from. Ideally, the instructor should have recognized my lack of knowledge and supervised the sparring to include specific techniques or concepts.

Learning involves more than listening to somebody telling you what you are doing right or wrong. Knowing what your mistakes are without knowing how to correct them doesn't help much. If your instructor points out that your punch lacks power and you should relax, just how do you learn to relax when the combat arts require a high degree of alertness? Identifying mistakes is only the beginning of the learning process, and might not be useful at all unless you can also bring about the corrective action. Knowing *how* requires intricate insight into the workings of the human body and mind. You must also have an idea of what you are capable of doing at your specific level. The information that the kick in a particular technique should be thrown to the head is not valuable unless you also have the flexibility and strength to perform it. Think about this: When your instructor tells you to kick higher or to work on your flexibility, what is she really telling you? Can you think of some efficient ways to increase the height of your kick?

If you lack power because you are tense, try some reaction drills with a partner.

1. Ask your partner to hold a focus mitt behind his back. Attempt to strike or kick the mitt as soon as your partner shows it to you. Shake out your arms and

If you lack the flexibility to kick high, try lowering your opponent's head through a sweep or joint lock and kick low instead.

legs between combinations of strikes. Caution: Be sure your partner does notremove the target suddenly. Doing so can cause you to hyperextend your elbow or shoulder when you miss.

2. Talk to your partner or have him ask you questions as a distraction while you attempt to strike the mitt. The purpose of this drill is to divert your attention away from being tense.

Let's say that your instructor observes you doing forms and brings to your attention that you are weak in the basics. You go home and practice the basics, but your instructor never provides additional feedback. What should you do? When I was studying karate, I wanted to learn a new and more advanced form. But my instructor told me to get back to basics and practice the old form until it flowed better. Although I understood the word *flow*, I didn't understand how it related to the form or how to bring it out. A good instructor does not give you an exercise without also giving you specific guidance and checking on your progress. If your instructor gives you a vague assignment, ask her to also give you a specific set of techniques to work on. Or ask her to show you the difference between what you are doing and what she wants you to do. Then ask her to provide you with some ways of reaching your objective.

Many students confuse the word *basic* with the word *beginning* and are reluctant to backtrack. But if you practice a stand-up art such as karate, the reverse punch may be your most-relied-upon technique and not something that you use just in the beginning stages. How to throw a punch without risking injury to your hand and wrist is also part of the basics. You can remain excited about basic techniques by understanding that they make up your foundation; they are the techniques that you will use the most throughout your martial arts career.

1. Brainstorm for specific benefits the basic techniques provide. Solid stances, for example, are basic because without a good stance you don't have balance. And without balance, you can't throw a powerful strike or kick or defend against an aggressive attacker effectively.

2. Explore how solid stances relate to effective techniques.

As you can see, learning is a lot about *how* to travel the road and not just about which road to take. As students of the martial arts, it helps to know how to be more efficient learners, how to solve problems and, in general, what it is that makes us tick.

Understanding the learning process

There is a difference between going through your paces and actually learning something. How fast or well you learn is not necessarily related to the intensity of your workouts. There are many ways to improve, but in order to be effective there has to be intent and not just drill work.

First, you must be motivated. Motivation may be your greatest driving force. Start by recognizing the martial arts as an activity that is unique. Just as the Marines go by the motto, "The few, the proud . . .," so should you think of yourself as someone special who will go where others have not gone. The fact is that it takes guts to learn the combat

arts. It takes guts to square off with another student, knowing that you *will* get hit. We will talk more about the learning process, motivation and goal setting in Chapters 6 and 8.

Getting organized

Many arts stress long and repeated drills that initially seem to lead nowhere. If you get bored and drop out of the class, others may think that you lack discipline. The martial arts do require a considerable amount of discipline, but that is not to say that practicing only the horse stance for the first six months is a good way to learn. If your instructor doesn't organize and articulate lessons in a manner that leads toward a tangible goal, you might need to re-evaluate your objectives and your method to achieve them. A good student stays on the path that leads him toward his goal. But he will only reach his goal if he studies with maximum effort and intent, and without wasting a moment.

Both adults and children need a structured classroom setting. If the lessons are haphazard, adults will quit and children will get bored. In order to teach a structured class, the instructor must be well organized and know exactly what he is to cover. You will do better and enjoy yourself more if a high level of performance is demanded. The demand for performance creates a competitive setting, you are thus more likely to work on your techniques at home. If your instructor fails to assign homework:

1. Find out what to expect for the next lesson and set aside a homework practice session prior to that lesson.

2. Do mental drills that allow you to consider new material that is to be learned, or discuss it with another student.

Both adults and children often act as if they don't have time to train at home. I think that this has more to do with a lack of interest and discipline than with a lack of time. As little as five minutes can be productive if you know what to work on. If your instructor is forgiving and doesn't check up on the assignments, you are less likely to follow through. But remember that you are not doing the assignments to please your instructor; you are doing the assignments primarily for yourself. It is therefore not solely your instructor's responsibility to assign homework. You can do a lot to cultivate the right mindset.

Since you are paying for instruction, you have a right to expect certain results, and lessons should never be cut short. Ideally, your instructor should start the lesson on time and display full focus on the lesson for the duration of the class. It is okay for the instructor to tell jokes or use anecdotes during the introduction to the lesson in order to gain your attention. But if she swerves off into other areas that do not relate to the material she intends to teach, you might feel short-changed. You can help keep your instructor on track by leaving personal matters at home. For example, avoid talking about what movies you watched last weekend or how tired you are from your job, unless it is absolutely necessary in order to illustrate a point about the material you are trying to learn.

In a private lesson, any conversation that extends outside of the martial arts adversely affects you alone. But if you engage in non-related conversation in a group class, valuable time is taken away from other students as well. Be respectful of your peers' time. Note that there are occasions when free talk or rap sessions can benefit you, but in general, they should be limited to before or after class. Martial arts lessons are primarily about learning and not about socializing. No matter how much you enjoy the class or your instructor's sense of humor, you should avoid accepting substandard performance in return for a friendly relationship.

 # SCENARIO 5

After warm-up, one of the students in your class mentions last weekend's tournament. The instructor starts to elaborate. You did not go to the tournament and have been looking forward to a productive lesson. What should you do?

1. Talk about the tournament.

2. Leave.

3. Ride it out and say nothing.

4. Interrupt and tell the instructor that you wish to get on with the lesson.

★★★★★

If one of the students starts discussing material that is not related to the lesson at hand, it is easy for the instructor to fall into the trap and end up teaching a less-than-satisfactory lesson. Although other students may seem to enjoy these rap sessions, there is always somebody who will feel short-changed. For example, if your work schedule limits you to attending one class per week, you want to ensure that you learn something constructive in each class. In high school, you might have looked forward to a day off, but when you pay for classes you don't feel that way. If this chatting is a one-time event, you may want to ride it out.

If your school is tournament oriented, however, you may want to pay attention to how organized the instructor is. Are there special days when you train to improve tournament skills? After a tournament, it is a good idea to review what took place, what you could have done differently, and how to prepare yourself for the next tournament. If your school is tournament-oriented:

1. Be prepared to participate in talk sessions. Critique your own performance, and then seek the critique of your instructor. An organized and constructive talk session does not include bragging or laughing about your opponent's misfortune.

2. Elaborate on the specific details of the tournament. If your instructor isn't doing this, steer him in the right direction by asking specific questions.

3. Think about what you want to discuss prior to coming to class.

For the opening night of the Jean-Claude Van Damme movie, *Double Impact*, my karate school had been asked to hold a demonstration at the local movie theater. Naturally, the students were excited. But to my disappointment, the time to rehearse our moves was limited to about 30 minutes on the lawn behind the theater. As a result, as a student of intermediate rank at the time, I felt almost embarrassed about my perfor-

Shorter talk sessions can prove beneficial if they focus on specific techniques or skills that have been learned or are to be learned in the upcoming lesson.

mance. Some drills were done with partners, and had we sufficient time to practice we could have fine-tuned our timing.

If you are participating in a demonstration at a public event and you have the opportunity to be part of the planning, try the following:

1. Suggest that the demonstration be varied. This creates a sense of intensity.

2. Suggest that you open with a group performance, with students punching and kicking in unison with loud *kiais* (shouts).

3. Suggest that each student performs one technique in the air or on a partner, while the other students stand back.

4. Suggest that one student does a short and powerful form.

5. Suggest that a couple of breaking techniques be demonstrated.

6. Suggest a strong ending with a short sparring match, for example, where students rotate (round robin) every few seconds.

The above is just a sample performance that could be done in about 10 minutes. A high energy level is likely to draw a lot of motivation both from the students, who will perform better as a result, and from the audience. Even basic techniques that are performed crisply will draw the audience's attention, and are something the beginning students in your school can participate in and enjoy as well.

– INSTRUCTOR TIP –

The martial arts are mainly practical. As your students gain experience, it is okay to include more theory in the lessons, but the theory should still relate directly to the particular technique or concept you are teaching.

– STUDENT TIP –

If you take private lessons, and especially if you have a good relationship with your instructor, it is easy to get sidetracked into friendly conversation. If you are a talker, you might be tempted to talk about everything from work to family (even in the middle of a round of bag work). This conversation invites your instructor to fall into the trap. If you can prevent nonmartial arts talk from originating with you, you can increase your chances of receiving a constructive lesson.

Showing interest

"You must crawl before you can walk," is a popular instructor reply when a student requests to learn a more advanced technique. But how do you determine how advanced

a technique is? Is the dance of death really more advanced than the single wrist grab? I believe that some instructors use the crawl-before-you-can-walk reply because they haven't really thought about and evaluated the learning process. There is also the possibility that they want to string students along by not giving them what they want all at once. The instructor's position brings her power. Be aware that she can use this power constructively in teaching others, or she can abuse it.

Some martial artists teach in order to satisfy their ego. Whom do you look up to? Who is the ultimate authority? Who is making the decisions? Who is exercising control? The instructor, right? The instructor can take on god-like qualities and seem almost invincible. She knows the answer to everything and is unbeatable in battle.

 # SCENARIO 6

You doubt what your instructor is telling you. What should you do?

1. Argue with the instructor.

2. Shrug and say that she is talking nonsense.

3. Explain to the instructor what she really means to say.

4. Ask the instructor to provide a more detailed explanation of what she means.

★★★★★

When I was a new student in karate, the

martial artist I idolized was also my worst instructor. After warm-up, he would stand in front of the group and rub his chin: "Well . . . let's see . . . what's next . . ?" Ideally, your instructor is in full control of the lesson. You have the right to expect this of him. If the leader doesn't know where he is going, how can he expect you to follow? The instructor who really understands the material he is teaching welcomes doubt. He sees the student with the inquisitive mind as being receptive to learning. A good student doesn't present his doubt as a challenge to the instructor's competence, but uses it as an opportunity to further his knowledge. Unfortunately, many instructors, students and martial artists in general are on a power trip. They degrade other arts and brag about which art, school or instructor is the best. It benefits both you and your instructor to talk about what other arts and schools have to offer. Keep an open mind without taking sides. Don't argue for the sake of arguing. Explore instead the pros and cons of all issues.

The more you can open your mind, the more others will come to trust and respect you. This does not mean that you should fail to support your ideas. If you are right, then defend your position if challenged. If you are wrong, admit it. If a person of higher rank disagrees with you, it is still appropriate to defend yourself. Rank might bring might, but it does not bring right. I recently met a renowned martial artist with whom I discussed the grappling arts. When I said, "If you let go of the control hold now . . ." he interrupted and said, "First of all, you *never* let go of one control hold to gain another." Since this martial artist was highly ranked in grappling, he assumed that I was

incorrect, without hearing me out or asking me to elaborate on what I meant. The point is that you should not use absolutes, especially not before you have heard the other person out. This principle applies to both students and instructors. It is easy to hear only your own thoughts and fall into the trap of assuming that other people's ideas lack merit.

Your instructor should be wiser and more knowledgeable than you, but you should not expect her to outperform you for time and eternity. If this were the case, her career would be short-lived. It is the years in the art that make her wise and able. As she ages, she may not be as flexible or energetic anymore, but she can still teach. Good instruction requires a deep understanding of the skills needed to master your art; it requires the ability to communicate those skills to the student. Your instructor's goal is not to make herself good, but to help make you good; to recognize when you are not performing correctly, to correct you, and to accelerate your rate of learning. The highest compliment you can give your instructor is when you outperform her. The best instructors can take you far beyond their own level of skill.

– INSTRUCTOR TIP –

Although you should be more concerned with the progress of your students than with your own progress, some show-off is appropriate. If your students are impressed with your skill, they are more likely to listen to and emulate you. If you are good at what you do, you will have your students' attention every time you perform.

A good instructor demonstrates a technique with precision, while pausing as needed to explain the intricacies of the art.

– STUDENT TIP –

A good student can see beyond the moment; he has vision and knows where his relationship with the instructor will lead. If ever in doubt, you should ask yourself, "Will this action help me learn?" If you answer "yes," you are probably doing the right thing. If you can keep this principle in mind throughout your martial arts career, you can with good conscience take whatever measures you need in order to increase your rate of learning:

Developing your attitude

I am sure there have been times when you have walked out of the training hall feeling totally energized, or have laid awake at night unable to sleep because of the martial arts thoughts that were racing through your mind. What triggers this feeling? What sets one class apart from the rest?

Attitudes rub off. The material taught in class is only a small part of learning. Your

level of success may have more to do with how you approach the lesson and how you carry yourself in front of others. If you portray a positive and dynamic attitude, others are more likely to follow and help set the pace for a constructive learning environment.

 SCENARIO 7

You are a prospective martial arts student in search of a school. You ask if you may observe a class. The instructor tells you that you must be a student at the school before you can observe a lesson. What should you do?

1. Sign up for lessons.

2. Go somewhere else.

3. Tell the instructor that you will sign up only after you have observed a lesson.

4. Ask what he is afraid of.

Should a nonmartial artist be allowed to observe the class? Why or why not? When I was a new student searching for a karate school, one of the schools I visited didn't allow me to observe the class. In fact, classes were held behind closed doors. The school owner told me that I had to sign up for classes before being allowed inside. Recently, at a different school, I had a better experience. When I asked if I could watch, not only did they invite me in and show me where to sit, they had me stand in respect with the rest of the class and asked if I would join in warm-ups. This etiquette gave me a great sense of belonging.

Parents whose children study the martial arts commonly want to sit in the audience and watch their kids in class. There may be specific times, however, when it is not in the student's best interest to have family or friends watching. One such time may be during a belt promotion. Although the promotion should highlight the student's career, and most of us enjoy showing off our skill in front of our peers, some students are very anxious about taking tests. I, myself, would not allow my mother to watch or even know of my kickboxing matches. Had she been in the audience, she would have worried that I would get hurt, which might have prevented me from focusing fully on the match.

When deciding on a future course of action for your martial arts studies, consider your prior experiences and decide what you liked or didn't like about them.

1. Were there many details skipped that you had to find out for yourself later?

2. Were you given too much information at once, or did you feel that too much time was spent on repetition? Personally, I enjoy a lot of repetition but think that it should be supervised. I dislike being left to practice alone for half an hour with no instructor stopping by to see how I am doing.

3. If you could have any instructor you wanted, what type of person would she be? How would she teach? Why would you enjoy her so much?

4. If you had this "star instructor," how would it change your attitude and learn-

ing experience?

In reality, it is not possible to decide how your instructor should behave, and we often have to accept the bad along with the good. But it is possible to decide how you are going to feel about the classes you attend.

1. Decide what type of learner you want to be and model yourself after this imaginary person.

2. After attending a class, mentally go through what happened. When were you able to be the kind of student you wanted to be? What could you have done better? What could you have handled differently?

3. When you feel that you did something right, give yourself credit. In what ways were your responses to problems appropriate? Make an effort to analyze your past.

4. Accept the fact that there are times when you will feel frustrated, proud, tired, motivated, or ready to quit.

Discipline and compassion

Your instructor should be a leader with clear objectives in mind. Teaching with authority is not unethical. The instructor's and the student's standings are not equal; the instructor has more knowledge and a longer background than the student, and teaching with discipline, adhering to rituals, or presenting a challenging workout is not the same as abusing power. Teaching with authority is not the same as being *authoritative*.

On the other hand, an instructor who uses

fear and intimidation tactics is not likely to be successful with students in today's society. Punishing a student with push-ups, for example, only works if the student sees the good in it and is willing. Any scare tactic is likely to fail. After all, you are paying the instructor, and you know fully that nothing is holding you in the class other than your own free will. It is also unlikely that scare tactics benefit children. While some children do well with punishment, it is harmful to others. If a shy or timid student makes a mistake and the instructor punishes him, it might have a negative effect on his future learning experiences. Observe how your instructor approaches other students. Is he cautious about disciplining a student before he knows how the student will react, or does he barge forward as if the student were just a number among a hundred others?

Some people think that we overcome fear by facing the fear and doing the things that we are afraid of. If you are afraid of sparring, for example, you should spar a lot to overcome your fear. If you are afraid of doing forms in front of the group, then that's what you should do. Something should be said for the fact that the more familiar we are with a subject, the less afraid we generally feel. This concept originates in the unknown; we generally fear what we do not understand. A good instructor, however, uses tact when making you do the things that you fear. The ability to use tact requires that the instructor knows something about you. In other words, she can't use the same tactics with everybody. Some students need to be eased forward more slowly than others.

1. How do you think you rank in relation to your peers when it comes to doing the things you fear? Can you push yourself beyond your fears and perform anyway?

2. Knowing how another person feels is often difficult. Are there particular students who shy away when you practice a technique on them? If this is you, what can you do to break this habit?

3. Is it possible that your fear will eventually make you stop coming to class? Do you ever rationalize why you should avoid certain exercises, such as sparring? If you look at your prior experiences objectively, how many times was your fear really warranted?

4. Recognize that everybody is different. Have patience with an instructor who uses a "softer" or "harder" approach than you would like.

The responsibility for good learning does not rest with your instructor alone. You must make the first commitment. If you are not serious about learning, you will be better off not wasting your time.

1. Understand the rules and abide by them.

2. Come to class on time, know when your payments are due and comply unless prior arrangements have been made.

3. If a uniform is required, but after two months you still haven't bothered to buy one, you are probably not very committed. The same goes for sparring gear.

Can two instructors of different philosophies teach at the same school and still be compatible? For example, one instructor may focus on tradition and the mental aspects of the art, and the other instructor may

How do you rank in comparison to your peers when it comes to fear? Do you shy away as soon as another student strikes at you, or are you able to hide your fear and portray an attitude of confidence?

be more like a drill sergeant. How would you deal with these different personalities?

There is seldom a single "right" way of performing a technique or exercise. I always found it difficult to learn from an instructor who would stand by and observe quietly, and then utter a loud "no, no, no!" Both you and your instructor must realize that students (particularly advanced students) often need to find their own way. At this level, your instructor should guide more than require absolute obedience. In fact, there are few absolutes in the martial arts. If you doubt it, just spend an hour with an instructor in the same art but from another school. You can be sure that she will teach the same techniques slightly differently.

Have a healthy respect for the inherent dangers associated with the sport. Take safety precautions, practice safe habits, and wear protection. Some instructors fail to live by their principles. For example, if you are required to wear headgear and a mouthpiece when sparring, but your instructor doesn't abide by the same rules, he will send a mixed message. If safety rules are broken in your school, keep in mind that nobody is invincible. Maintain a realistic view of the dangers associated with your art. Don't become complacent. Anybody can get injured, even if they have 30 years experience in the martial arts.

1. Do as your instructor preaches, not necessarily as he does. If your instructor doesn't live by his principles, it is still no excuse for you not to.

2. Listen to what your instructor says, and take the active approach to strengthen these principles on your own.

3. Practice your techniques with precision. If you frequently drop your guard in sparring because you feel that you are more experienced than your opponent, it may teach you a hard lesson on the street some day.

 SCENARIO 8

Your instructor is of small stature and frequently spars with students including you, who are heavier and stronger than she. Initially, the size difference doesn't matter. But as you gain experience, you begin to overpower your instructor. How should you handle it?

1. Slow down and exercise control.

2. Avoid sparring with your instructor, and spar only with other students your own size.

3. Compliment your instructor so she doesn't feel embarrassed about her performance.

4. Spar harder to see if you can beat your instructor.

★★★★★

As an instructor, I weigh 125 pounds and teach full-contact kickboxing. I frequently spar with students much heavier than I. I usually start by telling them that we will go light contact, which tends to escalate to medium or hard contact, when the pressure is on. On occasion, I have to remind them to back down on the power a little. When the instructor is in the middle of a sparring match, it can be challenging for her to separate her need to defend herself from her need to teach. At the higher levels of sparring, it is easier to be an effective instructor "from the outside."

Ideally, your instructor exercises good judgment and knows when to throw in the towel to prevent you from getting injured. Good work ethics are essential to learning, but your instructor should not require that you drive yourself to injury or exhaustion. Many students' egos and fighting spirits prevent them from quitting when the sparring gets tough. Your instructor must know when to call a break in the action. If he seems oblivious to how you feel, remember that ultimately you are in control of your own health and well-being. Consider at what point in

your training it is appropriate for you to avoid taking more punishment.

What would you do if your instructor were fighting in front of a large audience, and you were watching him getting hurt? Who would throw in the towel for him? How could you help your instructor quit and still save face?

Understanding that no one size fits all

In a group class, most instructors gear their lessons toward the average student. If your instructor teaches for the slow learners, everybody else will get bored. But if she teaches for the fast learners, nobody else will keep up. The problem with teaching for the average student is that she is teaching for nobody in particular. If teaching a large class, the instructor may utilize assistant instructors who can give students individual instruction based on their levels and abilities.

Not all students learn in the same way, and should therefore not be taught using the same approach. Children might need to be taught differently than adults. If you have a child enrolled in the martial arts, what can the instructor do to keep your child motivated without being intimidating or overwhelming? Ask your child what he or she likes. When I was a kid, I never liked participating in the all-kids classes because they often seemed unstructured and contained too much play time. Participating in an adult class made me feel more important and, therefore, more motivated.

Sometimes women need to be taught differently than men, although my experience is that the martial arts are not necessarily gender-specific. How you learn has more to do with your background and previous experiences than with your gender. Although different groups should be taught using different methods, it is dangerous to assume that children should be approached differently from adults or women differently than men. For example, in many contact sports, we tend to believe that women "can't take it" or that women should spar only with other women. But this is true only if the women have been conditioned not to take contact. However, there are women who are quite competitive, are in it for the sport aspect of the art, and are not at all intimidated by contact in either striking or grappling arts. The same holds true for the men. Many men are of the kinder and gentler type and are not particularly comfortable with contact sparring. When you first step into the martial arts training hall, and as you progress through your training, be attentive to what makes learning easier for you. Start out carefully and practice with a variety of people of both genders. A good student learns the technical details of the art, but a *great* student is in tune with his passions and capitalizes on his natural talents.

Your approach to learning will vary depending on your interests and goals. If you want to learn contact sparring, for example, but your school emphasizes forms, you will tire quickly. I knew a martial artist who went to other schools and asked for somebody who could teach him how to fight. Every school cannot satisfy the needs of every student. Most schools specialize either in forms, techniques or sparring. If you have taken the time to question your reasons for studying the martial arts before signing up for classes

Training with students of different genders, ages and builds allows you to discover when and how a technique works, and the factors that affect your success rate.

and continue to examine them throughout your career, you can tweak your studies and remain passionate about learning even if it eventually means leaving your school and going to the competition across the street.

 ## SCENARIO 9

You are working the roundhouse kick to the head, when another student tells you that you don't kick very well. What is your response?

1. You don't either!

2. You owe me 10 push-ups for that comment.

3. If *you* practiced a little harder, *your* kick would be better than mine.

4. I am doing the best I can.

5. Why not?

★★★★★

Many schools post motivational sayings on the walls, such as, "Don't use four-letter words," with the word *can't* circled and crossed out. Although motivational sayings are great, the problem is that they only work for those who are already healthy, motivated and physically able. You should therefore take these posters with a grain of salt. There are certain things that certain students really can't do. Be realistic and honest about your limitations. When you say "I can't," it is not necessarily due to a lack of confidence. However, another student's analysis of your technique should not serve to frustrate you or diminish your confidence either.

Note that much of this book is devoted to handling difficult or frustrating situations that occur within the training hall. But don't assume that these situations are the norm. Most students are not timid, do not have learning disabilities, are not afraid to get hit, are not lazy, and are forgiving and not apt to hold a grudge against you. Although you must be sensitive to your peers with special needs, you should not be overly cautious. Remember the Golden Rule: Treat others as you would like to be treated.

Consistency of behavior

Some people argue that it is more fun when a new technique is introduced suddenly, or when you are thrown into a test or perfor-

mance in front of your peers without prior warning. My experiences, however, tell me that most people enjoy stability far more; they like to see what's coming their way well in advance. In fact, we tend to feel that most of the fun is in the journey, in the anticipation of our goal. If you are learning the martial arts for self-defense, your instructor may need to throw surprise attacks simulations into the training. But you should still know when you sign up for the course, that it is part of the curriculum. Consistency of behavior brings stability to the learning process. When you know what to expect beforehand, you can prepare yourself better for the upcoming lesson.

Equally important is consistency in your behavior toward your instructor and peers. If you are a college student, you may have been immersed in a learning environment all day prior to coming to martial arts class at night. Or you may have had a trying day at your job that has left you tired and with a headache. Regardless of what the case may be, when you come to class after a full day's work and things don't go well, your patience may be tested. But your instructor and the other students are not responsible for what has happened to you earlier in the day, and they do not deserve to feel the effects of your bad experiences.

1. If you have mood swings, learn to control them while in class.

2. If you have a personal problem that affects your mood and that you can't control, consider taking time off until you have resolved your problem.

3. If you can't take time off, consider being up front with your instructor and peers

26

by telling them why you are acting strangely. In a recent martial arts class, one of the students got into an argument with the instructor. After the student and the instructor had spent a few minutes behind closed doors, the student came back to class and apologized for his behavior, explaining that he had just started taking a medication that left him grouchy. As a result of his willingness to explain, we welcomed him back to class.

 ## SCENARIO 10

Halfway through a lesson on kicks, you remember that the instructor promised last week to teach sweeps and throws today. She appears to have forgotten. What should you do?

1. Remind her of the promise and insist that she teaches sweeps and throws.

2. Ignore it, since you're having fun with the kicks.

3. Interrupt and tell the class how kicks eventually lead to sweeps, which eventually lead to throws.

4. Say, "I guess you've changed your mind. I guess you don't think we are ready for it."

Most of us have days when we just don't feel like going to class, or when we haven't had time to prepare ourselves sufficiently. This momentary lack of motivation happens to instructors, too. For example, if your in-

structor gives you an assignment and you prepare for it, but she forgets to follow up, you might get annoyed and feel that your preparation is in vain. There are times when I have come to class and the instructor has asked, "What would you like to do today?" I felt his question indicated a lack of preparation and interest; the instructor was relying on me, the student, to figure out what the lesson should be. Note that it could be appropriate on occasion to ask students which techniques they would like to work on; however, in general, lessons tend to be more constructive when they have been planned in advance. I have also come to classes where the instructor has walked in five or 10 minutes late and was yawning. The instructor isn't interested in hearing your excuse for being late. Likewise, you aren't interested in hearing the instructor's excuse.

1. If you are annoyed when coming to class, for whatever reason, try reviewing in your mind what you were working on last time. Remind yourself of what you did well and what made you excited about learning.

2. Rehearsing what you did last time gives you a goal for today and helps you focus on the lesson at hand. It may even help you get started on a new long-term goal.

Improving yourself

As a new student you have a natural tendency to repeat almost verbatim what he has been taught. From where else would you draw your knowledge? But as your experience grows, you should analyze what you learn and try to expand on the material. In order to move beyond rote (we will take a closer look at the definition of this term in Part 6), you must constantly think about your martial arts experiences and what you are learning.

Hopefully, you are learning techniques and concepts that are logical and useful. This may seem obvious, yet some things are taught because they have been handed down through tradition or because they were once useful. For example, some people claim that the flying sidekick was originally designed for kicking men off their horses. But few martial artists in today's society fight against horseback riders. Does this mean that the kick is useless? Not necessarily, but you should know the practicality of the technique, where it stemmed from and how to use it. For example, you may find uses for it as a head kick. Or you may find it a useful tool for refining your body mechanics, for learning explosiveness, or for exhibiting showmanship at a tournament. The uses should be stated so you understand the value of the technique.

Constantly look for ways to improve your skills and avoid being bound by tradition or prejudice. Learning everything about your art but then failing to train leads to stagnation, with your competition moving ahead. In order to stay with the times, you must consistently train for newer conditions as well as retrain to stay proficient at the old.

The frequency of training is more important than the length of training.

1. Remain proficient in techniques that you seldom use if they are to remain part of your repertoire.

2. When correcting a problem, know your art well enough to correctly define what is wrong. If not, seek help with the definition.

3. Take a minute to think about what needs to be done before jumping to conclusions. Don't feel forced to accept a challenge or to perform a technique that you are not comfortable with.

4. Don't place yourself in a situation that leaves you with no alternatives. Like they used to say in Driver's Ed, "Leave yourself an out."

So, there you have it! But as I've said, simply stating the facts does not a great student make. Now that we have talked about the tendencies you must be aware of in yourself and in your instructor, let's move ahead and further educate ourselves on professionalism, ethics and the learning process. Let's continue to look for the many potential pitfalls in training. Let's learn how to extract information from our peers in order to accelerate our own learning and retention.

2
Professionalism

WHAT IS PROFESSIONALISM?

Normally when we talk about professionals, we mean people who make money. Secondary are people who use agreeable manners and follow certain codes of ethics. A professional code of ethics for the martial arts student includes the following:

1. Take pride in yourself and dress appropriately for class.

2. Arrive on time, in good spirits, and prepared to learn.

3. Use appropriate language.

4. Live by your principles; do as you preach.

5. Have no hidden agendas or ulterior motives. When in class, your interest in learning should not come secondary to other activities.

6. Be a role model.

Note that role-model behavior can be somewhat difficult to define. For example, the school might define a role model as a person who abstains from drinking alcohol, smoking and other health hazards. But it is neither the school's responsibility nor its right to lecture you on what you should or should not do privately. In order to determine what role-model behavior means to you, you may want to take a critical look at how you lead your life and how you think others view you.

APPEARANCE

Your professional image, including your behavior and outer appearance, may determine how others feel about you. First impressions make powerful statements. As much as we would like to avoid prejudice, it is difficult to speak well of people who fail to follow certain standards. For example:

1. A student with awesome skill and a likable personality shows up to class in a *gi* (uniform) that is dirty and has a tear in the armpit. How does that affect his image? If a uniform is required, keep it clean and in good shape.

2. A female instructor in her early 50s is wearing too much make-up and two or three rings on every finger, including the thumb (or a man is wearing six gold chains around his neck and a ring through his lower lip). How does that affect her (or his) image? Most instructors tell us not to wear jewelry in class so that we don't injure ourselves and others.

3. A girl in her early teens is teaching a class to younger children. She is constantly yelling at her students, "When I tell you to do something, you do it!" Would you pay for your child's lessons at this school? A friend of mine enrolled his 6-year-old boy in karate class. After a few months, the boy quit. When I asked why he quit, he explained, "Because I am tired of being yelled at." Children, too, need to be treated with professionalism and respect.

Martial arts training requires fitness. Without it you can't perform at maximum intensity. Although some people have naturally heavier builds than others, excess weight alone does not determine your skill or dedication and should not cost you your peers' respect. The point is to be dedicated to the practice of the martial arts and make a commitment to your health.

COURTESY

Common courtesy is perhaps the most important personal habit a martial arts studentcam have. Others should feel welcome when they enter the school. Consistency of behavior is also important. It is difficult to associate with a person who is friendly one day and doesn't look at you the next. Although such a person's behavior may have nothing to do with you in particular, it does affect how you feel about him or her and makes it difficult to interact in class.

Many schools include the word *courtesy* in their creed. My experience is that although we generally respect other students within our school, we often don't extend that same courtesy to participants of other arts. I be-

lieve it is safe to say that few other professions spend as much time bad-mouthing and degrading their competition. For example:

1. You visit a rival studio to buy a *bokken* (a wooden sword). The school owner asks you where you are studying, then smirks and says, "Oh, your instructor charges too much, and his students always come in last in tournaments." You will probably not be very motivated to buy equipment from this school again.

2. You visit a grappling school. The instructor asks you which art you study. When you tell him you study kickboxing he says, "See those gloves I've got hanging above the fireplace? When people come in here and talk about kickboxing, I go a couple of rounds with them to humble them a little before I take them down and finish them on the ground." Would you be eager to recommend this instructor to your friends?

When Jeff Speakman starred in the movie, *Perfect Weapon*, a martial arts student said,

When your instructor or another student is speaking, listen with the intent of extracting information.

"Yeah, Jeff Speakman is a good brown belt!" Most of us know that Jeff Speakman left the brown-belt ranks eons ago. Watch your language. Derogatory remarks such as these do little to further your own good reputation.

SOCIALIZING

When going to the training hall, your main focus should be learning the martial arts, not socializing with others. If you steal time from the class by socializing with the instructor or other students, remember that somebody will always feel short-changed, even if they are courteous enough not to say so.

A fellow student regularly spent 20 minutes in the hallway engaged in conversation with the instructor. No matter how inspiring this conversation might have been to the student, when the instructor finally got back to class, I was cold, mad, and felt that I had been cut short. If you feel a need to engage in lengthy discussions, try to wait until after class. Yes, the instructor, too, is responsible for running an organized class; however, you can help by not trapping him in conversation.

PASSING THE BUCK

Ideally, your display of professionalism should transfer to the other students in the class. Few things are as pleasant as when another student compliments you in front of your instructor. Remember, too, that you represent your instructor and the school. If you behave badly at a tournament, it will reflect negatively on your instructor, even if she didn't teach or encourage these bad habits. Once you have been marked a troublemaker, it is difficult to regress and change how others perceive you.

Consider your instructor's professional re-sponsibilities toward you. An effective and professional learning environment requires an instructor who is well-trained and thoroughly prepared; she must understand her art well enough to provide explanations and demonstrations that make sense to the students. A credible instructor ensures that you:

1. Can use what you learn in a self-defense or tournament setting;

2. Practice according to safe standards; and

3. Perform and behave in a way that brings pride to yourself, your instructor and your school

Ideally, your instructor should also:

1. Know how learning takes place and be imaginative and creative in her thinking;

2. Know how to pave the way through definite exercises and timeframes that you can clearly see; and

3. Have patience and compassion, and persevere until the objectives are achieved.

Presenting a facade of infallibility does more harm than good. For example, some instructors (and students) want others to believe that the arts empower them with certain mystical skills. Other instructors teach randomly, without really knowing which elements to teach first and why. When I started in Aikido (the first art I studied), the vagueness of the instruction disappointed me. Techniques were demonstrated and we practiced with each other, but no in-depth explanations were provided. I believe this type of approach to teaching makes it difficult for beginners to learn. I decided that the martial arts weren't what I had anticipated. Shortly thereafter I hurt my knee and was unable to do many of the Aikido techniques. I took up karate instead. The school owner gave me my first lesson, which he cut from an hour to 30 minutes. It didn't impress me. The next day, I battled with the decision to go back to class or quit. I decided to give it one more chance. I was lucky enough to be introduced to another instructor, who remained my main teacher through intermediate rank. Immediately my desire to study the martial arts took a more positive direction. I can honestly say it is because of the good teaching abilities of my first karate instructor that I stayed in the arts long enough to want to make it a lifelong journey.

– INSTRUCTOR TIP –

Avoid mysticism or tendencies that lean toward secrecy. Help students develop proper attitudes toward learning by speaking openly and instilling respect for the many different styles of martial arts.

– STUDENT TIP –

Choose your instructor with care. Your first instructor may be the single most important factor in determining how far you will go in the martial arts.

3
Ethics

MISREPRESENTATION

Pick up a yellow pages phone book and look up *martial arts*. You will most likely find schools that advertise a blend of just about every art you can think of: karate, grappling, boxing, physical fitness, cardio-karate, weight lifting, weapons, street fighting, women's self-defense and so on. Although it may seem as though "the art for everybody" will attract more students, is the instructor really qualified to teach such a multitude of arts? Jiu-jitsu, for example, is a specific art and not a catch-all kind of word. What qualifies your karate instructor to teach jiu-jitsu? Is knowledge of a few arm bars and choke holds enough? If your instructor misrepresents himself as something or someone he is not, those students who don't know better will not get the best instruction for their money.

If you have taken first place in a number of tournaments, does it make you a champion, a national champion or a grand champion? Winning a national championship is not synonymous with being the best fighter in the nation. A tournament may simply be called "The Nationals." I am not saying that your efforts at the tournament should go unnoticed; I am saying that it is unethical to make certain assertions to the uninitiated. If you fight a person from a foreign country and you win, does it make you the international champion? If you lose and your opponent claims to be the international champion, would you think it fair?

Some martial artists have us believe that they are of the direct lineage of some ancient emperor of China, that they hold five world titles, or that they are undefeated in 200 street fights. Such claims, when unproven, do the martial arts community a disservice. How do you support a claim that your art is so superior that, after six months in your system, a student can beat anybody from any other system? Such a claim is not only disappointing when the truth is revealed, it may cost the gullible person his life! One student told me that his instructor *invented* grappling. A tiny bit of research will confirm that grappling can be traced as far back as 3400 BC. Some of the exact techniques used in today's grappling arts are painted on tomb walls in Egypt. New systems of martial arts are not really new; they are old ideas repackaged under new names. Avoid making or believing outrageous claims.

 SCENARIO 11

You ask your instructor to teach you a new technique, but she says that you are not ready for it. What should you do?

1. Bow and continue practicing the old techniques.

2. Plead with her to teach you a new technique, anyway.

3. Ask your more advanced buddy to teach you.

4. Go to another school.

5. Sign up for the black belt program to show your dedication to the art.

"Learn the basics first. When you get good enough, I will show you this new technique!" As a student in the martial arts, I find this type of answer frustrating. When you ask a question, your instructor should give you an answer—a straight and true answer. The opportunity to learn at a higher level often makes the lower level techniques come more naturally. An instructor who shares her knowledge freely is likely to make you more excited about learning. However, the instructor is not wrong when stressing that intellectual knowledge of a technique does not necessarily result in mastery.

Some schools teach techniques the "beginning way" and the "advanced way." I question whether this fosters learning. Why not learn a technique in its entirety early in the program? A good method may be to learn the basics first and then build on them with different scenarios and plenty of "what ifs:" What if my opponent steps forward when throwing the strike? What if I am unable to break the wrist grab with that specific technique? What if I slip and fall when I try to throw the kick? If your instructor withholds information without explaining why, you might get the impression that she is trying to string you along for economic reasons. It is also difficult to unlearn principles you have learned early in your training. Ideally, techniques should be taught and learned the way they are to be used.

 SCENARIO 12

You have seen the Gracies compete and want to learn some grappling techniques. You are taking karate and feel that your knowledge is lacking. What should you do?

1. Ask your instructor to recommend a good grappling school.

2. Tell others that karate is more effective than grappling, and that you can beat anybody in the Gracie system.

3. Pretend that grappling is more advanced than karate, and that it will benefit you to wait and learn grappling only after you have earned your black belt.

None of the above answers is very satisfying. Start by being honest about your desire to learn another art. If you have no knowledge of grappling, admitting that you have no knowledge should not make you feel inferior. Your mind expands when you allow yourself to be curious about other arts. Remember, a good instructor does not see an inquisitive mind as a threat to his authority. Curiosity about other arts does not mean that your current art lacks merit. Perhaps you just want to be introduced to the idea of fighting on the ground. Having knowledge of other arts is important even if you don't intend to pursue a black belt in more than one art. Understanding the gist of other arts allows you to hold intellectual conversations about them. Many of the wide variety of arts also employ similar principles. For example:

1. If you have never studied the Gracie system in particular, your art may still teach the principles of leverage and joint breaks. Discuss leverage concepts with your instructor and other students.

2. Try to relate the concepts of grappling to the concepts of stand-up fighting. If a choke is applied on the ground, can it also be applied when standing? If kicks are applied when standing, can they also be applied on the ground?

3. What are the strengths and weaknesses of each system, or of each technique as performed within that system? Avoid limiting your exploration to the strengths of your own system and the weaknesses of the other system. Explore both sides in order to acquire a more complete picture of the arts. Avoid making absolute statements such as, "Now that I have explored other arts, I know that my own art is superior."

If you really want to learn the intricate details of another art, it is okay to seek this knowledge regardless of whether or not others approve. Remember, your instructor doesn't own you physically, mentally or emotionally. It is better to learn from an expert than from somebody who has just dabbled in the art.

Leverage techniques are not exclusive to the grappling or ground-fighting arts. The principles of leverage apply also to the stand-up arts.

– INSTRUCTOR TIP –

Curiosity is a natural (and welcome) part of learning. The instructor's greatest objective is to educate and advance the student, even if it leads to the student's temporary leave from your school.

– STUDENT TIP –

Your desire to study another art can increase your insight into all arts. But you must be willing to explore both the pros and cons truthfully. Being a "dojo hopper" early in your training is unlikely to give you deeper insights into the great variety of arts.

HOW MUCH TO PAY

Professionalism can be defined in many ways, but most of us would agree that the professional knows how to reason clearly and intellectually. The professional makes sound decisions and is true to her beliefs. The professional is considered more experienced than the amateur; that's why she can charge for her services. In short, her services are her *profession*. However, as discussed in Part 2, your instructor can be professional even if she doesn't charge an arm and a leg, as long as she meets the other defining criteria.

 ## SCENARIO 13

You think that your instructor charges too much, so you send her an anonymous e-mail to the contact address on her website that reads, "Focus on training, not money." What does your message imply?

1. It is wrong for her to advertise her services on the Internet.

2. It is wrong to charge for instruction.

3. Money doesn't bring anyone happiness.

4. The instructor's website is lousy.

The main focus of this book is to help you become a better student, not to help you run a business. When discussing instructor responsibilities, with the exception of this brief discussion, we will follow the assumption that the instructor doesn't have to worry about the financial aspects of the school. However, many instructors are also school owners who can't separate themselves from the business and focus solely on teaching. Unless the school is well established, it is difficult for the instructor to make a living

on teaching. She might have to work long evenings and weekends in order to make ends meet. If she experiences too much financial pressure, she might even compromise her love of teaching for the opportunity to make more money. So how much should the instructor charge for lessons? The rental of the building and the utilities are expensive, right? Should that expense come out of the instructor's or the student's pocket?

The potential problem with charging for instruction is that the instructor might become a businessman rather than a teacher. His main focus has now shifted away from teaching. But somebody must run the business end of the school; somebody must recruit students and make ends meet. Any business deal is fine as long as it is honest. There is a problem only if the student is made to believe that he is learning from the master instructor, for example, when he is really learning from a number of assistant instructors. Learning from assistant instructors is fine, too, as long as there is full disclosure and you are at peace with the idea.

Assistant instructors commonly teach the less experienced students. Teaching is considered an honor and is often a requirement for a higher rank. Many assistant instructors are both professional and knowledgeable about the art. But if the assistant instructors teach all of the classes and the master instructor only oversees the operation, are you still paying for a "professional" service? It is not wrong for the master instructor to separate himself from teaching and employ assistant instructors; it is only wrong if he advertises himself as the main instructor. You should know what you are paying for prior to signing up for classes. Making money is not unethical, but *how* one makes money may be perceived as such. Learn how to recognize potentially destructive moneymaking ideas. For example:

1. You sign up for classes, pay a monthly fee, and are told that you may attend as many classes as you would like. When you have studied for three months, the school owner limits your attendance to two classes per week and imposes testing fees at belt promotions. Although most schools have testing fees, my opinion is that once a student has reached a level where she is ready to test, she should test without paying an additional fee. Why? Because the student should be rewarded based on her knowledge and ability. She has already paid for the instruction required to reach the next level. My opinion is also that tournament fees should be paid by the spectators, and not by the participants.

2. Many schools incorporate black belt programs. These programs are designed for students who want to commit themselves to attaining the black belt. When you sign up for such a program, you are expected to reach black-belt level within a certain time frame. Your participation and commitment to the program, in turn, motivates other students to work harder so that they, too, can be part of the elite group. Let's say that your school, after implementing a black-belt program and running it for six months, starts charging an additional fee for black-belt students. Rather than preserving the program as a specialty for the elite, the school is recruiting as many students as possible to the program. Aside from the fact that the extra fee may seem like questionable business ethics, the problem with everybody belonging to an elite program is that the program loses its meaning; it becomes just another class. If your school has a black-belt program, in order for it to remain effective, it should be reserved for a select few, for those who have demonstrated commitment rather than ability to pay.

3. Your school requires beginning, intermediate and advanced students to wear different-colored uniforms, and requires that you buy achievement patches at regular intervals. Recognize that these kinds of ideas have no instructional value and may be questionable financial ethics.

In the 17th century, the Japanese swordsman Miyamoto Musashi pointed out that "the field of martial arts is particularly ripe with flamboyant showmanship, with commercial popularization and profiteering on the part of both those who teach the science and those who study it." (From the *Book of Five Rings*, translated by Thomas Cleary, Shambhala, 1993). So now that we have established that it is ethical for the instructor to charge for his services, but unethical for him to misrepresent himself or to charge for unnecessary items, let's talk about why a fee is ethical and how to set an appropriate one.

Some instructors charge a ridiculously low fee, such as 10 dollars an hour for a private lesson. Although the low cost of martial arts education might excite you, my experience is that these practices often have an adverse effect. For example, if the student is not required to pay for classes in advance, there is no monetary loss to the student if he misses a few lessons. We also tend to question the knowledge of an instructor who fails to charge for his services. A highly educated person naturally takes pride in his knowledge and deserves some form of compensation. Are you being fair if you allow your instructor to teach you at no charge and when you have exhausted his knowledge, you go to another school and pay for lessons? Paying for lessons is not only ethical, it is necessary; it forces you to value the lessons more. It is unethical only if the fee is outrageous. Find out what the customary rate is for martial arts instruction in your area. No matter how good the instructor, nobody's lessons are worth 500 dollars an hour, because you cannot possibly digest 500 dollars worth of information in an hour.

Some students seem seriously interested in learning the martial arts, but they consistently fail to pay on time. Failing to pay for lessons is disrespectful toward your instructor. Claiming that you can't afford to pay for lessons is a poor excuse. If you want to study, you have to pay. A young man once asked me to teach him the martial arts, but then said that he couldn't afford it. At first, I considered giving him lessons for free. I believed that his financial situation shouldn't prevent him from benefiting from learning the martial arts. But when I saw him lighting a cigarette, I lost my desire to help him. I reasoned that if he could afford his unhealthy habit, then I would lose integrity if I gave him martial arts lessons for free.

So how much should you pay for lessons? Most group classes cost about 80 to 100 dollars a month or slightly more, and the instructor may or may not be an experienced instructor. Private lessons range from 30 to 500 dollars an hour.

– INSTRUCTOR TIP –

If students are consistently late with their payments, my advice is to dump them. They are not worth dealing with. A student who is serious about training has no problem paying for instruction. The exception may be if you are teaching in a very poor community. If you choose not to charge for lessons, you should do so with prior understanding that you are engaging in charity work.

– STUDENT TIP –

When deciding whether or not to sign up for lessons, consider both your instructor's martial arts background and his dedication to teaching. As already stated, the world champion martial artist may not be the world champion instructor. If you fail to learn what you desire to learn, no instructor is worth the expense.

WORK ETHICS

Your instructor's level of organization and his work ethics may determine whether or not you continue beyond the first few lessons. I once made the rounds to different schools and observed the lessons. One school in particular made a favorable impression. The instructor at this school displayed exceptional work ethics. He employed a high work tempo and took part in the exercises. He had students do kicks across the room while he held focus mitts for them, running from one student to the next. In contrast, I have met instructors who were tired of the exercise regimen. They instructed verbally and oversaw the lessons, but failed to participate physically. Granted, those of us who teach many hours a day, year in and year out, get tired and don't always feel like participating in the classes. I have met a few instructors who have failed to change to proper uniform. They show up at the last minute, hold the lesson in street clothes, and end the class five or 10 minutes early. One instructor gave the students an assignment to practice, and then left the room and talked on the telephone for 20 minutes. Another instructor went to the barber next door to get a haircut in the middle of class, and this was when I had paid for a *private lesson!*

Your instructor's work ethics help set the pace for your own. The opposite is also true: If you come to class excited and ready to learn, your instructor is more likely to follow suit. Some students don't want to participate in certain exercises. Undoubtedly,

Work ethics require a willingness to participate in class activities, and often involve direct instructor participation in specific skill-building exercises.

students don't always enjoy every aspect of the art, but this doesn't mean that they should sit out whenever they feel like it. Discipline is your greatest friend and protector. Pushing yourself to do the things that you don't really enjoy or feel like doing at the moment will bring you greater satisfaction later.

Your instructor can motivate you, but you can also motivate your instructor. If you don't show up for classes several weeks in a row, you might discourage an otherwise good instructor from teaching. When you don't show up for class, you are being unfair toward your instructor. Yes, we all need a vacation now and then, but remember that your dedication to the martial arts is your instructor's "food" for teaching. Without it, he is of little value.

LOYALTY AND PHILOSOPHY

Many schools expect loyalty from their students. When I studied Aikido, I visited a rival studio because I was unhappy with my own. When I stepped into the new studio, they asked if I had received permission to study there from my other instructor. This might be an extreme example of the expectation of loyalty between schools. In today's business world, it is more likely that the new studio would welcome you with no questions asked.

Some instructors expect you to be loyal also toward the instructor's personal philosophies. Although your instructor wears many hats—teacher, mentor, friend, disciplinarian, psychologist—the question is to what degree she should exercise these roles. Although your instructor should be a role model that you strive to emulate, she should know her boundaries and avoid crossing the line. My opinion is that the instructor should give you emotional support as it applies to the martial arts. For example, she should know how to handle students during an emotional low, as when you have failed an exam or lost in a tournament. But she is not a counselor or psychiatrist; she is first and foremost a martial arts teacher, and you should not expect more of her. However, some students who sign up for the martial arts are not looking for fighting or self-defense skills, but for inspiration, religion or a sense of belonging. If this is you, and you happen to meet an instructor who focuses on the mental aspects of the arts, you may set yourself up for a relationship where the instructor intrudes on your way of living outside of the training hall. If your instructor tells you (or even suggests) how to live, she has, in my opinion, gone a step too far. A good instructor discourages these sorts of relationships, even if it is you, the student, who seeks it.

 ## SCENARIO 14

You are required to read a creed at the beginning of each class. The creed states that you will avoid anything that reduces your mental growth or physical health. What does this mean?

1. You will refrain from smoking and drinking alcohol.

2. You will only eat healthy foods.

3. You will stay at home and take care of yourself when sick.

4. You will study hard in school.

How do you define *mental growth* and *physical health*? What if your idea of a healthy living differs from the instructor's? It is a good idea to talk about the exact meaning of the creed and not assume that you understand its implications. Although a creed and belief system is often used to strengthen the focus and unity of the school, there may be many different meanings that can be read into the creed. In order to find a valuable meaning that works for you, define the creed and relate it to your personal experiences.

It is appropriate for the instructor to give emotional support, for example, when you have lost in a tournament.

NON COMPETITION CLAUSES

Most schools employ assistant instructors, and many schools require that students teach in order to advance to higher ranks. Teaching is a great learning experience that catapults you to new heights. If you are asked to teach, make sure you do so with the right objectives in mind. For example, if teaching is a requirement for advancement, but you discover that your instructor uses you simply because he needs the help and doesn't want to pay for it, ask yourself if it is ethical. Why? It *could* be ethical, but you should know why you choose to teach and be at peace with your decision. One school owner tried to convince me to teach children's classes, even though I would rather teach adults. He told me that kids are more challenging, so teaching them would make me a better instructor. My belief, however, was that he asked me to teach these classes because the student base was mainly kids, and this was where he needed help.

When you have studied and taught the martial arts for a long time, you gain insight. The school owner might now fear that you will open up your own school and compete with it for students. Some school owners ask you to sign a non competition agreement, a contract stating that you will not open a martial arts school in the same city. However, before agreeing to sign such a contract, make sure you understand what it means and are at peace with your decision. Start by considering that these contracts are unfair for several reasons, including:

1. Often, you *must* teach in order to advance. In addition, you probably don't get paid for teaching, but you are still expected to pay your regular dues at the school.

2. A noncompetition agreement is unconstitutional and is not likely to be enforced by a court of law. The Constitution states that we have the right to life, liberty and the pursuit of happiness. A contract that interferes with our pursuit of happiness — in this case, the pursuit of running a business such as a martial arts school — is unconstitutional. When I was asked to sign a non competition agreement, the school owner called his instructors into the office one by one, I believe, because it is easier to influence somebody who is alone without the support of his peers. "You and I have known each other for a long time now," the school owner told me, and proceeded to explain why I owed it to him not to open my own school. I interrupted and said that I couldn't sign the contract. I gave him the reasons: I was not getting paid, I was not an employee of the school, the contract was unconstitutional, and knowledge that I had bought through my membership dues was mine to do with as I wished. The worst that could happen was that he would kick me out of the school. But who would be the loser then? I was still paying my membership dues *and* I was teaching his classes for free! As it turned out, I continued studying *and* teaching at the school, and we never spoke of it again.

3. Knowledge that you have acquired is valuable because nobody can take it from you. Moreover, if there is no exchange of services or money, you are not

obligated to make concessions. If you have paid for lessons that have led to the black belt you are wearing around your waist, then you have engaged in a fair business exchange. What you do later with your acquired knowledge is up to you. Don't sign your life away.

My advice is to never sign a non competition agreement. At the very least, take a few days to gain a proper perspective prior to signing. Ask yourself what you will gain by signing or lose by not signing the contract, and how you will feel about it five years from now. Remember, you may still have 70 good years ahead of you. Much can happen in that time. Don't gamble away your future when you don't have to.

SEPARATION, PREJUDICE AND STEREOTYPING

Many schools group students into separate classes. For example, they may teach adults, teens and children separately, or they may teach men and women separately, or they may separate students by level of achievement and have sublevels within these major levels. I am generally against separating males and females, or adults and children, unless, of course, you are unable to have a good mix. Obviously, a class with one adult and 15 kids does not benefit the adult. Many children enjoy learning in an adult environment. (When I was a child, I wanted to go to gymnastics class with my mom, and not with other kids.) Sometimes, we are under the impression that children should be treated as children, that they should have more fun, more play time, than adults. But the definition of fun is subjective and up for debate. Many children are very serious about their training and find play time silly

when in martial arts class. When kids reach adolescence, they often enjoy being treated as adults more than as children, and prefer to be grouped with adults. Many people also want the martial arts to be a family activity. If the class is mixed, the instructor must avoid making the lessons too kid oriented, or the more serious adults and children will not benefit.

Consider how your school groups the students for activities within the class. In what type of environment do you learn best: when students of similar rank spar with each other? When women spar with women only? When kids spar with kids only? When students of similar height and weight spar with each other? Generally, I believe in grouping together students with similar levels of experience. If one student is much more advanced than his partner, the advanced student can't benefit fully from the exercise. However, this type of grouping is okay on occasion, as long as the instructor

Younger students normally do quite well learning together with older students. Adolescents tend to prefer to go to adult classes rather than to children's classes.

also tends to the needs of the advanced student. Before deciding which type of grouping you like, make a careful analysis of the actual benefits. Don't accept a specific grouping system without considering the pros and cons. If you believe that the current grouping doesn't benefit you, find out if there is another class you can attend that is more in line with your needs.

 ## SCENARIO 15

Your instructor tells you to pair up with other students and practice. There is an uneven number of students in the class, and you are consistently left without a partner. How should you handle it?

1. Ignore it, because you don't need the help of others.

2. Accuse others of being arrogant and boring.

3. Tell the instructor that you don't have anybody to work with.

4. Ask another pair if you can rotate in with them.

Sometimes, for whatever reason, there might be one student with whom nobody wants to work. If a student consistently ends up without a partner in an uneven class setting:

1. Make an effort to break the pattern by asking her to work with you.

2. If others don't follow your lead, consider bringing the problem to the instructor's

attention in private after class.

If you're not careful, grouping naturally leads to prejudice. Although we like to believe that we avoid judging others based on their looks, gender, age or unrelated activities, it is difficult to completely avoid prejudice. Perhaps you find men with earrings and long hair distasteful. Or perhaps you don't think women belong in the martial arts at all. But the world is comprised of all sorts of people, and when you're in the learning environment, you must keep your prejudices to yourself. Personally, I don't believe in separating men and women. Even if they receive identical training, it still implies the "separate but equal" philosophy, which we long ago concluded doesn't work.

Let's say you see a sign that advertises self-defense for women. What indication does it give you regarding the instruction?

1. Does self-defense for women indicate that the training focuses on rape prevention, since women are more likely to get raped than men?

2. If a man were to get raped, how would his self-defense skills differ from a woman's?

3. If you were to attend a class on self-defense for men, in what ways would it differ from the same class held for women?

4. Why would men look for and use different weapons or different methods of defense than women? Would a technique that works for a man not work for a woman, or vice versa?

5. Do we stress self-defense for women, because we think that women don't like to take classes together with men, or vice versa?

★★★★★

I have heard it said that women are physically more flexible than men. My own flexibility is quite poor, however, despite the fact that I am female. I have also heard it said that men are faster than women. Perhaps most men are faster than most women, but some women are faster than most men. In general, it can be said that more men than women are interested in the martial arts. But this does not give anyone the right to assume that women are more timid or are slower learners than men. The same is true for older students or students with disabilities. For example, people in their 50s are not necessarily slower learners than people in their 20s, and people with physical disabilities will likely compensate for them in other ways. Educate yourself on yourself. How does your build, flexibility, strength, speed and aggressiveness compare to other students? Avoid assigning specific qualities to other students based on their gender or looks, at least until after you have conducted enough research to support your beliefs. If a woman is flexible she should be given credit, not because she is a woman but because she is flexible. If a man is quick he should be given credit, not because he is a man but because he has speed.

When I took my first karate lesson, the instructor asked, "Are you a dancer? I can tell because you are very coordinated." The fact is that I have never studied dance, and the times that I have actually danced can be counted on the fingers of one hand. In other words, I am definitely not a dancer. But since the instructor didn't give me the opportunity to answer his question, he misjudged the reason for my coordination. Over all, it did not matter. However, it is a demonstration of how we tend to stereotype for good and bad.

 ## SCENARIO 16

A female student in your class is determined to dispel the myth that women are not as strong or as good as men in the martial arts. This creates a problem for the male students, not because they want to prove her wrong, but because she really *isn't* as good as they are. The male students are afraid they will hit the cocky female student too hard when she comes charging in. You are a man. How do you deal with it?

1. Bring more attention to the female student to try to boost her confidence, so she will stop trying to prove something.

2. Quietly tell the other male students to play along.

3. Call the female student aside and ask, "What is your problem?"

4. Spar with the female student and hit her to show that she isn't so tough after all.

5. Ignore it, and let the chips fall where they may.

★★★★★

One of my fellow female karate students had a similar attitude problem. When I asked her to spar using light contact, she said, "I can't do that!" She was going to hit hard no matter what. Equality is a sensitive issue and a difficult line to walk.

– INSTRUCTOR TIP –

Rather than pairing up students for exercises, have them form a line or a circle, taking turns attacking and defending. In this way everybody gets an opportunity to work with everybody else, and nobody will feel cheated or left out.

– STUDENT TIP –

Although the instructor should treat men and women equally and give them the same opportunities, he must avoid doing so at the expense of the male students. If you are a male student and a female student gives you problems, bring it to the instructor's attention after class.

RESPECT AND DISCIPLINE

A martial arts instructor I know says respect is so important that if you hurt another student, you will not be allowed to spar again until that student's injury has healed and she has returned to class. Is this ethical? Is it proper? My belief is that injuries (although most are minor) are inherent to the martial arts, and to sports in general. If my workout partner were banned from the school every time I got a bruise, black eye or sprain, she would be years behind her current level. Hurting another student in anger is a different matter, of course, but there are other ways to deal with that.

Your instructor is a disciplinarian in the sense that martial arts training should be somewhat strict and organized. For example, it is common to have students do push-ups for failing to follow the rules and etiquette of the training hall. Push-ups may also be assigned if students talk when they are not supposed to, if they fail to maintain their stance or are off balance, if they train with weapons and lose a weapon, or if they show up late for class. Personally, I enjoy push-ups. I think that it is a mild form of punishment that also has physical value. The threat of push-ups helps me focus on the lesson. However, if your instructor uses this form of motivation, the intent should never be to ridicule you or the other students. The intent should always be to increase the rate of learning and to help you grow stronger. Discipline should stay within the confines of the training hall.

Discipline, rules and procedures should be established from the start. It is interesting how much the instructor's reputation can affect the way students behave. In high school, I had a German teacher who simply had to walk through the hallway to draw a hush from the students. That's respect! However, respect is not always beneficial. If it instills fear, you may not want to study with this instructor at all. Once established, the instructor's reputation is difficult to change, even if he changes as a person. As you grow in the martial arts, take care to establish the reputation you want. My kickboxing instructor, Keith Livingston, has a mixed reputation depending on the audience and the topic of conversation. Among students of kickboxing, it goes like this:

"Who trained you?"

"Keith Livingston."

"Oh, no wonder you're so good!"

Among students of touch sparring, it goes like this:

"Who gave you that black eye?"

"Keith Livingston."

"I should have known. He has no control!"

Good or bad? It depends on your audience. Just make sure that others perceive you as you intend and that you establish the reputation you want.

– INSTRUCTOR TIP –

Whatever punishment routine you choose, it should never be self-serving; it should never be used simply because it is something your instructor used on you and this is your chance to get even.

– STUDENT TIP –

If you believe you are unjustly punished and your confidence is dwindling, it is time to bring it to the instructor's attention. Make sure you understand the instructor's reasons for administering discipline. If not, ask him to explain.

RULES AND RITUALS

Many instructors try to mold the student's attitude into humbleness. Modesty, courtesy, integrity, perseverance, self-control, indomitable spirit — these words are posted on the wall where I train. However, sometimes words tend to lose their meanings, especially when we repeat them too many times. What exactly do we mean by *self-control*, and why would you want it? Might there be a time when it is better not to have too much self-control?

When I was studying Aikido, my friend brought his 14-year-old daughter to class. She asked why we were kneeling and bowing, then said, "If it's anything religious, I don't want to do it." There is a school in my area that insists that the students wear a *gi* (uniform) in the colors of a religious university nearby. Although the instructor may have gone to school there, his religious views have no place in the martial arts.

If there is a student creed in your school, it should preferably be as neutral as possible. If you find a particular part of the creed offensive, try to paraphrase it in a slightly different way. Doing so may help you find a meaning that works for you. If the creed states that you should develop yourself in a positive manner, what does this mean? Developing yourself in a positive manner can mean many things to many people. To you, it might mean that you should not drink or smoke, but to a smoker it might mean that he should love his spouse and be considerate of others. Because "develop yourself in a positive manner" is so nonspecific, it is a good statement to have in a creed (though it is still a good idea to talk about what it means). Had the creed read, "I will not smoke or drink," it might have offended those who like to have a glass of wine with their spouses over dinner.

Most students have no problem with repeating words or sayings. But consider what to do if your instructor defines a word with which you disagree.

1. Is it absolutely necessary that you agree with your instructor? For example, suppose that courtesy is described as being polite and not interrupting in the middle of a conversation. But what if others are rude toward you? What if there is an

emergency, and you need to get your message across? There might be a time when being too courteous is destructive. Being polite is normally helpful, but if you are polite to the point that others take advantage of you, it may have an adverse effect.

2. When your instructor defines the sayings and rituals, rather than simply learning the dictionary definition of the words try to discover what the principles mean to you in particular;

Bowing when stepping into the training hall, and bowing to the instructor and other students prior to sparring, is a common ritual in most martial arts schools. When a senior instructor steps into the training hall in the middle of class, you might be expected to face the instructor and bow to him. One student I know found the bowing excessive, even offensive. He believed that it marked him as a human of lesser value than the person he was bowing to.

Most students have no problem adhering to common martial arts rituals, such as brief periods of meditation at the close of a lesson. If you are uncomfortable with the idea, try to think of how the ritual may benefit you personally.

It is not possible to please the tastes and preferences of every student, and certain rituals must be adhered to. If you have a problem with bowing:

1. Try to think of it as a gesture of respect, similar to a handshake in our Western society. It does not give you a stamp of lesser value. In fact, you elevate yourself when you bow to another person without feeling inferior.

2. Name a few things that make a senior instructor worthy of your respect.

Etiquette is common in the traditional martial arts. In my Aikido class, the atmosphere was quiet and friendly. The instructor demonstrated the techniques without explanation while the students were kneeling and watching. The techniques were then practiced in silence four times, twice on each side, and no questions were asked. Aikido was the first art that I studied. Since I couldn't relate it to other arts and wasn't allowed to ask questions in class, I found that adhering to this type of etiquette was difficult. However, the positive part about etiquette is that it makes us feel as though we are part of something special. This feeling of belonging creates enthusiasm and pride which, in turn, enhances learning. But rules and rituals have little meaning unless they are enforced with consistency and equality among everybody. For example, if the instructor allows a friend to step into the training hall without bowing, what does this communicate to the rest of us? It communicates that there is one set of rules for the students, and another for the instructor and his friend. If the instructor steps into the training hall without bowing when he thinks that nobody is watching, he creates a double standard that is difficult to respect.

Great unity comes through regimented training. Standing in lines and doing the moves together on command creates a sense of belonging. Slackers can't hide. *Kiais* (shouts) help students harness the energy in the direction of the strike. Regimented training is great for drill work. However, some students don't learn well in this type of environment. Many adults don't like to be yelled at, and children get stressed, especially if they think they are being yelled at in anger. Loud yells do not help a student who is easily intimidated. Discipline and a regimen that helps bring unity and purpose are good, but your instructor should not use discipline in order to exercise her desire to control you. A balanced environment is needed in order for great learning to take place. When learning the details of a technique, a liberal approach that allows students to ask questions is normally better.

– INSTRUCTOR TIP –

A good instructor makes the rules of the training hall habits in her own life as well. You should not break the rules just because nobody is watching. If bowing is required when stepping into the training hall, bow even when you are alone.

– STUDENT TIP –

The martial arts school is not a democracy. The customer (you) is not always right. If you can't adhere to the code of your particular school, you might want to consider studying a different art at another school.

4

Educational Tools

FURTHERING YOUR KNOWLEDGE

The longer you train in the martial arts, the more expert you become. But you must still further your skills if you are to remain competitive. The science of martial arts, much like technology, advances at a fast rate. Techniques and concepts that were taught 10 years ago may not be as valid today. Crosstraining and open attitudes toward different approaches to training have become more common with the emergence of mixed martial arts tournaments. It is easy to resist change, however, and inadvertently allow your qualifications to lapse when you have trained in a particular art for a long time.

It is nearly impossible to be a master of all styles of martial arts, even if you hold numerous black belts. You may not perform as flawlessly in arts that you once mastered. There are, after all, only 24 hours in a day. However, your theoretical knowledge does not need to die. The first art that I pursued (after my short stint in Aikido) was Ed Parker's Kenpo karate. A few years later I left Kenpo and studied kickboxing. Naturally, as time passed, I forgot many of the Kenpo techniques and forms; I could not perform them to the same level of perfection anymore. When I returned to Kenpo after several years of absence, my consistent focus on principles rather than on techniques paid off and gave me a broader understanding of the concepts of Kenpo.

 SCENARIO 17

You have questions about techniques that you have seen elsewhere. Your instructor tells you that those techniques are useless. What should you do?

1. Stop worrying about what others learn, since your art is the "true way."

2. Study another art in secret.

3. Argue with your instructor.

4. Talk about your instructor behind her back.

★★★★★

Your instructor doesn't need to be expert in other arts, but she should recognize the value of other arts and respond to your questions. She should be able to elaborate and preferably offer some unbiased insight. For example, you may have questions about the differences between hard and soft styles, or how scoring in competition differs between styles. You will know when your instructor is ignorant (or worse, arrogant) of the many years others have spent learning their art. Educate yourself on the strong and weak points of other styles. If you don't have the time or opportunity to study other arts, at least read about them or watch videos to further your education.

No learning experience is complete without taking a critical look at both sides of the equation. When my 10-year-old cousin, who was studying judo at the time, learned that I was taking karate he said, "Also nice!" A simple comment, yes, but wonderful. Give others credit for their efforts.

GATHERING INFORMATION

Passing the black belt test is not the end of your journey. As you advance through the ranks, you must constantly look for ways to improve yourself. Times change and new arts are introduced. A good student stays abreast of these changes. The UFC (Ultimate Fighting Championship) may be as far from traditional karate as you can get, but the contest's popularity has led many students to crosstrain in other arts. Although the introduction of new arts does not mean that a student of a traditional art must deviate from his fundamental beliefs, it does mean that he must be knowledgeable about other arts. If he ignores his education, he will cheat himself out of meaningful information. In order to stay competitive, we must embrace change. The same applies to instructors. Instructors are authorities. They, too, must know about new safety gear, new arts and new tournaments, and keep students informed. Consider using these information sources:

1. Books, videos and the Internet are great sources of information. Many websites include information about other arts and inform us of competition results.

2. Emailing other martial artists allows us to exchange views, training tips and information.

3. Visiting other schools and observing a lesson or two helps us understand what other styles have to offer.

4. Going to competitions and sitting in the audience allows us to gain perspective by observing techniques and behaviors from a distance.

5. Reading popular martial arts magazines helps us stay informed of the newest champions in each style and division.

6. Attending seminars helps us gain insight into our own art and sharpen our skills.

7. Fellow students with backgrounds in other arts can provide us with new techniques or old techniques presented in a new light.

GOING ON FIELD TRIPS

The field trip is a good educational tool. Prior to competing, attend a tournament as a spectator, or visit a school that teaches a different art than yours and sit in the audience and observe. The outside observer, especially one who has some experience already, can gain many benefits from watching others train so long as she has specific objectives in mind. When taking the role of observer, know what to look for and be ready to discuss your findings afterward. For example:

1. Look for ways in which the roundhouse kick differs between arts.

2. Look for ways in which strikes and kicks can be used in a grappling situation.

Most schools are accommodating once you have explained the reason for your visit. Ask your instructor if you may invite the students of another school to your school for a similar exercise.

If possible, allow field trips to coincide with the task you are currently studying. If you are preparing to attend your first tournament, observe a similar tournament a month or two in advance. If you are preparing for a belt promotion, observe a promotion a month or two prior to your own test. Some instructors prefer to keep the promotion a secret ceremony and are reluctant to allow students to observe. While the purpose of observation is to gain motivation to train and prepare for the test, not all instructors will allow you to take a seat in the audience.

When observing a test for a higher rank, the purpose of training will become more evident. Prior to my yellow belt test in karate, I had nightmares because I didn't know what to expect. When testing for orange belt, I observed the more advanced students test for purple and brown belts, and I was in awe. Upon returning home that day, I set my priorities straight. I knew what I needed to do to reach the higher levels.

Two of my kickboxing students are almost ready to test for a higher level, but one of them is more ready than the other. Since both take private lessons, they have never seen each other. I would like to bring the

When visiting other schools, observe how specific techniques are practiced. For example, if you normally apply the full Nelson from the rear, can it be done also from the front or from kneeling?

"slower" student in to observe the "quicker" student training, in the hopes that the exercise will give the slower student motivation to train harder.

– INSTRUCTOR TIP –

The requirements for a particular award should be clear. Students should know what the requirements are, so that they can prepare for the test. If a less-skilled student observes a more-skilled student training, make sure the exercise serves the intended purpose: to benefit the less-skilled or slower student. The observation should not act as a deterrent that causes the student to quit.

– STUDENT TIP –

When you get home after observing a belt pro-

motion, do a self-evaluation of your own readiness to test. Write a list of techniques and concepts that you need to practice.

USING EDUCATIONAL AIDS

It has been suggested that about 75 percent of all learning comes through visual observation. A smaller percentage comes through hearing and doing (we will elaborate on these ideas in Part 2). Martial arts lessons should include plenty of demonstrations and practice, and talk sessions should be kept to a minimum. If your instructor holds a half-hour lecture on what to do after you have unbalanced an opponent and taken him down, you are not likely to learn as much as if he actually shows you takedowns and allows you to practice the techniques. Verbal descriptions sometimes create different meanings in different people's minds. Visual demonstrations help decrease this tendency (although they may not eliminate it entirely), and ensure that the instructor and students communicate on the same level. Keep the following items in mind if your instructor uses visual aids:

1. Stand so that you can clearly see what he is showing you. Some schools require students to stay in their lines. If you cannot see the details of a demonstration and you are not allowed to move, ask the instructor to position himself in such a way that everybody can see.

2. The person who holds the demonstration may be required to assume different positions, depending on the particular technique she is demonstrating. For example, a demonstration of a joint lock against the wrist may require a different position than a demonstration of a kick.

3. If your instructor uses a student as a visual aid, try to position yourself so that you are not standing directly behind the instructor. Also, be aware that your position may block the other students' views of the technique.

4. If your instructor chooses to use you as a visual aid for his demonstrations, be aware that you may miss many of the details of the technique. It is often better to be an outside observer than to actively participate in a demonstration. If possible, ask to observe another pair of students doing the technique before you engage in partner practice.

Instructor demonstrations on a live person are normally helpful before the component parts of the technique are taught. You now have a mental picture of what is happening. Live demonstrations can also be done to show simple one-step techniques, such as the reverse punch. For example, a demonstration of the target, or a demonstration of the optimal distance between yourself and your opponent, will give you a point of reference when you practice the technique in the air later. Visual aids are also great tools for holding student attention. A long lecture will make less-attentive students drift off in thought. A visual demonstration, on the other hand, is likely to hold their attention and allow them to recall the technique later.

Educational aids, such as heavy bags and dummies or weight-training sets, should be used to enhance the learning process. Mirrors are great tools for fine tuning stance, positioning and technique. For example, you can use the mirror to correct a stance that is too upright, to correct the defensive position of your hands, or to widen or narrow your base for greatest mobility. A mirror eliminates doubt and confusion by showing you the exact position of your stance. If your instructor uses mirrors to correct your technique, make it a habit to correct yourself each time you come to class by standing in front of the mirror. Such self-evaluations are likely to make you more aware of future mistakes.

– INSTRUCTOR TIP –

Educational aids are great teaching tools but should not take precedence over good teaching technique. The person or equipment used for your demonstration should be an aid, *not a substitute for good instruction.*

– STUDENT TIP –

How good do you need to be? Do you need to be good enough to beat the toughest person in your school? If you are already the toughest, you will have little motivation to increase your skill. Another person's skill level can serve as

An explanation of the tool (fist) and target (nose) through a visual demonstration on a live person will help you develop a mental picture of the technique.

a catalyst for your own. Your peers are therefore good visual aids.

KEEPING RECORDS

When your instructor has provided you with the tools and training you need to practice your art, you may want to go a step further and consider how to make your own life easier beyond a particular lesson. Consider keeping a record of what you have learned, for the following reasons:

1. It helps you remember what you learned last time, and helps you think about issues you want to discuss in your next lesson.

2. It reminds you of your attendance, and makes it obvious if you cheat or cut classes. If you are often absent from class, you may want to talk with your instructor about setting some goals.

3. It helps you establish your credibility when it is time for a promotion to a higher rank.

4. It helps you create a manual of knowledge that is unique, that is truly yours, and that you can use to build lesson plans for teaching later in your career.

Record-keeping takes work, but it is well worth the effort. Not only will it help you clarify techniques and concepts, it may even allow you to accumulate enough information that you can organize it into an instructional book some day.

5

Practical Matters

STUDENT AND INSTRUCTOR LIABILITY

The instructor must exercise good judgment. He must know how to practice safe habits and how to handle difficult students. He must respect the needs of the more sensitive students. The instructor's and the students' personalities, stress levels, attitudes or health conditions can interfere with their respective ability to exercise good judgment. Judgment should be learned as part of the curriculum. It can be learned concurrently with technique training and sparring.

Unlike many teaching professions, the martial arts instructor does not need a license to teach. The unregulated nature of the martial arts is beneficial in the sense that everybody can share information freely without being held back by regulations, costs and time requirements that third parties can profit from. The martial arts do not relate directly to safety (not in the way driving a car or flying an airplane do), nor are martial arts skills required in order to get the job you want (at least not generally). A license that grants a person permission to practice the martial arts is therefore not essential. The diversity of the martial arts also makes it difficult to teach an instructor how to teach specific techniques. An additional problem with licensing martial arts instructors is that instructors teaching other instructors for cer-

tification may take financial advantage of their position. As a prospective student, ask for the instructor's credentials. Many martial arts instructors post their certificates on the wall and display their trophies in the window.

Both you and the instructor would be wise to learn about the legal system as well. For example, how much physical contact should the instructor use without risking a lawsuit? If he does get sued for hurting a student, how can he justify his position? When I was substituting for my kickboxing instructor a few years ago, I did some light contact sparring with the new students. The students seemed upbeat at the end of class, and I was under the impression that I had given them a constructive lesson. The next day, one of the female students — a good friend of a male student with whom I had sparred — requested to talk to me. To make a long story short, I got a verbal reprimand for using excessive contact and making the male student feel uncomfortable. I talked to some of the other students to get their input. In the end, the issue was never discussed again; however I could have supported my position by demonstrating that I was only half the size and weight of the student who complained. No blood or bruises had formed. Nothing had been said during or after the sparring session to alert me of his distress.

There was a sign above the door that read, "Full Contact Kickboxing," and it would have seemed unreasonable if the sparring had involved no contact.

As an instructor, I find it useful to keep records of how frequently students come to class. For example, if a student has come three times a week for the last two years and then gets a whiplash injury, it may be useful to show a record stating that she has attended class consistently for a duration of time. I also keep a record of how long I have been teaching, where and how I have gained my experience, and whether any complaints against me have surfaced. Some students give gifts or notes of thanks to their instructor upon passing a belt examination. I save any correspondence between my students and myself.

It is unlikely you will remain completely injury-free in any sport in which you participate for a long duration of time. In case of injury, negligence needs to be proven. Remember, however, that you are supposed to work together with your instructor, not look for opportunities to sue. Should anything questionable happen, make sure you record what happened, when and how it happened, who was involved, and whether there were any witnesses.

HOW OFTEN TO TRAIN

Practice is important, but you can reach a point where more practice may be harmful. The martial arts should not take over your life, and your instructor must be sensible when assigning homework. So, how often should you train?

People are individuals, and the amount and frequency of your training depends on your lifestyle (home conditions, work conditions, etc.) and your physical and mental characteristics. I see no harm in training every day, as long as you enjoy it and it benefits you. But if you get burned out or reach a plateau, this schedule may not be for you. On the other hand, taking Sunday off every week may work for some students but not for others. Which day of the week you take off, or even if you take a day off, must be decided individually. Some students may benefit from two or three long workouts a week, while others do better with seven shorter workouts. However, there is a point at which practice should be stopped. When I was new in the martial arts, I was eager to improve rapidly and believed that the more I practiced, the faster I would improve. I kept track of my practice sessions on a sheet of paper taped to my wall and tried to outdo my friend in time and frequency. It got to the point that I would get home from work at 11 p.m. and put in an hour or more of practice time. This was in addition to the practice session I had already completed in the morning. The next morning, I would get up and practice some more.

If you practice too much, other areas of your life may suffer. Eventually, training may become the same mundane grind every day, where you practice more out of guilt than for true improvement. Rather than keeping track of the number of hours you practice, a better way may be to set specific goals and work on specific tasks to accomplish these goals. For example, it is better to train for 45 minutes four days a week than to train for hours every day. If you can establish a concrete workout plan, 45 minutes are more powerful than long hours of boring work. Shorter training segments also give you time to accomplish your nonmartial arts activities.

Too much training can be an obstacle to learning. If your only goal is to test for a higher rank, as is often the case in the early stages of training, you may feel tempted to come to class both in the morning and in the evening. I have heard stories of people in China and Japan training all day from 5:00 in the morning until after sunset, while living on a meager diet and getting little sleep. This sort of discipline may be useful if you want to find your limits, but I question whether it really hones your skill (plus, I don't know if the stories are really true). A balanced schedule of three to four times a week, in addition to a half-hour practice at home before or after class to review techniques, should be just about optimal for most students. My opinion is that it benefits you more to go to class twice a week and practice at home once between classes than to go to class five times a week and not practice at home at all. Too much information, especially in the early stages, is difficult to digest. It is better to limit the number of new techniques and spend some time to refine them on your own.

Underscheduling classes is not good, either. You need to review material and have the opportunity to ask questions before too much time has passed between training sessions. If two to three weeks pass between lessons, it may be difficult to remember where you left off. Your instructor may also resist recommending you for a promotion if you only come to class twice a month. There should be a certain commitment in order for you to advance. Part of proper scheduling is the instructor's responsibility, but you can help by having the right

mindset. You are wasting your time and money if you come to class haphazardly. If you have financial problems, I recommend talking to your instructor about the possibility of taking lessons in spurts. For example:

1. Come to class twice a week for a month, then take a month off and practice at home. Then come back to class twice a week for another month. This type of scheduling allows you to work with your instructor on specific short-term goals.

2. Keep a record of what you learn as a reminder of what to practice at home during downtime. When you come back to class, your instructor can give you a mini-test on the material to further motivate you to continue practicing at home.

3. Your instructor can help motivate you by calling you once a week to check on your progress and to answer any questions you may have.

DEALING WITH INJURIES

Although the training conditions should be clearly stated and agreed upon by both instructor and student, you must understand that some injuries are inherent to all sports. Be honest with yourself on the subject of pain and injury. After all, you are learning a fighting art. It is unlikely that you will go through your career as a fighter without sustaining any injuries. Take precautions and give your injuries proper care; use protective equipment (pads, braces and tape) to protect an already-injured limb. Be aware that jewelry can get in the way and injure you or your workout partner. Look for rings, wristwatches, bracelets and necklaces on your training partner, as well as ankle bracelets and earrings that hang from the lobe. Today, with body piercing so popular, students may be wearing jewelry that is not visible but that can nonetheless cause problems.

Your instructor has an obligation to supervise sparring and partner drills. But many instructors fail to supervise heavy bag or mitt work. If the mitt holder holds the mitts incorrectly, injury can result both to the holder and the practitioner. When striking mitts, pain is usually an indication that you are not hitting the device correctly.

1. When punching, your wrist should be straight and your fist tight. When kicking, your toes should be curled back or extended, depending on the type of kick you throw.

2. If you use a *makiwara* board for striking, you will get a visible indication of whether or not you are striking the board correctly. The straighter the strike, the less abrasive effect the board has.

3. Correct striking technique is important, not only to avoid injury, but also to attain power. If a strike skids on impact, power is decreased.

4. Correct distance is crucial to power and injury prevention. If you are too far away from the target, you risk hyperextending the elbow joint. If you strike a swinging bag and your fist isn't tight when the bag swings toward you, the additional impact may buckle your wrist.

5. It is easy to jam the fingers when working finger jabs on a bag or shield. A piece of paper or thin cardboard may be a good device for practicing finger jabs.

6. Consider how to position your hand when using *shutos* (knife hand) and ridge hand strikes. How can you avoid injury to your hand or wrist?

Your instructor should not leave classes unattended for even short periods of time, and should ensure that the equipment is in good condition. You can help by checking the equipment before using it. A good equipment check includes examining hinges on heavy bags and checking carpet and floor areas for evenness. I once stepped off the edge of a grappling mat and twisted my ankle. When kicking a freestanding heavy bag with a Thai-attachment, a fellow student of mine slammed his foot against the metal pole in the middle of the bag. Luckily, he didn't break any bones, but he got a significant lump on his instep. Point out potential hazards to your instructor and peers.

Tell your instructor about any previous injuries so that you can avoid aggravating

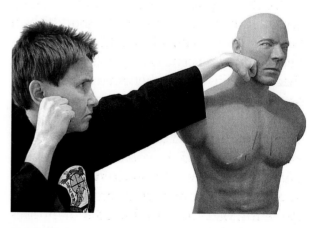

Having a bent wrist when you impact the target may cause injury to your hand.

them. Knowing first aid is advisable. You should at least know how to treat minor injuries, such as nosebleeds, and be able to help your peers recover when getting the wind knocked out of them. One of my fellow students was taken off balance through a foot sweep and banged the back of his head against the carpeted floor. When questioned, he said he was okay. But soon thereafter he started complaining about a headache and blurred vision. It is recommended that you see a doctor for any head injuries.

What about noncontact training? Noncontact training is fine, if that's what you believe in. But if you are training for self-defense, the ability to develop realistic skills requires training with at least some contact. Training to hit real targets allows you to work on penetrating power and target accuracy. It also teaches you to take a strike without getting stunned from the blow.

Pay attention to how capable you are of working the exercises that your instructor assigns you. I once took lessons from an assistant instructor who had students of all ages and backgrounds doing back flips. This instructor might have been to a tournament and seen musical forms with back flips, or he might have seen a Jackie Chan movie, or he might have been a gymnast. The point is that if your instructor doesn't use common sense, then the burden falls on you. If your instructor tells you to do 50 push-ups but you are ready to faint from exhaustion when you have done 25, listen to your body and take a break, even if you draw attention to yourself. On the contrary, a slower or weaker student should not be allowed to hold back the whole class. Martial arts are about com-

bat and traditionally the instructor would push students to the breaking point. Just make sure that when the instructor pushes, he is knowledgeable and pushes you for the right reasons.

 SCENARIO 18

Is it a good idea to bring a water bottle to class and pause frequently to drink?

1. Yes, if you are careful not to spill the water.

2. Yes, as long as it is really water in the bottle and not coffee.

3. Yes, if you bring enough for the rest of the class.

4. No, you should wait until after class to drink.

5. No, not unless the instructor offers the other students a "drinking pause."

Is it a good idea to drink water during workouts? Some schools discourage drinking, either because they don't want the distraction or they see it as a sign of weakness and working through the uncomfortable experience makes us stronger. Others claim that water settles in your stomach and makes you sick during training. Some schools believe in raising the temperature in the training area by a few degrees so that students sweat more and "burn more weight." I do not recommend training in excessive temperatures. Heat, along with exercise and protective gear, is not a good combination.

In rare instances, heat exhaustion can kill you.

Research has demonstrated that it is good to drink before, during and after exercise. Furthermore, you can be dehydrated before you feel thirsty. If you participate in a less-strenuous lesson, however, you can drink before the start of the lesson. If you do a lot of bag work, heavy sparring or grappling, you should consider drinking during the workout or between rounds as well. Drinking often in small amounts keeps you hydrated and makes you less likely to get sick than if gulping down a gallon of cold water all at once.

Finally, speak up if you are getting hurt. As an instructor, I like to ask my students if they want the tough workout or the wimpy one. They know that they have to choose the tough one, of course, but if your instructor appears too tough, you may not have the courage to tell him when you are hurt. In a class I taught, I had the students hold kicking shields for each other. I had neglected to tell them how to properly hold the shield, and one lady got hurt because she was leaving a gap between the shield and her body. I had no idea she was hurt until the next day when another student brought it to my attention. The lady was new to the class and fearing she would appear wimpy, had not dared to speak up. Some students are also afraid to ask questions during class. If you know of common mistakes that less-experienced students make, you may want to volunteer the information before the need to ask arises.

– INSTRUCTOR TIP –

Pay attention to your students' physical health. Not everybody who says, "I can't!" *says so out of laziness or lack of confidence. Tell students that it is okay for them to ask questions about their health.*

– STUDENT TIP –

It is okay for the instructor to push you to your limits, as long as she knows where those limits are. She should be careful with pushing you past your limits. Injuries are destructive to future practice. Telling your instructor that you are hurt does not indicate a lack of "heart." Ultimately, you are responsible for your own health.

SUMMARY OF A NEGATIVE LEARNING ENVIRONMENT

Before we move on to the next section about the principles of learning, let's summarize what constitutes a negative learning environment. Understanding the negative aspects gives us insight into the positive ones. If you can meet your instructor halfway, you have taken a step on the road to becoming a better student. If you dislike your instructor, you are not likely to continue studying under him. Although the instructor cannot please every student, both the instructor and student should be aware of certain ethical and instructional issues. To summarize:

1. Some instructors are reluctant to teach the "real thing," especially to kids. But it is difficult to break years of bad habits if the instructor has taught a watered-down version of the art. If the instructor is concerned that students will hurt each other, she can be selective with the techniques that she teaches. But kids and beginning students should still be taught the real thing, in order to give them a healthy foundation for learning of techniques and concepts in the future.

2. Some instructors teach extremes: "*Never* do this," or "*Always* do that." Let me give you a couple of nonmartial arts examples. I have been teaching people to fly airplanes for many years. There are many ways to position the airplane when doing the run-up of the engine prior to takeoff. Some pilots like to turn the nose into the wind. Others like to position the plane so they can see the approach path to the runway. Both are correct, but circumstances such as wind speed could affect one's decision. During a flight review I conducted with another pilot, I sensed a defensive attitude from the start. While taxiing to the runway, he asked how I like to position the aircraft during run-up and explained to me his method before I had time to answer his question. In a writing class I took in college, we were to be evaluated by our peers. One student said, "Never, *ever* end with a preposition!" Yes, one should normally not end with a preposition, but never *ever* is a step too far. More than one path leads up the mountain, and your experience and personality traits give you many ways in which to reach your goals. You can communicate more clearly when you allow yourself to break the rules on occasion. Avoid using extremes. Zero tolerance fails. Following perceived absolutes hinders performance.

3. Miscommunication or comments by people not schooled on the subject can be misleading. For example, when there is an accident in aviation, the news reporters often say, "The pilot did not file a flight plan." The general public does not understand that most pilots who fly for their personal enjoyment often do not file a flight plan when flying in the vicinity of the airport or on cross country flights in good weather. Filing a flight plan is neither required nor needed. Despite the fact that a flight plan was irrelevant to the reported accident, to the uneducated person it appeared as though the pilot was careless. Few things are black and white. How and what we do is often governed by the circumstances.

4. The instructor should recognize when a student's behavior will help and when it will hinder. In a kid's class, a little girl about six years old was beating another student of about the same age in sparring, and enjoying every bit of it. This girl had all the elements required of a great kickboxer, and I thought that somebody should talk to her parents about the possibility of giving her special training. But the instructor kept stopping the sparring (even though nobody was getting hurt), telling the girl that her fighting was "garbage." The point is that when a student has a special talent, this talent should be recognized and built upon rather than discouraged.

5. Students are interested in their own progress when they come to class (they have a right to be), and not in the martial ability of the instructor. A seminar is a great opportunity for the instructor to place his skills on display. Although the instructor's demonstration is an indication of the *instructor's* ability in the art he is practicing, it does not really do much to help the student improve. The primary job of the instructor is to enhance

the skills of his students, not to place his own skills on display.

6. Many assistant instructor-students lack knowledge of how to teach. They have only been told *what* to teach, not *how* to teach. The resulting instruction is thus disorganized and unsupervised, conducted by an instructor who is merely a student himself. Assistant instructors should be educated. When you become one, do your best to seek information about the martial arts and particularly about *teaching* the martial arts.

7. The instructor should avoid making unreasonable demands. She should not ridicule the students, for example, by walking away shaking her head when your technique is unsatisfactory. The task the instructor assigns you should be difficult enough to present a challenge, but enough to attain within the scope of your training time and experience. Impossible goals, at any level, retard learning. Sarcasm should be avoided; it can be misunderstood. For example, if the instructor says, "Great kick! Keep kicking like that, and you're likely to kill someone!" is she being sarcastic or is she giving you a compliment?

8. Instructor and student impatience retards learning. If instruction is geared toward the slower student, the quicker students are likely to get frustrated. One instructor said that he wouldn't teach anybody anything new until all students had caught up, so that they could learn together. But martial art training, although conducted in a group setting, is an individual activity. When you attain

a goal, you should be encouraged to advance to the next step regardless of where your peers are in the learning process. You sign up for classes because you have a desire to learn, and when you have a desire the doors should be open.

9. Learning cannot be forced, or as has been said: "You can lead a horse to water, but you cannot make it drink." In order for learning to take place, you must be ready to learn. An instructor who claims that she can't teach a particular technique because you are not ready for it is giving you lip service. If you ask to be taught a new technique, you probably have the desire to learn it. If you have the desire, you are most likely ready and should therefore be taught. If you really aren't ready, it is the instructor's job to get you ready. Both the instructor and the student must work toward the goal of improving the student. The best instructors are in it for the journey, and not for a payoff in personal gain.

10. Many students develop a friendship with their instructor. When socializing outside of class, you may see the instructor in a less-than-admirable light. This may complicate the relationship to the point that you lose respect for your instructor. When respect is lost, the learning process is harmed. I married my flight instructor. But once we were married, I prefered flight lessons from somebody else.

As you can see, your relationship with your instructor and peers can be complicated and require many skills beyond martial arts or athletic ability.

Part Two
Principles of Learning

6

Principles of Learning

LEARNING GOOD SKILLS

Many adults marvel at the way a small child can repeat the alphabet, or point to the many countries on a world map and name them all correctly. But would it be fair to say that this child has developed a skill? Suppose the same child comes home from school one day and says, "Mommy, Daddy, I can read!" You get the books out of the child's backpack and listen as she reads out loud to you. Has the child developed a skill? Today, when reading is second nature to you, how many times have you caught yourself reading a paragraph and having no idea what you just read? Does merely *being able* to read make reading useful? Does the ability to name the countries of the world evoke insight and understanding of the people who live there? Anyone off the street can imitate the roundhouse kick on her first try, with just the slightest amount of coaching. If you spend one week with this person and teach her to memorize 100 techniques, would it be fair to say that she has developed the skills of self-defense?

It takes time and opportunity to learn. Your primary responsibility as a student is to learn good skills until you understand your art completely: every movement, every concept. Part of learning encompasses mechanics of technique; the other part encompasses proper thinking. If you simply learn technique, you will never understand your art completely. When you truly understand technique *and* concept, you are indeed a rare individual.

WHAT IS LEARNING?

Learning can be broken down into the following stages:

1. Rote

2. Understanding

3. Application

4. Correlation

Rote: The first stage of learning is called *rote*, also referred to as the *mechanical* stage. When you have reached this stage, you can repeat information by memory without understanding or being able to apply the information properly. Performing mechanically is necessary in the early stages of training before you have gained insight into the art you are studying. You must have at least some experience before you can start learning concepts. Learning specific defenses to specific attacks may work well in a classroom setting. But if one element changes, such as the speed with which the attack occurs, or if there is a sudden distraction or a different target becomes available, the mechanical stage is insufficient.

Understanding: The second stage of learning is called *understanding*. When you reach this stage, you can explain how to do a technique and why, but you are not necessarily proficient in its execution. Your instructor should not assume that you understand the technique just because you were present when he taught it. Your instructor can gain an indication of your understanding by asking you to explain as much as possible about the technique; he can prompt you by asking why and how a technique is to be done. You can use this same method to enhance your own learning process. Whenever you have learned a new technique, take a few minutes after class to paraphrase the technique in your mind. Dissect the technique by asking yourself "why" and "how."

The study of martial arts is not a mindless act. Good understanding evokes insight; it gives the techniques meaning and eliminates simple imitation of performance. When you have gained a basic understanding of the art you are studying (after having received instruction in particular techniques), try to explain these techniques to one of your peers before you execute them. A good way to acquire an understanding of techniques and concepts is to teach them to other students.

1. Regardless of whether or not you intend to pursue teaching, explaining to others how and why a technique is done is a good learning tool, even at the beginning stages.

2. Teaching others forces you to think. If you are unable to answer a question someone poses, you must find the answer through independent study or by asking someone else.

3. When you can explain techniques correctly, you have demonstrated evidence of understanding.

4. When you reach the intermediate and advanced levels and assist teaching, you may be able to explain the concepts of a technique you have not yet learned, simply because the technique is similar to another technique you have already learned.

Theoretical understanding alone may not enable you to perform the technique. Proficiency in performance comes over a period of time and practice. But proficient performance without understanding is mechanical and useless in a situation that requires adaptation to the circumstances. Understanding and performing therefore go hand in hand and should be nurtured together. Generally, you can perform a technique with reasonable proficiency before you develop insight. The reason is because you are learning by rote initially. Occasionally, a few students develop a very good understanding of the techniques but lack the motor skills to coordinate and perform them with proficiency.

Application: The third stage of learning is called *application*. When you reach this stage, you can perform the technique nonmechanically in sparring or in real life. But don't assume that you can apply a technique under changing circumstances just because you demonstrate understanding. Knowing and learning are different things. Anybody can recite a series of techniques, but true learning takes place when the techniques become meaningful and you can apply your knowledge. You must progress beyond rote in order to use a skill; however, it is not always obvious when this progression occurs. Since many martial arts are comprised of long sequences of moves, it may seem as though you can apply your skill when you have really only memorized the moves. You can test your understanding and ability to apply the techniques by demonstrating your skills under less predictable circumstances, and by asking yourself the "W questions":

1. **W**hat is the purpose of the technique?

2. **W**hen would I use it?

3. **W**ho would I use it against?

4. **H**ow are the moves put together?

5. **W**hy this way?

6. **W**hat if . . .?

Many instructors don't go beyond the application stage of learning; they feel that the student has now reached his goal. Even more common may be the instructor who doesn't know how to take the student beyond the application stage. You must therefore make an effort to take yourself beyond this stage, and to extract additional details from the information the instructor has already given you. At the advanced levels, the instructor-student relationship should change into mutual learning and exploration. The goal should be to analyze and discover together.

Correlation: The fourth and highest stage of learning is called *correlation*. When you reach this stage, you understand how the material relates to other material that you have not yet learned. You can now use what you have learned from one technique and apply it to another. Or you can use what you have learned in a stand-up art and apply it to a grappling art, and vice versa. For example, if you study karate and a student of grappling suddenly takes you to the ground, using your striking techniques along with your understanding of balance and leverage to subdue your opponent demonstrates that you have reached the correlation stage of learning. You can now teach yourself new techniques and concepts and answer questions about techniques that you have never practiced or experienced. When you understand the underlying principles of learning, you will begin to see similarities between different arts and will come to appreciate other arts more.

Application = Give a man a fish, and he will eat for a day.

Correlation = Teach a man to fish, and he will eat for life.

You can reach the correlation stage of learning by constantly exploring how one technique or concept is similar to or relates to another technique or concept. For example:

1. When learning the horizontal elbow strike, start by reviewing the hook, since both strikes follow the same *striking pattern*.

2. After learning the horizontal elbow strike, learn the related downward elbow strike, since both strikes utilize the same *striking weapon*.

Correlation also takes place when you relate the current week's lesson to the previous week's lesson, or when you put theory into practice. For example, rather than practicing aimless heavy bag work, be conscious of what is happening around you. Ask somebody to provide distractions to show you the effects of frustration and split focus.

FACTORS OF LEARNING

Why do you study the martial arts? When you sign up for a program, take some time to determine your goal.

1. Is it physical fitness?

2. Is it self-defense?

3. Is it discipline?

4. Is it personal growth?

5. Is it competition?

Traditionally, the martial arts are learned in a formal setting. Moves are performed in unison, questions are not asked during class, and rituals are adhered to. In this type of environment, you learn through repetitive drill work and through the instructor's skill at presenting the material. In contrast, many of the modern arts encourage student participation. The classroom setting is more relaxed and students are likely to participate in discussions. Although discussion and active student participation create a good learning environment, it is not always appropriate for the martial arts.

You will progress faster if you have is a reason to learn. You create purpose when you stress the value of what you have learned and set goals that you want to achieve. Belt promotions and tournaments may serve this

 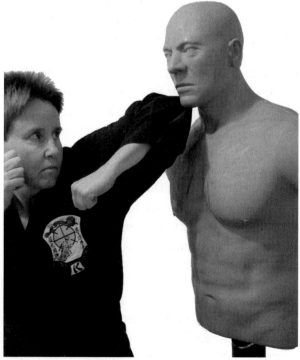

A hook (left) and an elbow strike (right) follow the same striking pattern. When would you use either technique? When would you use the roundhouse kick versus the hook?

purpose. Intermediate steps, such as a "half-rank" or an extra stripe on your belt, are often desirable because they help you to see your progress clearly. Goals, regardless of whether they are short-term or long-term, need to be tangible (clearly defined) throughout the learning process. New material should be related to the goals you have set. You must also be ready, willing and able to learn in order for learning to take place. Merely complying with the instructor's desires, without displaying your own true desire to learn, will result in little retention. The best learning happens when you can meet the instructor halfway.

Lessons that evoke insight stimulate learning. Insights eventually occur to some degree, whether or not the instructor is present. But if you learn by trial and error you are likely to experience frustration or feelings of defeat. You can speed up the learning process by using a number of tactics that make you more receptive to learning.

1. **The first thing learned is normally what you will remember best.** It is difficult to unlearn mistakes, so take great care in learning the basics correctly from the start. Introducing complex material before you have mastered the basics may be confusing and lead to poor habits. However, we tend to categorize material as "beginning" and advanced, without really analyzing whether the "advanced" material really is more complex.

2. **Interesting lessons increase the hunger to learn.** If the lesson is boring, little progress will be made. However, you may not realize that it is the instructor who is boring and not the material pre-

sented. If this is the case, you will leave class believing that the martial arts are not for you. Too much talking at the early stages may also be destructive. It is better if lessons are dramatic and allow you to experience the martial arts firsthand.

3. **You will learn more when you are active than when you are passive.** There must be some activity in order for learning to take place. Listening, to be productive, must also be active. You can listen actively by taking notes, asking questions and participating in discussions.

4. **Practice is essential to learning.** When a new technique is introduced, it is important that you to practice it right away while the material is still fresh on your mind. Perhaps the greatest value of practice is when you learn how one move or technique relates to another. When you are able to discern relationships between moves or techniques, verbal instructions will come to mean more.

5. **Realistic situations reinforce learning.** You can remain challenged and motivated by working on activities that allow you to apply your knowledge and skill. When you have learned a new technique, seek additional applications on your own to stimulate learning.

6. **Having a plan helps you learn.** You are more likely to remain interested when you know where you are headed. Make sure you have a clear understanding of what is expected of you and the standards you are being measured against. Good performance should be recog-

nized. Learning is reinforced when others notice your efforts.

7. **Overcoming learning plateaus counters feelings of frustration.** A learning plateau, where the rate of learning has slowed or ceased completely, is a common phenomenon. Learning plateaus normally happen to most of us at some time in our training. The instructor can help you break through the plateau by finding a more efficient way of teaching. The problem may also be that your interest has declined or you have reached some personal limit. If you have reached a limit in your physical capacity – for example, you are unable to attain the flexibility needed to execute a particular kick – try to divert your focus to another area that allows you to make progress.

8. **How quickly you learn depends to a degree on your past experiences.** If you can relate the new material to something that is familiar to you, learning will come more easily. For example, I speak three languages: English, Swedish and German. Since most languages are related in some way, when you know three languages, learning a fourth language is relatively easy. For example, the first word in a sentence written in an unfamiliar language may be similar to Swedish, the second word may be similar to English and German, the third word may be similar to German, and the fourth word may be similar to Swedish and English. The same principle applies to learning the martial arts. Students who have achieved a black belt in one art can normally achieve a black belt in a different art more quickly than their peers.

 SCENARIO 19

Should the wheel that squeaks get the grease? If your instructor thinks you have an ego problem because you always want to be in the spotlight, what should he do?

1. Tell you that satisfaction should come from within.

2. Pair you up with a more advanced student to give you a humbling experience.

3. Brag about you in front of the other students.

4. Promote you to assistant instructor.

Learning good skills requires more than a physical ability to perform them. Improvement doesn't happen by itself. Your instructor must clearly intend for you to improve. He must recognize your mistakes, make an effort to correct them, and constantly work to maintain your motivation. Your instructor must take a personal interest in your progress and deliberately plan for you to succeed.

– INSTRUCTOR TIP –

If your student squeaks for more information or is overly anxious about showing you what she knows, give her a more challenging technique. For example, if she can throw a great spinning back kick, show her the jump spinning back kick and ask her to demonstrate three uses of the kick at the next time.

If you are hungry for more information, consider what you can do to draw attention to your skill during the next belt promotion. For example, make up your own form and ask your instructor if you may demonstrate it the next time you test for a higher rank.

TRANSFER OF LEARNING

Lessons should be organized so that the material is taught in a logical sequence. A common method is to go from the simple to the complex. You want to find a path that logically helps you climb higher. But if you practice a technique only once or twice before moving on, you are not likely to develop proficiency with the technique. Learn a few moves first, then practice on bags or with your peers, then learn more moves, and finally tie them together. Mixing different practice drills can help you avoid boredom. If you participate in a large class or practice the same technique for 20 minutes or longer, and the instructor doesn't help you or give you advice, speak up and ask a particular question to get your instructor's attention.

Learning the complex before the simple has been mastered may interfere with learning. But we must first define simple and complex. For example, is a doctor's job more complex than a nurse's? Is an airline pilot's job more complex than a flight attendant's? Perhaps a doctor and an airline pilot would like to have more complex or more advanced skills, but do they really have them? A nurse is in a different profession than a doctor, and a flight attendant is in a different profession than a pilot. Consider this: Which is more complex, a spinning back fist or a reverse punch? Most people would say that the spinning back fist is more complex. However, sometimes what we learn last seems more complex, regardless of the type of move. Thus if we learn the spinning back fist before learning the reverse punch, the spinning back fist might seem like the less complex of the two. When you want to learn a technique required for a higher rank and your instructor tells you it is too complex for your level, is she speaking the truth? She *could* be speaking the truth, but is she necessarily doing so? A better way may be for your instructor to explain that you need to pass the yellow belt level before she will

Which is more complex: a spinning back fist (left) or a reverse punch (right)? Why?

teach you techniques for the blue belt level, in order to ensure that you don't neglect training in the basics.

It is also important to differentiate between basic and beginning. A basic technique is a technique that all other techniques are built upon. For example, the front kick is a basic technique because it is straight and relatively easy to learn, but more importantly, because the mechanics of the front kick are used for most other kicks as well. When you throw a roundhouse or side kick, for example, you start it the same way you start the front kick: by raising the knee high. But although the front kick is a basic technique, it is not necessarily a beginning technique. The front kick is used consistently throughout your training and in the highest forms of competition. We must therefore be steadfast and practice it with consistency. I remember a student of intermediate rank who was offended by the fact that he was trained in the same techniques as the beginning class. He misunderstood the word *basic* by *equating* it to beginning.

Although the front kick is basic, it is one of the most versatile of techniques. Name a stand-up art that doesn't teach it.

But what about reversing the procedure and going from the complex to the simple? Sometimes it helps to know at least what the complex technique looks like.

1. Ask to see a technique in its entirety before learning the individual moves. Getting the full picture early in your training might help you know what you are trying to achieve. It might also instill motivation.

2. Break the technique down into smaller segments. When you have learned one segment, ask your instructor to illustrate that segment again so you can see how it fits into the technique as a whole.

HOW WE LEARN

People respond differently to the methods of learning. While some students want a lot of verbal background information, others need hands-on experience early in their training and only a few verbal commands. Since most martial arts instruction involves teaching many students simultaneously, finding a learning situation that helps all students in the most efficient way may prove difficult. If you ask the right questions, you might alter your instructor's teaching style so that it benefits you in particular. But in order to do this, you must be aware of how you learn. Generally, it is not enough to ask yourself whether you learn better by listening, seeing or doing, because most people are not aware of which method works best for them in particular. I know from past experience that I am primarily an auditory learner.

Learning by listening: If you learn well by listening, you will benefit from an instructor who gives you specific verbal commands. For example, rather than showing you which direction to step in a form, she might tell you, "Step forward and strike with an inward *shuto* to the forearm." As an instructor, I have found that many students like to break a technique into its component parts. Therefore, I like to number each segment and call it out — *One, one-two, one-two-three,* etc. — until the students can perform the whole technique smoothly. If you learn by listening, it is also likely that you will ask questions or verbalize the techniques. Since I know that I learn best by listening, I have found it helpful to talk to myself while learning. I don't necessarily talk out loud, but I do like to paraphrase each step to myself: *Use the hand on the opposite side of the grab, the leg that is closest to your opponent is the one that steps,* etc. I even do this with my eyes closed to cut out the visual sense. Or if I keep my eyes open, I often don't register what I see.

Verbalizing the material may be an invaluable learning tool, because it forces you to think through each step of the technique and pay attention to detail. Explain the technique to a friend at home. If you can do this in a way that makes sense to a nonmartial artist, it is an indication that you have gone beyond rote learning.

Some students verbalize in the middle of the instructor's demonstration. As long as it doesn't interfere with the lesson (if it is a private lesson, for example), the instructor should allow the verbalization to continue, even if it seems as though you are interrupting her. If verbalizing helps you learn the technique, the instructor (not you) should adapt. Explaining the technique to your instructor or to a fellow student can also be

effective, and may eliminate the need for you to talk to yourself during the lesson.

Learning by seeing: If you learn well by seeing, you may find it confusing if your instructor talks each time he demonstrates a technique (as one of my private students pointed out to me). If possible, try to position yourself so that you can easily see what your instructor is demonstrating. Many martial arts schools position students by rank. Thus not every student is in the ideal position for observing techniques. If you learn best by hearing, you may not mind being placed in the back row, as long as you can hear what the instructor is saying. But if you learn best by seeing, you may want to suggest that the instructor allow students to position themselves so they can easily see the demonstrations. It is also a good idea for the instructor to both show and tell, so that the majority of students can benefit.

Learning by doing: If you learn well by doing, it won't matter how many times your instructor shows you the technique, or how many times she says, "I've *told* you a thousand times . . ." If you don't actually get to do the moves, you won't learn. Students who learn best by doing sometimes mimic the instructor's moves while she is demonstrating the technique. Although this may seem disrespectful, a good instructor avoids punishing or scolding the student until she knows the underlying reasons for the behavior.

Many people believe that everybody learns best by doing, but this is not the case. How we learn is an individual matter. Few people, however, use only one method of learning. Most of us learn through a combination of listening, seeing and doing.

When you have discoverd what type of learner you are, you must then decide you process information. Some students learn "from the inside out," while others learn "from the outside in." In simple terms, this means that some students want small bits of information which they can put together to form the full picture. Others need to see the full picture first, so that they can break it into its component parts. When learning forms, for example, the instructor might teach each segment separately, without telling you how long the form is or demonstrating it in its entirety. Or he might demonstrate the full form first to give you a feel for where he is taking you, and then teach each segment separately. I used to think that the latter was the better approach, but this is not necessarily true. Students who favor the latter approach may argue, "What's the joy in learning if you don't know where you're

If you learn well by doing, experiencing the technique and touching each target may help accelerate your rate of learning.

going?" Students who favor the former approach believe, "Inch by inch, it's a cinch . . ." One of my students used the analogy of the turtle: No matter how small your steps or how slowly you move, as long as you are persistent, you will get there. Others may find this approach boring. The point is that both approaches are correct, but people are different.

 ## SCENARIO 20

When the instructor tells you, "You must learn to crawl before you can walk!" what does she mean?

1. One technique is a building block for another.

2. You have to lay a strong foundation before you can build a high rise.

3. You must learn the small steps before learning how they relate to other techniques.

4. Don't be so impatient! One thing at a time!

★★★★★

While sequential learning may seem theoretically sound, it does not necessarily benefit every student. An instructor who has good people skills and is patient still might not be a good instructor, unless she also understands the many different ways in which people learn and knows how to adapt her lessons.

If you are the type of student who learns from the outside in (by seeing the whole first), when practicing the basics you should pay attention to how they relate to other techniques. If your instructor fails to relate the basics to the whole, you may feel as though he isn't explaining the techniques thoroughly. It is possible to lose interest because the instructor fails to adapt his style of teaching to your style of learning. However, if you don't understand the learning process, you may not be able to pinpoint the problem. You may simply be bored, or feel that the martial arts aren't right for you, even though you can't say why. Understanding why you do things a certain way may help the learning process. For example, rather than simply learning to pivot on your supporting foot when throwing the roundhouse kick, ask your instructor to explain the purpose of the pivot (for extension and follow-through in the hips).

On the other hand, if you are the type of student who learns from the inside out (through small steps, one at a time), you may feel as though your instructor is giving you too much information when she demonstrates the full technique. This type of student often enjoys learning *what* she is supposed to do, rather than *why* she is supposed to do it. Inside-out types of students will learn the technique until they know it flawlessly, and fill in the details later.

Again, one type of student is not better than the other, and both have the potential to become great martial artists. If your instructor is the type of person who learns by seeing the whole technique first before breaking it into its component parts, she might think that a student who prefers not to know everything from the start is boring, not as smart, or unable to process a large amount of in-

formation. Likewise, if your instructor is the type of person who likes to learn bit by bit, he might think that a student who wants everything from the start is careless, sloppy or inattentive. Neither is a correct analysis.

Those who learn from the outside in are likely to want to discuss and experiment with how one technique relates to another. The instructor should therefore not leave these students alone to practice the same move over and over. Such students are also likely to get bored, to stop and seek conversation with another student, or to start practicing something else. These types of students require a lot of attention and interaction. In contrast, those who learn from the inside out normally work great alone and for long periods of time. They like lessons that are very organized and don't mind spending a great deal of time on the same technique, perfecting the details. The inside-out types of learners often want to be assured of a technique's validity before spending a considerable amount of time perfecting it. But once they start working on it, they are organized and relentless in their pursuit. They always achieve their goals one step at a time, and they pay great attention to detail. If you are this type of learner, your instructor must ensure that the details he gives you about a technique today is the same as the details he will give you tomorrow.

Personally, I am leaning toward being an inside-out type of learner. When I was a new student in karate, I attended a class not taught by my primary instructor. This instructor demonstrated the upward block slightly differently from how I had learned it. It bothered me. Since martial arts are seldom black and white, both blocks may have been correct. But I did not know this, given my very limited experience of the arts. A different type of learner might not have even noticed that there was a difference between the blocks, but would have been more interested in how he could use the block regardless of the exact angle of the forearm.

Students should be aware that not every instructor teaches every technique in exactly the same way. Sometimes the details of a technique relate to the situation at hand, and students must learn to adapt. As an instructor, I like to teach what I call the "bone" of the technique. This is the basic framework that students learn before they know anything else. Once they master the bone and achieve good balance and smoothness of movement, I elaborate and present different variations.

If both you and your instructor favor the same approach to learning, you will be in tune with your instructor and will probably like her. However, if you favor opposite approaches to learning, you may feel that your instructor is not the right person to teach you. Therefore, the quality of instruction is not necessarily objective. If your instructor makes an effort to adapt her teaching methods to your particular approach to learning, the next student that steps in the door may think the instructor is uninteresting. One reason it is so important to be aware of the different methods of learning is because it allows you to seek the kind of instruction that benefits you the most.

– INSTRUCTOR TIP –

If you and your student favor opposite approaches to learning, you might worry that your student is getting bored. But this may not be how your student feels. Search for clues as to how particular students learn, and make an effort to vary your teaching style enough that most students can benefit.

– STUDENT TIP –

Do you learn best by hearing, seeing or doing? Can you pinpoint your method of learning immediately, without giving it much thought? Learning can be physical, as when you punch and kick, or psychological, as when you gain a better understanding of yourself. Can you think of situations where you felt that learning was fun? What made it so? This may be your first indication as to what type of learner you are.

LEARNING THROUGH VISUALIZATION

If you have the ability to use vivid visualization techniques, you can create a feeling of familiarity with the subject. You will also create some muscle memory. Although the visualization exercises do not include actual technique practice, your muscles still respond to vivid images. Martial artists who say they are "in the zone" or "can feel the ch'i," are in a state where their physical and mental preparations coincide. Prior to testing for my blue belt in karate, I desperately wanted to be told that I was the top student. Visualization exercises helped me train with a greater intensity. As a result, I received the "most outstanding student" award. Technique only gets you so far; attitude takes you the rest of the way.

Note that not everybody has the same ability to visualize techniques. I recommend that visualization exercises be done before and after training, rather than during training.

Too much thinking may interfere with performance.

BENEFITS OF EXPERIENCE

If you were learning how to repair a photocopy machine, which type of instruction would be more interesting?

1. Your instructor requires you to memorize a technical service manual.

2. Your instructor shares a story of when he was on his knees, spilling toner on his new $300.00 suit and the grouchy office lady walked into the room, breathing garlic down his neck and telling him that the last technician couldn't fix the machine *either!*

Any field of expertise involves more than just the ability to understand the technical workings of your craft. The unforeseen problems and the solutions to them, bring insight into the field. When learning the martial arts, you must elaborate on each thought. Your prior experiences are not compilations of facts; they are unique. Insight occurs when you can relate your new experiences to something that you are already familiar with. Think of it this way: Is it easier to memorize a list of foreign words you don't understand, or to memorize a list of words you are familiar with? The words you understand and are familiar with are easier to memorize, because you can relate them to specific experiences. The foreign words, however, cannot be related, because you don't understand their meanings to begin with.

Your instructor's background and prior experiences can help her present interesting lessons. If she can present a personal story that you can relate to, you will be more apt to listen and remember the material later. Although it has been said that there is nothing new under the sun, there are a thousand new ways to express an idea. Just think about all the songs that have been written about love. Lessons can be presented:

1. Isolated from the actual environment (in the classroom). This gives you and your instructor privacy to discuss and explore techniques and concepts.

2. Within the actual environment. This gives you hands-on experience with real stresses. This could be either a tournament setting or a seminar setting.

Two students who are taught the same lesson may learn different things, depending on their personal experiences. It is therefore useful to learn from your fellow students as well as from your instructor. A good exercise is to talk about your experiences with others. Soon one student's experience will build on another student's, resulting in a myriad of learning from even the simplest techniques. This incidental learning helps you develop a fuller picture. Both adults and children have a broad background of experiences which you can use to build valuable lessons for yourself.

When learning a new technique or concept, where do you begin? Many of us feel that the simplest way is to begin at the beginning; to start by breaking the technique down into smaller segments. But sometimes you may benefit from starting in the middle or near the end. I call this *reverse engineering*. How is it done? Let's say that your instructor teaches you, a novice, about grappling. Perhaps you are a forms practitioner who wants to broaden your views. Or perhaps you are new to the martial arts and just happened to choose a grappling school. To reverse engineer the lesson, the instructor will start without giving you any information at all; he will simply tell you that you will grapple with him for three minutes and use whatever techniques you can come up with. The purpose of this exercise is to allow you to experience the situation as a whole, before learning the details, and to give you certain insights from the beginning. For example:

1. You will immediately experience the difficulties of a grappling situation.

2. You will understand the importance of physical conditioning.

3. You will feel the effectiveness of joint control techniques.

4. You will begin to understand balance.

When learning the specific techniques later, you can relate them to this initial grappling experience. If your instructor chooses this reverse-engineering approach, he should explain that your performance in this first practice session has nothing to do with your ability to succeed later. It is merely intended to introduce you to the experience of a grappling situation.

Experience makes you grow. The security of the training hall and an imaginary fight under pressure are not substitutes for the real thing. What should be learned from competition, for example, is not who is better or how it feels to win, but rather how you react when under pressure and how far you are capable of going when tired, hurt or scared.

Your grappling instructor can reverse engineer your first lesson by placing you in a choke hold and allow you to experience the choke, before teaching you how to defend against it.

Some martial arts award black belts in one or two years, others take seven to eight years to award them. Either approach may be correct, as long as it coincides with the requirements of the art. However, both the student and the instructor should understand that learning is based on experience. Information that is simply told to you does not transfer into meaningful experiences. You must be given sufficient time to learn, absorb the material, practice it, and relate it to meaningful situations. This is why a black belt student with a year and a half in his art is usually not as good as a martial artist with ten years experience, regardless of the color of his belt.

Most people will agree that they learn more quickly if the experience is enjoyable. But enjoyable should not be confused with pleasant. Sparring, for example, is seldom pleasant. Sparring is challenging, frightening and painful. But if practiced under the tutelage of a good instructor, sparring is a rewarding experience that you will remember for a long time. It is only when the experience creates frustration, anger or defeat that it tends to inhibit learning.

You have gained a new skill when you can perform the techniques consistently in different situations. But learning doesn't end here. You must now continue to build on your established platform. Since all martial arts have similar uses, if you have studied and gained proficiency in one martial art, it is easier to gain proficiency in a second art.

– INSTRUCTOR TIP –

Don't underestimate the student. Constantly challenge the student to think for herself and build on previously established scenarios.

– STUDENT TIP –

An experienced student will look at a situation much differently than a new student. When you have gained some experience in the martial arts, you might learn more than what your instructor is attempting to teach you. Learn to draw your own inferences based on prior knowledge.

7

Methods of Instruction and Learning

INTRODUCTION AND EXPLANATION

An organized lesson can be broken down into the following segments:

1. Introduction and explanation

2. Demonstration

3. Application

4. Summary, review and evaluation

In any learning situation, the most critical phase may be the introduction, because this is where interest is aroused. The introduction should cover what the lesson is about. It may be helpful to clarify what it is *not* about as well. The introduction should *introduce*; it should not include the whole lesson or everything you have experienced in the last 20 years.

Before you can learn anything at all, the instructor must gain your attention and organize the instructional material carefully so that you can relate to each step along the way. If the instructor chooses to introduce the lesson by talking about the material, he must present it with passion and clarity. A good way to introduce a lesson might be to state two or three points of importance, give a brief example of each, and then answer questions.

Since it is not possible to learn a technique perfectly in only one lesson, as an instructor I normally state what students are expected to know when the lesson is over. I also tell them that the technique will be part of their repertoire for years to come, and that we will build on it next time. The introduction might also be a good time for the instructor to stress why it is important that students come to class regularly.

DEMONSTRATION

The demonstration method is often desirable when presenting a new skill. Lessons can be made more intense by relating different concepts to one another.

1. When using the demonstration method, your instructor explains the technique followed by a demonstration. This method allows you to use your visual sense along with your audio sense. How much time your instructor devotes to demonstrations depends on the complexity of the techniques and your level of learning. In general, a good amount of practice should be mixed in with the demonstrations. For example, when your instructor has shown the technique in its entirety and you know where you are headed, she can demonstrate the component parts separately. Practice these smaller segments and ask your instructor to fill in the details later.

81

2. If you, the student, already have some background experience, the teaching situation can be switched so that it allows you to explain the technique, while your instructor simultaneously demonstrates to reinforce learning. When I was studying karate, students would line up in rows with the instructor in front. Whenever he demonstrated a new technique, he would first turn his back toward the students so he was facing the same direction as they were. This strategy made it easier for students to imitate the technique. I recommend that the instructor demonstrate techniques this way initially, but then face the students so that they can also see how the technique looks if done by an opponent coming toward them. Your instructor might also want to demonstrate from a side view, especially with kicks, in order to demonstrate such things as chambering the leg.

3. A third way to learn is for you (the student) to explain the technique and *also* demonstrate it. This kind of paraphrasing generally aids your understanding of the material. Discuss the purpose of the technique. Is it a set-up or finishing technique? What are the targets? Without talking about these things, the technique will simply be a set of meaningless moves. How useful is the technique? Are there other ways to handle the given situation? Ask your instructor to demonstrate the results of different combinations of moves. Explore how a partial technique can be used to defend against an attacker. How can you use just the first move, just the middle move, or just the last move of the technique? You are not aiming for

mastery at this point, but for understanding. Practice the techniques on another student.

Note that if you are a new student in the martial arts, you need to learn proper mechanics before all the details will make sense. Your instructor should be a little conservative with the amount of detail she includes in the demonstrations.

The martial arts are physical in nature and therefore present an opportunity for interesting demonstrations. Rather than simply naming the target areas, explore how an opponent might react when struck. Work on target accuracy. Decide which weapon to use for each target and why. Reciting an answer is not sufficient, unless you can also see the correlation. Are there different ways in

Explaining a technique and simultaneously demonstrating it on the instructor or another student is a good way to reinforce learning once you have acquired basic knowledge of the technique.

which to accomplish the same thing? For example, a forward step synchronized with your strike increases your momentum and therefore the power of the strike. But if you time the strike to your opponent's forward motion instead, he will step into the technique and accomplish the same thing. If you have problems:

1. Ask the instructor to demonstrate the technique again, breaking it down into its component parts.

2. Work on one segment of the technique at a time.

3. Observe your fellow students. Observing from the sidelines gives you a better perspective. This may be especially true when the action is chaotic, which is often the case in self-defense and combat scenarios.

If you are participating in a large class, not all of the students may be able to spar, for example, at the same time. When you are not sparring, take advantage of your downtime by observing others. Your instructor should talk to you about what you should observe. For example:

1. Is one fighter more aggressive than the other? What benefits does it give her?

2. Does she use set-ups? Do they work?

3. Do the fighters switch stance, or do they stay in the same stance the whole time?

4. Do they seem to use one technique repeatedly or exclusively?

5. Do they use mostly punches or mostly kicks?

Make sure that you stand so that you can see the technique clearly when your instructor demonstrates on another student, or when you observe your peers from the sidelines.

6. If you were fighting these people next, what would you need to be careful of? What kind of strategy would you use?

A good exercise is to break into groups of three or four students, where one or two students observe the other two students sparring. Those who are not sparring know that they will soon go up against one of the students they are observing. When you observe your peers, look at their strategy and consider how you can set them up or avoid getting tagged when it is your turn to spar. If you don't understand the purpose of your observation, you will derive little benefit from it. Pause frequently to ask questions. You can also do an observation exercise at home with the help of the TV. When I was a new student in kickboxing, I didn't find it particularly interesting to watch kickboxing matches on TV. However, a few years later it became very interesting, because I had trained myself to be observant and look for strategy that I could later apply in my own sparring.

You can learn a great deal from your instructor's demonstrations. However, since you perceive what your instructor does as correct, he must evaluate a situation beforehand and decide whether it really is a good learning experience. He must be watchful and exercise good judgment when deciding how far to let you go when performing incorrectly. Having permission to make mistakes can speed up the learning process, as long as the mistakes are analyzed and corrected.

 SCENARIO 21

Your instructor demonstrates a technique that requires a moderate degree of contact. How should this be done?

1. One student should act as the opponent, while the instructor demonstrates the technique at half speed so that nobody gets hurt.

2. The technique should be demonstrated with full speed and power on a heavy bag.

3. The instructor should demonstrate the technique on a student, using reasonable contact and full speed.

4. The instructor should explain the technique, and then have an advanced student demonstrate it on the instructor.

★★★★★

It is better to give than to receive; it is more fun to hit than to get hit. When you practice with a partner you may feel tempted to let him take all the hits. But if you do so repeatedly without trading off, your peers will soon figure out that you are taking advantage of them. When practicing with a partner, give him his fair share. Your partner, too, is eager to learn new techniques.

– INSTRUCTOR TIP –

Some instructors are more intent on showing off their own skills than teaching their students. But remember, many students learn best by doing. Keep demonstrations short and allow students to practice, while you observe and make suggestions.

– STUDENT TIP –

When your instructor demonstrates techniques, look for common factors that tie the moves together. For example, which is more valuable: learning how to throw or defend against a punch after you have seen a demonstration of a punch, or practicing kicks after you have seen a demonstration of a punch? Learning how to throw or defend against a punch is more valuable, because it relates directly to the demonstration.

APPLICATION

Application generally follows the explanation and demonstration phases. Since the first thing learned is normally what we fall back on when under stress, it is important to perform the technique correctly the first few times. After your instructor has demonstrated the technique and talked briefly about its uses, she should give you the opportunity to practice it in the air or on focus mitts to learn proper mechanics. When you have achieved good form, practice the technique with a partner. Your instructor should supervise, make corrections and guide you to the right decision, rather than telling you the correct answer outright.

When you associate new information with a particular experience, you gain a deeper insight than when you examine the steps alone. You will also become very good at anything you do frequently. If you jump rope a lot, you will become very good at jumping rope and your endurance may seem phenomenal. But this does not necessarily mean you can run a mile without huffing and puffing. The reason we become good at what we practice frequently is that we teach ourselves to relax. However, if you do a lot of bag work, it is unlikely that you will excel at sparring. If you want to excel at sparring, you should spar often.

You can increase retention if you use your knowledge as soon as possible after learning a new technique. For example:

1. Practice the technique in the air or on a bag and talk yourself through the moves to stay on track. Try short instructional phrases that command action, such as,

Partner practice that allows you to touch the targets and that helps you see other subtleties, such as your opponent's movement and positioning, helps reinforce learning.

"Step forward! Reverse strike! Move!"

2. I recommend getting started in sparring early. Free sparring gives you the opportunity to apply the techniques and see how they work in real time. Even if you have learned only stance and basic movement, you can still pair up with another student and work on how to move and manipulate distance.

3. As you advance in the martial arts, try *progressive overload*. With this concept you set goals that are consistently out of reach, and that force you to rise to a new level. When you reach your goal, immediately set a new and higher goal to prevent stagnation.

SUMMARY, REVIEW AND EVALUATION

At the end of the instructional period, emphasize what was covered in class. Review and evaluate the material to reinforce learning and improve retention. There are two ways in which you can debrief after a lesson.

Debriefing Method One

1. Review the important points together with your instructor. Keep it brief.

2. Ask specific questions to determine how much you have understood.

Debriefing Method Two

1. Emphasize one important point only.

2. Your instructor can prompt you by asking questions.

Testing is a valid method of evaluation. Tests can be used to determine your readiness to move to a new level. Your instructor can also use tests as a self-evaluation tool to discover deficiencies in her instruction.

 ## SCENARIO 22

When a critique is included in the debriefing, how should it be phrased for greatest effect?

1. We worked on kicks today and some of you did okay, but most of you still have a lot of work to do.

2. Good job! I really didn't see any problems.

3. Kicking is about strategy, not only about power. Next time, we will look at how to use a kick to set up a punch technique.

4. I like low kicks better than high kicks, because you don't expose your groin as much.

★★★★★

A good critique should be specific. If your instructor simply tells you that you did well or poorly, you don't really gain new insight. The critique should also give you something to think about until next time. Forewarned is forearmed. You can now get excited about the next lesson. As already stated, it is important that your instructor teaches what he said he was going to teach. If he tells you, "We have now learned how to fall without getting hurt. Next time we will start practicing some simple throws," but next time he forgets his promise and starts teaching kicks instead, you may get disappointed and feel that any mental preparation you have done is wasted (at least for the time being). Already-developed lesson plans can help your instructor stay organized and teach the material in a logical sequence. We will discuss the value of lesson plans in Chapter 10.

STUDENT INTERACTION

Learning is an active process. If you want to reap the rewards, you must make an effort to learn. Don't expect the information to be handed to you; don't expect to be spoon fed. Learning takes work. Most people don't inherently dislike work as long as there is a clearly stated purpose. Active participation and interaction with others make lessons more meaningful. For example, if your instructor relies too heavily on the lecture method, you may get bored or drift off in thought. Retention is better if you can discuss and ask questions and debate a variety of issues. Students also tend to learn more from their own ideas than from the ideas of others. Paraphrasing new material and talking about it with others allows you to develop a deeper understanding and gain new insights.

CONCEPTS AND EXERCISES

Clarity of instruction: Knowing what is expected of you increases your ability to learn. Your instructor must remember the end objective of the lesson and take you on a straight path toward the goal. Instructor inconsistency and unclear communication send mixed messages that can confuse and hinder learning.

Exercise 1

- A new student observing a black belt martial artist may find the journey toward the black belt overwhelming and discouraging. To avoid negative feelings, break the material down into smaller parts and have a definite plan for reaching each intermediate goal.

- Identify your needs and interests and develop a written plan for reaching short-term goals. Estimate the time needed to reach the goal.

Exercise 2

- Lessons that are haphazard may result in frustration. Make sure that you understand what is expected of you as an instructor. It is a good idea to post the plan on the wall so that both students and instructors can view it.

- If you fail to follow the plan without prior consent from your instructor, there should be some form of penalty. A list of appropriate motivational penalties can be posted on the wall as well, as long as it is adhered to.

Human personality: Many students are emotional or sensitive. A teaching technique that works well with one student may not work with another. Your instructor must be tactful in order to prevent emotions and negative feelings from interfering with the learning process. Although he may be a superb martial artist, he may not be the best instructor for *every* student who walks in the door.

Exercise 1

- Note when your emotions seem to interfere with learning. How can you deal with frustration? How can you help resolve an argument between two of your peers? What can you do if a fellow student brings his personal problems to class?

- How can you handle a situation where the instructor has an off day and brings his personal problems to class?

- How would you handle a personality conflict between you and the instructor?

Exercise 2

- Some students have outgoing personalities and are aggressive, while others are more timid or laid back. Some students like group work and others don't. Should your instructor accept you as you are, or are there times when he should push you out of your comfort zone and make you partake in activities that do not fit your natural personality? Give an example.

- If a fellow student suddenly fails to show up for class, is there anything you can or should do to help bring him back? Give some examples.

Hunger to learn: In order to make progress, we must seriously want the subject taught. Otherwise, progress will be difficult and slow. When progress is slow, we lose motivation and it is more difficult to learn. Your instructor can give you the hunger to learn by eliminating boring lessons, by letting you experience the value of the technique taught, and by setting short-term goals that help you see your progress.

Exercise 1

- When you notice a lack of interest in a peer student, what can you do to motivate her? Some students need more personal attention than others.

Exercise 2

- What can you do to avoid getting bored with the lessons? Your instructor could easily become stale when she teaches the same thing day in and day out. Try to extract new information from your instructor by asking appropriate questions and considering what excites you. We will talk about the art of asking questions in more detail in Chapter 13.

- Keeping you on your toes with a variety of exercises helps alienate boredom. A funny story or the opportunity to laugh may lighten the atmosphere.

- Make sure you understand the value of the lesson taught. Techniques can be made more graphic by relating them to real-life scenarios.

Gaining insight: Insights occur when you practice the techniques realistically. Insights help you see the relationship between the material taught and the situation to which it applies. Seeking other applications on your own fosters insight and deepens your understanding of principles and concepts.

Exercise 1

- Practice the technique in situations that are as realistic and unrehearsed as possible.

- Explore a variety of scenarios where the technique can be applied. Experiment with the validity of each case and discuss it with others. Talk about what to do if the technique fails.

Exercise 2

- When you have gained some background knowledge, come up with techniques and situations without your instructor's guidance. You will likely gain deeper insights when experimenting with your own techniques than with somebody else's.

Knowing vs. learning: Most people can memorize moves without understanding the application of them. They can answer questions correctly without understanding the answers. But remember, you haven't *learned* simply because you *know* or can imitate what you have been shown. How much you have learned can be tested through your ability to analyze a problem, arrive at a conclusion, and demonstrate your skill in a variety of unrehearsed scenarios.

Exercise 1

- When faced with a problem, asking *what if* is excellent for analyzing the problem and coming up with a solution.

- Test the validity of the solution in an unrehearsed scenario.

Exercise 2

- If you can talk about a technique but have difficulty applying it, what can you do to get past this learning plateau?

- Sometimes too much work on one technique without realizing results can make you lose confidence. Try leaving that particular technique for a while and move on to something else.

Learning with intention: In order for improvement to occur, you must clearly intend to improve and must persevere until the objectives are met. Your instructor, too, must intend for you to improve. When he evaluates or critiques your performance, unless the critique helps you advance toward your goal, it is useless and should not be given. A good critique should be precise with clear suggestions for improvement.

Exercise 1

• Note when your mood or feelings seem to interfere with your ability to learn. What about your instructor's mood or feelings? Does he ever cut a class short because he simply doesn't feel like being there?

• If you ask for extra help after class, does your instructor make an effort to accommodate you? If not, what might be the reason?

• How does your instructor's personal appearance (the way he dresses and acts) affect his mood and the mood of the students? Is it important that the instructor changes to a proper uniform when teaching, or is it enough to come to class in street clothes? Why?

Exercise 2

• When your instructor evaluates or critiques your performance, do you understand what the critique is trying to accomplish? Is it a good idea for you to critique yourself? Why or why not?

• What are the benefits and drawbacks of students critiquing each other? When critiquing your peers, be tactful so that the critique doesn't result in loss of confidence or hurt feelings.

8
Motivation and Goal Setting

DEFINING GOALS

When I started in karate, the school had me fill out a questionnaire about why I wanted to study the martial arts. This is a good idea if it helps you define your goals and understand how martial arts training will benefit you. It also gives your instructor an indication of what motivates you. However, if the questionnaire is simply a formality that is thrown carelessly on a desk or filed away in some dusty archive never to be looked at again, it is a waste of time and a disappointment to the student. If you are asked to fill out a questionnaire, you have the right to expect some feedback; you should not have to wonder whether somebody read it or even cared.

How quickly we learn depends on our goals and motivation. If the material taught coincides with your goals, you are more likely to stay in class than if you are learning material that interests you less. Questions about your expectations should be detailed enough to create a clear image of what you wish to achieve.

At the extreme ends of the spectrum, there are two types of students: those who would rather go all the way to black belt without ever squaring off against an opponent in sparring, and those who get bored to death

with forms or technique practice and could live on sparring alone. How does the instructor keep both types of students motivated simultaneously? Some students don't really know what their goals are when they first sign up for martial arts training, and many students change their goals as they progress through the course. Initially, I was more interested in techniques training than in free sparring. After a few months my interests changed. Now, after more than 20 years in the martial arts, I have come full circle and am again interested in studying techniques and principles.

 SCENARIO 23

You are a white belt student who is bored with the lessons and wants to get started with sparring. Normally, your instructor doesn't allow students to spar until they have achieved intermediate rank. What should your instructor tell you in order to preserve your motivation?

1. You need to get your purple belt first.

2. I can give you some private lessons in sparring. They're $50 an hour.

3. Buy some sparring gear and we can get started today.

4. We normally don't spar at the lower levels, but you can come and watch others spar.

★★★★★

Your instructor might want to start by considering how strong your desire is for sparring and how long it would take for you to achieve the required belt level. If it is a matter of a few months, waiting to spar may serve as a motivator. However, I believe that most students can get started in sparring very early in their training, as long as they start at a comfortable pace and with good taste. As an instructor, I like to build on my students' natural desires, because this is where I am most likely to find their talents. When I have found their talents, I know what avenues to take in order to accelerate their learning process. If you desire to spar and your instructor tells you "no," but your buddy at another school is sparring, might you be tempted to join the other school? I am not suggesting that your instructor should let you decide the curriculum. However, he can build on your natural enthusiasm, for example, by giving you a few minutes of private instruction after class, or by providing specific exercises that prepare you for sparring.

When I entered the training hall for the first time, my eye caught the different-colored belts hanging on the wall in ascending order. Throughout my training, these belts gave me an indication of my position on the road to black belt. But it often takes more than a visual indicator to motivate students to progress toward their goals. In order for a goal to truly serve as a motivator, it should be clearly defined, with the exact steps stated and organized. You should be able to visualize each step and understand the importance of each higher belt. If you adhere to the plan, attaining the black belt should not only be a possibility; it should be a certainty. If you are under the impression that it will take a specific number of years to attain a black belt, and when those years have passed but your goal is still looming in the distance, the motivating steps will lose their meaning. Your instructor should therefore be specific when stating the requirements for each belt level.

When you reach a goal, you should be rewarded and a new goal should be set. Polishing the details indefinitely will not make you a better martial artist; it will only make you frustrated. Changing the requirements in midstream is not a good idea, either. At one school where I trained, the instructor frequently changed a complicated form, adding little insignificant details and requiring students to master the new version before allowing them to test for a higher rank. His teaching methods gave me the impression that he didn't want students to progress.

Goals should be short-term and long-term. Short-term goals help you see your step-by-step progress toward the next higher belt. Long-term goals help you continue past the belt promotion and motivate you to proceed toward the next short-term goal. So, in a sense, it can be said that short- and long-term goals act as catalysts for one another.

– INSTRUCTOR TIP –

A written plan not only organizes the instructor, it also organizes the student. In order to provide students with a meaningful experi-

ence, the skill learned must be appropriate to their expectations.

INSTRUCTOR MOTIVATION

Why are you taking this class? This is a common question college teachers ask students on the first day of class, perhaps hoping for that miracle answer "Because this subject is absolutely fascinating!" However, a more likely answer is, "Because it is a requirement for graduation!" If you were the instructor and all of your students gave you this answer, how enthusiastic would you be about teaching? "Isn't anybody here because it might benefit you later in life?" you may ask. "Isn't anybody here for the pure joy of it?" Too often we take classes that we have no interest in taking, simply because it is a requirement for whatever degree we are pursuing. But how do the instructors feel? If you asked your instructor why he is teaching the class, what would be his answer?

Perhaps the greatest obstacle to student motivation is when the instructor lacks motivation. If the student is the primary beneficiary of the student-teacher relationship, then one might wonder what motivates the instructor. Does she teach because it is a requirement for getting her black belt? Does she teach to supplement her income, but as soon as she wins the lottery she'll never set foot in the training hall again? Does she teach because she is the owner and sole operator of the school and *somebody* has to teach? Or does she teach because of the joy of it? As an instructor, most of my motivation to teach comes from the excitement of others. When I show students a new technique and their eyes light up as if to say, "Wow, that's really cool!" then my eyes (and heart) light up, too.

When the instructor is with her students, she must portray an attitude of enthusiasm and competence. An instructor who teaches simply because she *has to* is likely to fail severely in motivating her students. Your instructor can show motivation by:

1. Being on time, taking charge and having a definite plan; and

2. Being on a mission that is so important that nobody wants to be left behind.

Your instructor's facial expressions will communicate to you whether he enjoys teaching or is just trying to get through the day.

SCENARIO 24

You are consistently late for class and give your instructor every imaginable excuse: your kid was sick, you were sick, you had a bad day at work, your mom was in town... What should your instructor do?

1. Start being late for class.

2. Charge you a "late fee."

3. Ask if there is anything he can do to help.

4. Tell you that you won't be promoted to a higher rank unless you start coming to class on time.

5. Have you do push-ups in the back of the room.

It is appropriate to require that students do their part. You should be held accountable for the fact that you are studying the martial arts. Slacking off, showing up late, not doing your homework, and not applying yourself properly are unacceptable student behaviors, despite the fact that you are paying for lessons. When you are held accountable for your behavior, you are more likely to pay attention during lessons and will therefore learn more. However, your instructor should avoid lecturing you on personal matters. Before offering solutions to your problems, he should consider that nobody knows one's life better than the person who has to live it. For example, if you tell your instructor, "I don't have time to do my homework," and he tells you, "Everybody has 24 hours; it's just a matter of how you plan your time," he is attacking you personally. He is saying that you are a poor planner when, in fact, he doesn't have a clue about your schedule. You will know when your instructor doesn't know what he is talking about. Furthermore, not everybody's obligations to home, family and job are the same and can't be resolved with an easy one-size-fits-all type of policy.

STUDENT MOTIVATION

Motivation may be our strongest driving force. The hungry student realizes the value of the material taught and is therefore receptive to learning. In the martial arts, contributing motivational factors range from a desire to learn to protect oneself, to a desire to attain a higher level of fitness, to a search for comradeship and belonging. Initially, while the material is still new and exciting, you will progress quickly. During this mechanical stage of learning, most students are easily motivated. Once past the mechanical stage, you can perform the acquired skill with less conscious effort. When you attain your black belt, learning is more refined and focuses on adapting to different environments, conditions and situations. Because the skill is so highly refined, noticeable improvements in performance come at a much slower pace. You must now find new ways to stay motivated.

SCENARIO 25

You question for how long you will have to practice the horse stance. What should your instructor tell you?

1. Until you get real good.

2. Until it becomes habit and you don't have to think about it.

3. For another six months.

4. Don't question. Practice!

★★★★★

In karate, the horse stance may be the most basic technique taught, which is why we often hear how, in the old days, the horse stance was practiced for six months straight before the student was allowed to learn anything else. One of the reasons this approach is not readily accepted in today's classes is that it isn't the best way to learn. Practicing only the horse stance for six months will not improve your martial arts skills. Aside from being discouraging and boring, this sort of practice also prevents you from adjusting to the new demands placed on your body. Even basic techniques should be taught with depth and insight.

Beginner student motivation

Much motivation comes from knowing where you are going. Sometimes the objectives of the lesson are not obvious; you don't see the value of what is taught from the start, so you don't appreciate it. Your instructor can alleviate this problem by avoiding drills that don't contribute directly to competent performance. Learning the horse stance, without also learning the value of a good stance with all of its many facets, has little value. I believe that the integrated method of instruction, where you learn the application from the start, is the fastest way to learn.

Basic techniques, such as the upward block, can be learned from a variety of stances and does not need to be practiced from the horse stance only.

We have an enormous capacity to absorb information, especially when the information is presented with forethought and the appropriate pacing. The more your instructor can simplify a lesson without sacrificing insight, the more information she can impart in a given time frame. Although some people may argue that the "old school" allowed the instructor to determine who was worthy and disciplined enough to follow "the way," the instructor's responsibility is still to teach and, in my opinion, to teach techniques rather than morals. When you are a new student in the martial arts, you need to feel that you are making regular progress.

Intermediate student motivation

In Western society, we tend to question rather than go with the flow. In a particular school I attended, a new rule was added whereby students had to earn two stripes on their belt before being allowed to test for a higher rank. The change was implemented suddenly while I was on vacation. When I came back to class, most students had already been given one stripe on their belt. Because of my dedication and aptitude for the arts, I expected to be given a stripe that day. When nobody approached me about it after four weeks passed, I was bothered. After all, I always did my homework, I came to class many times a week, and I assisted with teaching. Had they simply forgotten about me? Or were they trying some kind of reverse psychology?

If your peers advance at a faster rate than you, you might get frustrated, especially if you don't understand why. If you get overly frustrated, you are likely to lose motivation.

But many of us don't consider that failure, because it is unpleasant, can also be a motivator. Nevertheless, when you fail, you should understand why. If you fail consistently, you will find little reason to continue learning. Your instructor should never fail you when you deserve to succeed simply because he doesn't like you, your attitude, or the fact that you are moving ahead of your peers. If you fail a belt exam or if your instructor is reluctant to recommend you for an exam, make sure you understand the reasons for it. If you understand the reasons without having to ask for an explanation, your instructor is probably judging your performance soundly. If you don't understand the reasons, you might want to question your instructor.

One of my instructors enforced the acronym TEAM (Together Everybody Achieves More). This instructor insisted that all stu-

When learning stance and movement, do you learn best by watching your instructor demonstrate the movement or by listening to him explain it?

dents test at the same time. No student was allowed to move ahead of the group. The concept of teamwork is noble, but since martial arts are an individual activity, each student should be allowed to progress at his or her own rate. The reason you are ahead of the others may be that you have worked harder than your peers, come to class more often, and applied yourself better. Your efforts should therefore be rewarded.

Learning rates differ among students. The insightful instructor tries to find ways to help students progress. But in order to do so, she must identify why students learn at different rates. Learning is often enhanced by building on the student's current interests; however, don't count on this approach always working for you. I have a student who is an expert dancer but is unable to co-ordinate her hands and feet when learning a new technique or form. Her problem might be that she is trying to learn by listening when, in fact, she is the type of person who learns best through feel.

 ## SCENARIO 26

You are a new student and you ask your instructor for private lessons. From a motivational standpoint, what should she tell you?

1. Private lessons are great even though they are expensive, because you get the instructor's full attention throughout the lesson.

2. The instructor would like to give you private lessons, but she has so many students that she simply doesn't have the time.

3. Private lessons are for the advanced students only.

Students in a group class automatically help motivate each other. Nobody likes being less skilled than her peers, and when a student starts lagging behind she will work harder to catch up. In private lessons, there is no other student who can act as a motivator. Motivation must therefore come from your instructor. However, your instructor's un-divided attention in a private lesson may not outweigh the benefits of the peer pressure you receive from group instruction. When you already have some background knowledge, a private lesson will mean more and may be a great way to fine-tune your technique.

– INSTRUCTOR TIP –

Progress brings motivation. It is therefore wrong to hold back those students who are ready to advance. The instructor who presents the TEAM concept may get verbal approval from his students. But keep in mind that few students are ready to argue with the master instructor, especially in public. Students may therefore not give you a true indication of how they feel.

– STUDENT TIP –

From a learning standpoint, a variety of skill levels within the group tends to motivate the slower students and help them rise to the occasion. Approval from our peers increases motivation. Take advantage of situations where your instructor tries to build enthusiasm by helping you perform successfully in front of your peers.

Advanced student motivation

Learning physical skills is often easier than learning mental or social skills. Receiving a list of techniques to learn for your next belt level is more concrete than being told, for example, that you must learn self-control. Learning and measuring physical skills work well in the lower ranks when the higher-ranking students serve as motivators. But what should you do when your instructor has no more new techniques to teach you? Well, you refine those techniques you have already learned. When you reach this stage, you should remember that your progress won't be quite as apparent. You will also start identifying more errors, and may therefore feel as though learning has slowed or even reversed. Some higher-ranking students open their own schools at this point. Other students have more abstract goals that help them stay motivated. However, after our initial motivation has faded, most of us need some sort of concrete goal.

Staying motivated to pursue the study of martial arts is a tough venture. Your instructor must constantly help you progress. An advanced student might stay motivated when he starts teaching his own class. Since your skills are honed, your instructor should give you some leeway about *how* to teach, so that you can take ownership of the class. Special assignments, such as acting as a judge at belt promotions or tournaments, or assisting with seminars, may also be good motivators.

Let's say that your instructor demonstrates a difficult jump kick in an attempt to motivate you. Good or bad? If your instructor wants to impress you in order to build ex-

citement, he should show you a technique that is relatively difficult but still within reach for your experience level. He should then teach you at least the first step of the technique. Although your instructor should demonstrate proper form, showing off excessively is hardly ever needed in order to gain a student's attention.

– INSTRUCTOR TIP –

Never use your student's lesser experience to boost your own ego. When demonstrating a technique to the class, it is better to ask for the assisting student's cooperation than to use excessive force in order to prove a point.

– STUDENT TIP –

You may feel as though you are working for a higher belt, certificate or trophy, but it is really the higher skill that is your goal. The award is simply an indication that you have achieved the higher skill.

TEN MOTIVATION TIPS

1. **Motivation gives you a reason to learn.** Your instructor can get your attention through a story, anecdote or interesting demonstration. When introducing the lesson, he can also review previously learned material. Sometimes, for example, showing you his belts and trophies and talking about how he won these awards might do the trick.

2. **Motivation comes when you define your goals so that you can see your progression clearly.** Knowledge heightens your awareness and curiosity and makes you look forward to future lessons. When I was a kid, knowing a month in advance where we were going on vacation was more fun than having it sud-

denly thrust upon me. Sometimes you will learn material that does not seem to lead anywhere at that moment. But knowing that this material may be a requirement on your next test may help you retain your motivation.

3. **Learning material that is useful and relevant increases motivation.** When I took a course in aviation in high school, we spent almost the entire semester focusing on the history of flight despite the fact that students were interested mainly in getting their pilots' licenses. History, although fascinating, is irrelevant to the skill of piloting an airplane. The instruction therefore did not contribute directly to motivating the students. Unless you are enthusiastic about learning, little improvement will be made. Your instructor can help you build on your natural enthusiasm. For example, if you want to learn *nunchakus* as your weapon of choice but your instructor insists that you learn the *bo* staff instead, your natural enthusiasm will likely be dampened. Likewise, if you want to compete in free sparring, your instructor will not keep you interested in the martial arts by requiring you to do a year of forms practice before allowing you to spar. Although forms practice teaches many useful concepts, such as balance, flow, visualization, preplanning, etc., you are not likely to find value in these concepts or discover how they apply to sparring if it is really sparring that excites you. If you must learn forms as part of the curriculum, then you must also find a way to change your perception of what you find valuable.

4. **In order to improve, you must clearly intend to improve.** A commitment to learning means that you recognize mistakes and make a conscious effort to correct them. Critique increases motivation, but only if you take the critique as intended and see the value of it. If you consistently fail or are always negatively critiqued, it is unlikely that you will remain dedicated to the martial arts. Sometimes small failures may help motivate you to study harder. But since success is more pleasant than failure, success is more likely to keep you in class and make you come back for more training.

5. **Assignments should be attainable.** Friendly competition is often a good motivator. Sometimes just observing a higher skilled student is enough to motivate you. If you are the best student in your class, you have no role model to emulate; if you are the worst student in your class, you will likely get discouraged. The ideal learning situation is somewhere in the middle. As you climb the ranks, be aware that the lower ranking students observe the higher ranking studentsand are influenced by them. High-ranking students should therefore behave appropriately, so they can serve as good role models and motivators for the less experienced students.

6. **Motivation needs constant reinforcement.** Many students take a break following a belt promotion, perhaps because they feel that is a good time for that well-earned rest. I have seen students take breaks that last up to six months! In my opinion, it is a bad idea to hold a belt promotion or contest on

the last weekend before the holiday season. After a belt promotion or tournament, you should be given the opportunity to capitalize on what you learned. If you did well, it will motivate you to continue. If you did poorly but the situation was handled correctly, it will also motivate you to continue. When I lost a kickboxing match, I was disappointed not because I lost but because I didn't know when my next match would be. I needed to work toward a new goal. However, training must go in cycles to fit the human body and mind. Nobody can continue at full pace without a rest. Generally, you will feel energetic when working toward a specific goal. But when you have achieved this goal, you should be given the opportunity to slow the pace and replenish your energies. When you come to class after a tournament or belt promotion, try changing direction slightly by learning something new.

7. **Winning is always better than losing.** When you succeed, you are generally motivated to continue learning. Awards of recognition give you an experience with success. Tangible returns such as different-colored belts, trophies and certificates are usually helpful. The same principle is true in competition. Permanent score cards tend to create greater motivation than having to start over each time. Your last achievement should serve as a stepping stone for your next achievement.

8. **Consider your most immediate needs.** For example, you may attend an ongoing class that randomly teaches the techniques required for the next promotion. Or there may be free sparring every Thursday. But as you get close to rank promotion or competitive sparring, you may need to focus on your immediate needs. If a tournament is coming up next month, find out who is competing and in what divisions, and try to set some short-term goals. If a rank promotion is coming up, spend time reviewing the techniques on which you will be tested. Try starting the review when you are close to your peak performance. If the school curriculum is built so that the most urgent skills are practiced when you are ready to peak, you will perform better during the event, and motivation is increased. If the same material is taught for several months, you might lose enthusiasm. Timing is therefore critical.

9. **Study your competition and strive to be a bit sharper than them.** Much of your school's reputation is built upon how students perform in front of strangers. When your instructor's name comes up in conversation and a stranger says, "Yeah, I studied with her for a while, but she just didn't do much for me," you may question the validity of the instruction. What standards are other schools adhering to? If your school awards black belts in a year and a half but other schools take five years to do so, what does this mean? Does it imply that you are much better than others because you get your belt sooner, or does it mean that others train according to stricter standards?

10. **Pride increases motivation.** Pride comes from a sense of belonging. The better a school is in comparison to its counterparts, the more pride the members will feel. Wearing a uniform helps you identify with your school, its goals and accomplishments. Pride also comes when you feel you know something that others don't know, when you have earned the right to wear the uniform, to belong to the team, or to call yourself a black belt or a champion. Pride makes you stand up for and support your school. Your instructor should prioritize the development of pride.

Wearing uniforms and patches creates a sense of belonging and accomplishment and, therefore, pride.

9

Student Performance

STUDENT DIFFERENCES

Although the martial arts are often taught in a group setting, training is still an individual activity. Students advance at their own pace and many skill levels are mixed in the same class. To the instructor, this type of environment creates the challenge of teaching a group while at the same time attending to each student's individual needs.

Students have both physic1al and mental needs. For example, since most of us are right-handed, the instructor might be tempted to teach the techniques from a right stance. Other physical differences are in size, strength and flexibility. Not all students perform the same tasks to the same degree of expertise. For example, some students need to practice the spinning back kick for months before they can apply it in sparring. Others are reasonably proficient after the first lesson. The faster learners should be taught specific uses for the kick, while the slower learners may need to practice on a bag or smaller target in order to gain proficiency. If you have trouble performing a specific technique, however, you are not necessarily less skilled than your peers. In fact, you will probably excel in other areas. Perhaps if the material were presented differently you might suddenly succeed. If you progress faster than expected at your level, your instructor should have a back-up plan so you can move ahead to the next step when you are ready. If your rate of learning is above average, it is only natural to get bored and frustrated if you are not allowed to advance to the next technique or concept when you are ready to do so.

Just as physical aptitude varies among students, so does mental aptitude. A student who does well mentally may not be the greatest athlete physically, and vice versa. However, it should not be assumed that this is always the case. People have many different talents and characteristics, and although few of us are equally skilled at everything, some of us do very well both physically and mentally. Recognize and acknowledge differences between yourself and your peers, and focus on building your strengths rather than imitating your peers or trying to eliminate your weaknesses. For example, I have only mediocre flexibility in my legs, which limits the height of my side-kick and spinning back kick. It also limits how far I can stretch. Others are often amazed that I am unable to do the splits, considering my many years of study. Although I practice the martial arts and stretch every day, I realize very little, if any, improvement in flexibility. I would therefore be offended if someone told me that I just don't work hard enough. If you are unable to improve in a specific area, the problem might lie somewhere other than in work ethics. In other words, your inability to improve may not be due to laziness or lack of confidence.

SCENARIO 27

Your instructor teaches you the same technique over and over, but you still don't seem to get it. What should you do?

1. Shrug and say, "It will come."

2. Argue that some people just learn faster than others.

3. Tell him that you are bored and would like to do something else.

4. Ask for private lessons.

5. Quit.

★★★★★

Sometimes you may fail to improve even in simple techniques and concepts. You must now determine the cause. As an instructor, I have found that if a student is simply hurried and doesn't pay attention, threatening with push-ups works well. For example, one of my students consistently dropped her hands low in sparring, even though I reminded her every ten seconds to keep her guard up. When I told her, "If you drop your hands again, it will cost you ten push-ups," the problem miraculously disappeared! However, the push-up threat only works if the problem is due to a student's inattentiveness. Other causes must be treated differently. If your instructor threatens with push-ups for every "offense," the threat be-

comes annoying rather than helpful. You should generally not worry about short learning plateaus of a few weeks. But if you seem to stagnate, your instructor should help you determine the cause and assist you in moving forward.

SPECIALIZED TRAINING

When you have mastered the basics, you may want to diversify and learn special skills. A school where I studied karate added a weapons class for those students interested in pursuing special skills. If you attend such a class, is it proper for the instructor to require that you learn the weapon of his choice, or should he allow you to choose freely the weapon you want to specialize in? The school where I studied required that every student learn the *bo* staff and one other weapon of choice. I chose the short sticks. But a few weeks into the training I discovered that stick fighting didn't interest me after all, and I would rather learn the *nunchaku*. But the instructor frowned on my suggestion and thought I lacked perseverance. Unfortunately, sometimes you might not know where your interests lie until you have gained some background experience. In my case, I resolved the problem by going to another school to study the *nunchaku*. However, I didn't tell the instructor or any of my peers for fear of disapproval.

If your school provides specialized training, your instructor should make an effort to keep it "special." If your school runs the special classes on a seminar or short-term basis, when you finish the class you should feel that you know more than those who didn't attend. The material you can learn in a special class is almost infinite and is up to your instructor's imagination. You might want to suggest the following:

1 How to perform spinning and jump kicks;

2. How to win in tournament competition;

3. How to be a good referee or judge;

4. How to implement weapons in the techniques you have already learned;

5. How to speed up your hand techniques;

6. How to manipulate your opponent's balance;

7. How to fake and attack;

8. How to be a good counterstriker;

9. How to use stand-up skills on the ground; and

10. How to use grappling skills when standing.

Special classes might have a test associated with them. A colored stripe for your belt, a patch for your uniform, or a certificate to hang on your wall is a good alternative to a test. The classes may also be held without a specific pass/fail requirement. Whatever the case, when you have finished the class, you should have gained insights that your peers, who did not take the class, lack. The insights you gain should move you a step ahead of your peers.

CORRECTING ERRORS

Some instructors are quick to point out everything you are doing wrong. But remember, anybody can do that, whether an intructor or not. When your instructor tells you what is wrong with a technique, she should also provide you with a way to correct the error. For example, saying that you are telegraphing the techniques is useless, unless she also explains why you are telegraphing them and what you can do about it. These sorts of "failed instructions" can be particularly bothersome if you are more advanced than your instructor. If your instructor doesn't make an effort to learn about your background, you must tell her about other arts you have studied so she can tailor the instruction and not waste your time by having you "reinvent the wheel."

When problems develop, it is useful for the instructor to know how to respond to each particular problem with physical assistance and, later, with reminders. When your in-

Share special skills, such as knowledge of handguns, with your peers.

structor understands the common student errors in advance, he will also know what to look for and will therefore be of greater assistance. For example, common errors for the spinning back kick are:

1. Extending the kicking leg too soon and before you can see the target; and

2. Over-rotating or losing balance because your upper body is leaning instead of rotating around a vertical axis.

The sidekick and spinning back kick rely on essentially the same body mechanics for extending the leg and impacting the target. Common errors with both of these kicks include failing to chamber the leg prior to kicking, and bringing the leg up straight from the floor to impact the target at an upward angle. Proper chambering of the leg ensures power through a longer travel distance and decreases the risk of your opponent countering the technique with kicks or sweeps to your supporting leg. Chambering the leg also allows you to extend the kick straight (horizontally) into the target.

When throwing the spinning back kick, perhaps the most common error is failing to bring the head around prior to extending the kick, thus failing to see the target and missing it. The spinning back kick can be practiced with varying degrees of spin. Ask another student to hold a kicking shield directly in front of you. You must now spin 180 degrees in order to land the kick. Next have your partner hold the shield directly to the side, so that you only have to spin 90 degrees. Then have him vary the angle from directly behind (this will be more of a back kick) to a 45, 90, 135 and 180-degree angle. You can also go past 180 degrees, but be

aware that the kick tends to get impractical if you have to spin much more than 180 degrees. A roundhouse kick may now be a better option.

Another common error for the spinning back kick is to swing the kicking leg out wide, over-rotating and striking the target from the side rather than straight. A wide kick is also slower than a tight kick because it has more rotational inertia. Your balance might therefore suffer, or you might inadvertently telegraph the kick. To ensure a tight kick, stand with the side of your body against a wall. When you start rotating for the kick, the wall provides a barrier and reminds you to keep your leg tight throughout the spin.

 SCENARIO 28

In sparring, you notice how your opponent displays nervous traits: wiping his palms on his pants, fidgeting and slapping his gloves together. What should you do?

1. Tell him to keep his guard up.

2. Ask if he is afraid.

3. Show him a way to use these idiosyncrasies as fakes.

4. Whisper that you will take advantage of him.

Nervous behavior (past the initial learning stages) that interferes with your ability to perform the techniques should be brought to your attention. These kinds of traits can give a fighter away. If allowed to continue, unnecessary moves may become habit even after you get over your nervousness. For example, if you are in the habit of touching your gloves together prior to throwing a punch, the idiosyncrasy might tell your opponent what to expect (a punch). Your instructor or partner should bring the problem to your attention and remind you whenever it is happening. If reminding you doesn't fix the problem, you must actively work on eliminating the trait. Ask a partner to hold focus mitts for you. Focus on throwing your strikes without any prior movement in your hands. Have your partner tell you every time he can "read" your intentions, until the new habit overtakes the old.

– INSTRUCTOR TIP –

Allowing students to commit mistakes can speed up the learning process, as long as the mistakes are analyzed and corrected. Good judgment must be exercised when deciding how far to let students go when performing incorrectly.

– STUDENT TIP –

Although you may be wearing a white belt in the art you are currently studying, you might still be experienced in other arts. If you are an experienced martial artist and do a technique differently from how your instructor would do it, you might want to volunteer an explanation of your background experiences.

STUDENT AND INSTRUCTOR SUGGESTIONS FOR CORRECTING ERRORS

1. If your instructor notices an error, she should correct it. If the error is common,

she should bring it to the rest of the class' attention as well. If many students perform the same error, it may be appropriate for the instructor to call a time out and give group instruction, re-explain the technique and give students some extra practice time. The benefit of having a seasoned instructor is that she will see the same problems over and over. When the instructor knows where you are likely to stumble, she can develop a plan that will take you through the difficulties smoothly. Although nearly everybody may be having problems with a particular technique initially, your instructor should not assume that every student is the same. If, by chance, you do not have a problem where everybody else does, your instructor should not create one by giving you instruction on how to correct it.

2. When learning a new technique, you should be allowed to practice it a few times before the instructor corrects you, in order to get your body accustomed to moving in a new way. Then, with the instructor's help, make minor adjustments to fine-tune your technique. Small errors can be pointed out early in training. As long as you are aware of the errors and understand them, you should not worry that they will develop into habits that are later difficult to break.

3. When learning a new technique, specific details should be introduced and discussed after you have acquired a basic understanding of the technique. If details are discussed too soon, they will not make much sense because you will not yet be able to relate them to the technique

or situation you are practicing. Similarly, instructors can discuss and correct errors as ou make them and as you learn more about the technique. For example, your instructor should wait until you perform an error, then point it out and discuss it immediately. If he tells you all the common errors prior to letting you practice the technique, the corrections will make little sense.

4. When you have difficulty remembering a specific technique, your instructor should not rush in and help prematurely. It is better that she prompts you, forcing you to think rather than simply imitate. You should be allowed to make mistakes and should be given sufficient time to think about what went wrong and how to fix it. This problem-reflection-fixing strategy is part of an active learning process.

5. If you perform only minor errors, your instructor may not want to stop and make corrections at that time. It is better that he mentions only the errors that are consistent and obvious, and gives you specific details to work on until next time. For example, you may perform 10 excellent kicks, only to throw one lousy kick. Is this worth mentioning? More than likely, you will be well aware of which kick had the error in it. Nothing may need to be said as long as your overall performance is helping you progress. If you repeatedly throw good kicks followed by one bad kick, it may also be because you are overtraining and are getting fatigued. In this case, it would make little sense for the instructor to correct you. Fatigue often leads to poor per-

formance in spinning techniques where you have to factor in the risk of getting dizzy. Rather than throwing 10 spinning kicks in a row, you may want to alternate between lefts and rights, or throw five kicks, break for a minute and focus on something else, and then throw five more kicks.

6. If you are having problems with a specific technique, don't let other techniques suffer while you try to attain perfection with the one that is troubling you. Since most techniques are related in some way, you will be returning to the problem area plenty of times through the use of other techniques. In addition, it might be beneficial to get away for a while from the technique that is causing you problems.

7. Your instructor should avoid simply *telling* you what to do. She should ask and answer questions, but should not get sidetracked onto irrelevant issues or give you the answers outright. There are times when you will listen to what your instructor is telling you, acknowledge what she says but still continue to make mistakes. In this case, you may not clearly understand what your instructor wants you to do. She can test your understanding by asking specific questions that relate to the technique or concept. She might ask you to show her how to perform a specific segment of a technique, or to explain the differences between the concepts. These sorts of questions will test your knowledge and understanding. Moreover, you might not know when you perform correctly unless your instructor tells you so, or un-

less she shows you the difference between the correct and incorrect technique.

8. Force yourself to think about the particular move you are practicing at the moment. It is easy to get ahead of ourselves and focus on a move that is three or four moves away. For example, if the technique calls for a parry followed by a sidekick and you focus on the sidekick, the mechanics of the parry will suffer. Without a properly executed parry, you will be unable to use the sidekick effectively in this particular combination. There is a fine line that needs to be observed. If you are too tied up in every little detail of a technique, you will try to do everything and will be able to do nothing. Sometimes it is better to "just do it," without thinking too much.

9. When you are aware of your mistakes, making the correction on your own does not only help you remember it the next time, but it also eliminates most feelings of frustration. Your instructor should allow you to practice a few times uninterrupted while he is watching. This teaching strategy helps him determine whether or not you have the insight required to make corrections on your own. It also helps him determine to what degree you have understood the technique. When you start making corrections on your own, without prompting from your instructor, you are on your way to the application and correlation stages of learning. When you reach this level, it should reflect positively on your instructor. Your corrections may not be perfect, but the fact that you recognize the need to make a correction tells your instruc-

tor that you are beginning to discern relationships between techniques.

10. Your instructor should not nit-pick in the days prior to a promotion. It is better to catch and correct errors as they occur, before the problem has become a habit. By asking questions pertaining to the technique, your instructor can determine the depth of your understanding. For example, in the first lesson he might talk about how wide apart your feet should be in your stance and why. In the next lesson, he might ask you to assume a stance and then check it for correctness. If it is correct, he should ask you to explain why. Your explanation assures him that you didn't just end up this way by chance. If your stance is incorrect, he should also ask you why. Or he should correct the stance and then ask why it is better. Some sample questions include: "How did we decide to position the feet? Do you remember how we tested the width of your stance? Why is it a bad idea to assume a stance that is too narrow? What is bad about a stance that is too wide? Name three ways in which you can use your stance to strengthen your fighting ability." When your instructor asks you to explain what is wrong with a technique, try to give him only one exact answer. If you give him 10 different answers, it is unlikely you have gained true understanding. You might just be guessing or repeating what he has told you on an earlier occasion.

11. You won't perform perfectly every time. It is okay to make mistakes. You should be more concerned with your progress as a whole than with your performance at the moment. Try to find a trend: Are

you attending class regularly? Can you stay focused during training? Are you even-tempered? A person's temper may not seem to have much to do with learning, but it is my experience that those who are even-tempered normally have more endurance when it comes to completing a program. Persistence and consistency win the game. It is not necessarily the most talented students who go to the championships, but rather those who have persevered and continued training and competing on a regular basis. Those who are slow learners initially often progress faster once they get over the first hump.

12. Some students are those rare types of learners who do everything correctly from the start. It might now be tempting for your instructor to correct techniques that don't really need correction. For example, a common error for the roundhouse kick is to neglect chambering the leg prior to kicking. Since this is a problem that tends to occur with almost every student initially, your instructor might be tempted to correct those students who are chambering their leg correctly as well. Drawing attention to common errors is good, but only to those which need to be corrected. In a case like this, your instructor should draw attention to the fact that you did perform the technique correctly. If you are not aware of your performance, a good kick might have been coincidental. But if your instructor draws attention to what you did correctly, you will have something to think about when you analyze your techniques later.

13. At the end of the lesson, your instructor should give you some form of encouragement:

Bad: *"I told you last time to use a set-up technique and not just blast the kick out there! You're never going to land it that way!"*

Good: *"I can see that you have practiced the sidekick, because you're doing much better extending the leg and kicking through the target. You should now work on increasing your speed during the set-up phase of the kick. The reason you're getting countered is because you're not concealing the kick well. Here is something to think about . . ."*

14. When you are ready to move ahead, move ahead. Few things are worse than having the same material rehashed with no progress in sight, particularly when both you and your instructor know fully well that you are ready to move ahead. In order for you to retain excitement about learning the martial arts, your instructor must constantly present you with new challenges.

BUILDING CONFIDENCE

Confidence is desirable, but you must also be truthful about how far you have come and what you can really do at your stage of learning. Some students appear overly confident, when in fact it is a facade used to hide a lack of confidence. Others may appear slow or less smart than their peers. But this outer appearance can delude you as well. Although first impressions are powerful, they can be faulty. Your instructor must therefore take time to re-evaluate your progress against measurable standards. For example, if you are slow at learning a new technique, your instructor's first impression might be to give you more instruction. However, the reason you are slow may not be that you lack knowledge or confidence. The problem may also come from factors, such as an argument at home that inhibits learning at a particular time. In the weeks following the sudden and premature death of my brother, I would suffer from mental standstills where I was unable to remember names of techniques or moves that I had been practicing for years.

Sometimes the apt students are the most difficult to teach. When few corrections are needed, the instructor must look for new ways to challenge you. Sometimes the apt students don't take criticism well because they are used to scoring straight A's. Your instructor must handle these situations delicately. Even when you perform flawlessly, your instructor should still debrief you or offer suggestions that will further challenge you. Once she gets to know you better, she will also learn more about your personality. This knowledge will help her develop either a more aggressive or more delicate approach to training, as needed.

 SCENARIO 29

You are having problems with a particular technique. When you see your peers plowing ahead, you get discouraged. How should you handle it?

1. Go home and practice until you get it right.

2. Take a week off to rest and think about it.

3. Ignore it, because the problem will most likely go away by itself.

4. Ask for private instruction after class.

5. Suggest that the whole class goes back to basics.

The more you stew about your problem the less likely you are to learn, because when you are angry or frustrated you also get tunnel vision and are therefore not receptive to learning. So this is not the time to practice until you "get it right." Nor is it the time to take a week off to think about it. You are worried that you will never catch up to your peers, so taking time off will only make it more difficult to do so. In a situation like this, your instructor should help you build confidence rather than correct a specific technique. For example, learning a more advanced technique may allow you to feel that you know something the others do not know. This extra knowledge may boost your confidence and free your mind to focus on correcting the initial problem.

It is often more productive to go between or around the obstacles than through them. Distancing yourself from the technique that causes you problems allows you to progress by focusing your efforts elsewhere. When I was learning how to fly sailplanes I often bounced on landing, and my instructor was constantly nagging me about it. But when I flew from a different field where nobody knew me, I could suddenly make perfect landings.

How do you know when you are ready to move ahead? Waiting too long may result in boredom and discouragement, while moving ahead before you are ready can lead to frustration. A sign of readiness is when you respond quickly and confidently to your instructor's commands. Even if you don't display complete competence, moving ahead to the next stage may still prove beneficial because:

1. Moving ahead provides variation and can help you overcome learning plateaus;

2. Moving ahead suggests progress and is therefore a natural confidence-builder; and

3. Moving ahead can help you increase your skill and may motivate you for further practice.

When your instructor watches your technique closely and offers suggestions, do you feel you can progress faster, or do you feel he is nagging you about your performance?

– INSTRUCTOR TIP –

A student asks about his performance and you tell him, "I have nothing to say. You were perfect!" What is wrong with this statement? If you have no comments about your student's performance, he may think you are either uninterested or lazy. Talking about what took place, even if no corrections are needed, helps the student retain what he has learned. Talking about what the student did right helps him capitalize on it the next time.

– STUDENT TIP –

When I was a student of intermediate rank, a beginner student kicked me in the head in sparring. The instructor didn't see the incident, but when he asked later how we had performed, a little boy who was about six years old pointed at me and said, "She was awesome!" Although my own assessment of my work was less encouraging, the boy's comment made my day. When you see one of your peers getting discouraged, try to emphasize the good things he or she did, preferably in front of the class. How we feel about ourselves has a lot to do with how we think others perceive us.

OBSTACLES TO LEARNING

A year has passed since you first stepped into the training hall. You have trained enthusiastically four or five days a week and have progressed through one rank after another. In fact, you just passed your brown belt test. But now you feel as though you are rehashing the same material. Lessons seem geared toward the beginning students, and even in the advanced classes you don't feel as though you get enough one-on-one time with the instructor. You have lost sight of your goal. You have stagnated and lost your zest for learning. You are thinking about taking a leave, maybe even quitting.

When you seem to stagnate for a long period of time, you may have reached a learning plateau. If you are not aware of what is happening, you could end up a statistic; a student who shakes his head years later and says, "Yeah, I used to be a martial artist..."

A variety of emotional and physical responses can interfere with learning. The main obstacle to learning is a lack of desire. Without a true desire to learn, you are likely to quit before reaching any significant level of expertise. Your instructor must therefore help you preserve the hunger to learn, so that you look forward to the next lesson. Your instructor should assign you enough tasks or exercises to help you maintain interest. But he should not assign so many that you get overwhelmed. Many factors, in addition to a lack of desire, can create obstacles to learning. Be cautious of the following:

1. **Unfair treatment**. It is difficult to learn when your instructor fails to treat everybody with fairness, or if she critiques you unfairly. Fair treatment, however, does not mean *identical* treatment of everybody.

2. **Instructor lack of interest**. An instructor who appears uninterested could damage your desire to learn. If your instructor has other things on his mind, he must still make an effort to appear interested in order to help you maintain interest.

3. **Physical discomfort or illness**. It is difficult to learn when you are sick or have worries on your mind. Sometimes you simply have an offday. When you are

not feeling well, physically or mentally, you have a harder time concentrating on learning.

4. **Apathy caused by inadequate instructor preparation**. When you are bored, your mind begins to wander and your focus is not on the material presented.

5. **Impatience to proceed caused by boring lessons or a feeling of being held back**. Activities, such as friendly competition and challenging problems, can help you break through this obstacle to learning.

6. **Worry or anxiety**. When you are afraid, you are unable to learn because you are unable to relax. Your instructor should avoid surprises; she should tell you what to expect beforehand.

7. **Instructor lack of sincerity**. If you feel that your instructor is not taking your efforts seriously, learning will be difficult no matter how much you desire to learn.

BATTLING LEARNING PLATEAUS

Learning that has already taken place — including learning bad habits — is difficult to undo. If you become a "dojo hopper" and try to learn several arts too early in your development, you may get confused when one instructor tells you one thing and another instructor tells you something else. One of the greatest responsibilities of the professional instructor is to recognize problems that may lead to learning plateaus and to help you break through this critical phase of learning. Let's look at some ways in which you can teamup with your instructor and help him help you overcome plateaus.

Move ahead: Learning plateaus are recognized by a sudden stagnation, which, in turn, leads to frustration or skipping classes. At this point, it is tempting to take a half step back to where you were still making progress, and polish the basics. However, it is my experience that a learning plateau is not necessarily due to your inability to grasp more complex techniques. Rather, it may be because you are tired or have lost your enthusiasm. This happened to me shortly after I reached intermediate rank in Kenpo karate. I took a six-week leave and even considered quitting. (Six weeks may not sound like much, but it is six times longer than any leave I have taken since.) Instead of going back to basics, ask your instructor to give you more-advanced techniques. The introduction of new material might help you to get excited about learning again. Your instructor can also push you to test for a higher rank, even if you don't want to test or aren't quite ready. Achieving a higher rank may help you rise to a new level mentally, and therefore rise past the learning plateau. Or take a shorter leave, such as two weeks, to replenish your energies.

Be innovative: A subject that is presented in a way different from the norm can help you overcome obstacles. For example, you don't learn to kick harder by listening to your instructor telling you to kick harder. You don't necessarily learn to kick harder by learning proper kicking mechanics, either. When you have difficulty learning a particular technique, ask your instructor to teach you a technique that is more difficult but along the same path. For example, if you have problems with the sidekick, learn the spinning back kick. Or your instructor can try giving you a distraction that briefly removes your focus from the technique you are trying to do. For example, if you have problems with the spinning back kick, throw a roundhouse kick followed by a spinning back kick. Or throw a spinning back kick followed by a sidekick. Or try decreasing the size of the target. Too much focus on one technique can also make you tense. The more information you have to keep track of, the less concerned you will be with each individual move. Speeding up sometimes produces better results than slowing down, because you don't have as much time to think about the technique and will thus be forced to make the necessary adjustments. A simple technique often comes easier when reintroduced after a more complex technique.

Delete four-letter words: Some schools have inspiring signs that read, "Four-letter words are forbidden. *Can't* is a four-letter word." But just how do you remove the negative from your vocabulary? Rather than insisting that you can't do a technique, explain to your instructor what you *can* do. For example, if you can't do the roundhouse kick because you have a limitation in your hips which prevents you from pivoting, explore how much you *can* pivot your hips while explaining the problem to your instructor. Paraphrasing your problem can help you discover a solution more easily.

Go to a substitute instructor: Sometimes the instruction goes in one ear and out the other. Ask your instructor to recommend another instructor who presents the subject slightly differently, and who would welcome your attendance for a lesson or two. Receiving another person's view may instill new insights that can help you break through barriers. If your instructor is reluctant to send you to another instructor, suggest someone she knows and trusts. Or attend the class of another instructor within the same school.

Be unique: It is not absolutely necessary that everybody develop the same skills beyond the basics. Having a special skill makes you unique. If you know more about weapons than your peers, for example, or more about grappling, you will feel that your individualism counts. Ask to demonstrate your special skills at a belt promotion or during a seminar. Doing so gives you something particular to work toward.

Capitalize on your strengths: It is all too common for instructors to emphasize the weaknesses: "You need to work on the height in that kick!" Once you have reached intermediate level and have determined that you do not have the same athletic ability as other students, start focusing on your strengths. Ask your instructor to show you how you can defeat a high kicker, for example, by kicking your opponent's supporting leg. Explore the advantages of the lesser effort, greater speed, and better deception of the low kick. Since low kicks are not as tiresome as high kicks, emphasizing the low kick may also enable older or weaker students to outfight younger, stronger or more athletic students. Note that high kicks may be flashier and more difficult to perform than low kicks. But since you can also reach your opponent's head with your hands, you have not eliminated the high target by kicking to the legs; you have merely reworked

your strategy to fit your personal characteristics and strengths. Many people also have a preconceived idea that jump kicks must be thrown to high targets. But a secondary purpose of the jump is to create more power by enabling faster and easier turns of your body in the air. Learn the value of jump kicks low to the legs or midsection, rather than to the head. If you are smaller or weaker than other students, ask your instructor to demonstrate strategic strengths, such as leverage, fighting at close range, footwork, etc. Learning strategy gives you greater benefits than simply being told to work on stretching for greater flexibility, or to weight train for better strength. Focusing on your strengths instead of your weaknesses allows you to realize immediate results.

Capitalize on your natural enthusiasm: When your natural enthusiasm is nurtured, it will grow and enable you to reach heights much greater than what may be called for in your current rank. When you are enthusiastic about learning, your instructor should nurture it even if the source of your excitement is a technique or concept you are not supposed to learn at this time. Perhaps a more advanced student showed you an easy way to render a bigger opponent harmless. You are now excited about learning more. Ask your instructor to elaborate on the technique. In other words, he should give you the advanced technique and maybe a little more. Acquiring knowledge that is more advanced than what your current rank calls for does not mean you must sacrifice the material you are supposed to learn at this level. Natural enthusiasm can also appear in areas other than technique. Pay attention to what you enjoy and are good at.

Perhaps you have exceptional communication skills and enjoy assisting less experienced students. Perhaps you have organizational skills and enjoy helping in tournaments. Perhaps you excel in individual activities. Being quiet and disliking games or competition does not mean you have a social disorder. For example, you may be an excellent speaker as long as you have something important to say. You may be cut out to be an instructor or to lead a seminar.

Understand your background: A student with less experience or a lower educational level may not learn as fast as the rest of the class, which is not the same as saying that such a student lacks intelligence. Likewise, a student who is highly educated and more experienced than the instructor may find the lessons utterly boring, because she has already heard it all before. Your instructor must therefore be informed about your knowledge and background so that he can avoid teaching lessons that are either too complicated or too boring. The rate of learning can be enhanced by building on your current knowledge and prior experiences. Experience, or more specifically, *common* experience, is important to learning. For example, if this is your first exposure to the martial arts, you may still have certain common experiences with your instructor and peers because of your background in police work, the military, contact sports, etc.

Take a blind shot: When you reach a plateau, consider whether something unusual or dramatic has happened in your life. When we change jobs, get married or break up with our spouse, start school, or have a baby, our lives change and with them our priorities. Sometimes taking a break is good for you. But you can also try reworking your schedule. Perhaps two morning lessons will work better than four evening lessons. If you can't identify your problem in specific terms, taking a blind shot and changing your schedule might just work.

Break through learning plateaus by being unique. For example, develop a special skill such as knife defense, which you can demonstrate to other students during a belt promotion.

 SCENARIO 30

You are slow and hesitant and have problems performing the simplest techniques. What can your instructor do to help you?

1. Make you work more on the simple techniques.

2. Tell you to relax and speed up.

3. Introduce a more advanced technique.

4. Require you to spar often, forcing you to use the techniques in real time.

★★★★★

116

If your instructor holds an object in her hand and asks you to reach out and grab it, you will do so automatically without putting much thought into it. But if she tells you to throw a punch and you think of every detail involved in throwing that punch, your technique will be stiff, slow and uncoordinated. When you are hesitant, speeding up rather than slowing down may help you get over this hurdle. Rather than telling you to take your time with every move, your instructor might want to give you special commands such as, "Go! Again! Faster!" When speeding up, you don't have much time to think about the technique and your body is forced to make the necessary adjustments. Your instructor might also want to introduce a more complex technique whenever you have problems with a simple technique, and then reintroduce the simple technique later. Getting through or around an obstacle is sometimes a matter of diverting your attention away from the obstacle.

10
Lesson Plans

THE BENEFITS OF LESSON PLANS

Improving your skill takes a dedicated, well-planned effort. This chapter on lesson plans will further help you understand some of the things a good instructor does to help you progress. Lesson plans can be considered blue prints to ensure that no part of the material is left untaught. Since learning rates differ between students, the lesson plan need not be followed precisely, but should function as an outline — a loose plan of what the lesson is to cover. Well-written lesson plans make each lesson economical and eliminate duplication of lessons. When several instructors are teaching at the school and everybody follows the same lesson plan, all students are moved toward the same objectives. The lesson plan for the week (or month) can be placed on the counter or posted on the wall. When the evening class instructor comes in, he can teach the same lesson as the morning class instructor. Lesson plans ensure uniformity among instructors and keep the school organized. Lesson plans that are posted also help you (the student) prepare for the next lesson in advance.

When your instructor has developed lesson plans for an entire course, she can place them in a binder and use them over and over. She can also keep a log of which lesson plan she is teaching to a particular group of students, date it, and use it as a reference to refresh her memory later. Lesson plans assist the instructor not only with the present lesson and student group, but also with new students who come for instruction the next year. The act of writing lesson plans ensures that the instructor gives the lesson sufficient thought; that she has, in fact, taught herself the lesson first. Lesson plans for specific lessons can be written several days in advance. The instructor can now gain focus quickly when the lesson starts.

Since attaining a black belt requires a long-term training program, it is essential to break it down into several shorter segments. If you want to know what is being done to help you achieve your goals, the lesson plan can tell you what you have done so far, and what you are doing next month. However, lesson plans shouldn't remain static and unchanging for many years. Your instructor may discover, due to his own advancement, that what worked well last year may not work this year. When the objectives change, so should the plan. As your instructor discovers new and pertinent information, he should add it to the appropriate lesson plan and delete information that he has determined is no longer needed. Over time, this process creates a highly refined system of teaching and learning that wastes a minimal amount of time and effort.

While lesson plans are intended to keep the instructor focused on the lesson, they are not intended to take away her creativity or flexibility with the lesson. Initially, lesson plans should be fully developed to ensure that your instructor has thought about what she is to teach. Later, when she gains more teaching experience, lesson plans can be made simpler or even written on some scrap paper.

An instructor who is a proponent of lesson plans will take a few minutes to familiarize himself with the plan prior to teaching. This familiarization prevents him from having to refer to the written plan throughout the lesson. However, the lesson plan should not be so detailed that the instructor has to spend five minutes reading every statement before teaching it. Rather, he should be very familiar with the content of the plan before the lesson begins, and rely on key points to support his presentation. It is okay for the instructor to deviate from the lesson plan if needed in order to serve a greater objective, but he shouldn't deviate so much that irrelevant material is introduced. The lesson plan should not be "mechanical." Your instructor must still think about what he is teaching. Lesson plans are not substitutes for proper preparation. A lesson plan that doesn't seem to help students reach the desired objective should be modified. A lesson plan written for a particular student group may not have the same effect on a different group.

When developing lesson plans, the instructor must consider what students already know. For example, if you already understand the mechanics of the front kick, your instructor may want to give you some warm-up exercises for the front kick instead of going over its mechanics again. You will then work on kick application. Repetition is good, but only if it actually helps you progress. Some new material should be taught in every lesson. You should also be given plenty of opportunity to practice this new material. Note that plenty of opportunity is not the same as plenty of time. Practicing a single technique for 30 minutes may not be as beneficial as practicing the technique in shorter segments using different scenarios. The more varied the practice methods are, the more insight you gain into the different uses of the technique. Most students agree that at least some variety makes training fun. Your instructor must also consider the size of the group she is teaching. Teaching a group of 20 students requires a different approach than teaching one student privately. Lesson plans:

- Help your instructor think about what is important to teach;

- Help your instructor stay on track and teach the material in a logical sequence;

- Help your instructor check on your progress and look for errors;

- Help standardize instruction;

- Can be used by other instructors;

- Can be saved and reused the next year; and

- Can be used to inform students, parents and others about the program's methods and objectives.

WHAT THE LESSON PLAN SHOULD INCLUDE

A lesson plan can be a simple list of techniques required for the next level, or it can be a more complex list of specific skills or concepts, such as how to control the ring environment or how to apply angled attacks effectively in sparring. However, in order for a lesson plan to be effective, it should clearly state the objectives to be attained, the content to be learned, the means by which the objectives are achieved, and the skill acquired (or the completion standards). Lesson plans should also include common errors, facts and principles or concepts relating to the material taught.

A complex lesson should be broken down into its component parts, and your instructor should specify how to achieve each objective. This breakdown is particularly important if the objectives are abstract. If your instructor tells you that you must master defense, for example, the image it creates in your mind and the image it creates in your instructor's mind may not be the same. Your instructor must therefore identify what is involved in "mastering defense." Does it mean you can execute specific blocks? Does it mean you can move out of harm's way? Does it mean you can use offense defensively? How?

The objectives must also be specific and attainable within the allotted time. The objective "to become the world champion," is not only too vague to be valuable, it is unrealistic. Although becoming the world champion may be a goal worth striving for, the objective should be a little more concrete; something that you can achieve in a shorter time. Let's look at how to break down the lesson plan.

Objective: This is a clear statement of what the lesson is to cover. In order to specify the objective, your instructor must analyze the course he is to teach and break it into its component parts. The objective keeps your instructor on track and helps him select the best method for teaching the material. The objective can also include a description of the conditions during which the techniques should be done, and the standards that must be met before the objectives are achieved.

1. Objectives should be challenging. When you reach the objective, you should feel a sense of accomplishment.

2. Objectives should be useful. You will be more excited about learning if you can use what you have learned early in your training. For example, if reaching the objective allows you to compete in your first tournament, and competition is your goal, then the objective is useful.

3. Objectives should be measurable. When you have reached the objective, it should be clear that you are ahead of those students who have not yet completed the lesson.

Content/Instruction: This part of the lesson plan should include a step-by-step analysis of how to teach the material that is to be covered in the lesson, including specific tips that help students learn. This section can also include the time that should be devoted to each exercise, and how your instructor should present each element. For example:

1. Should the material be presented by lecture or demonstration? Or should it be a combination of both?

121

2. Should the material be presented by letting students practice on bags, on each other or in the air?

A number of key points will help your instructor stay on track and is usually better than a hard-and-fast plan. Your instructor should elaborate on each step. For example, if she is to teach the front kick, the roundhouse kick and the sidekick, and she simply demonstrates each kick and lets you try 10 kicks with each leg, she will run out of things to say after 10 minutes. In addition, you will not increase your skill simply because you have been introduced to basic techniques without application. To help you think of additional things to capitalize on, your instructor should give you exercises employing scenarios rather than having you kick only the air or the bags.

Common Errors: Identifying the most common student errors for each specific lesson will help your instructor know beforehand what to look for, and will therefore help him correct the majority of errors early in the lesson. He should explain not just what the common errors are, but also why they occur. Knowing why helps him tell you how to apply the corrective action. For example:

1. A common error when throwing a reverse punch is to lean your upper body forward, compromising balance. This error occurs because you push with your rear foot against the floor, straightening your leg.

2. The corrective action is to "set down" in your stance: to bend your leg rather than straighten it, thereby lowering your weight. This action eliminates the balance problem and the potential power

loss because you avoid jamming your own technique.

Completion Standards: This is a statement specifying the standards of performance that must be met before you can move on to the next lesson. Your instructor should evaluate you against the objective and receive feedback to help her plan future lessons. Feedback could be either verbal or physical, but you should provide some kind of evidence that you have mastered the material.

When the lesson is complete, your instructor might want to write down any student reactions that she observed. For example, how did the students feel about the lesson? What questions did they ask? How interested were they in the subject? How well did they perform? This analysis helps the instructor modify the lesson plan for future use.

If the completion standard states that you must be able to control your opponent through the use of a joint lock, then you must demonstrate control and not just the mechanics of the technique.

122

The instructor should avoid asking open-ended questions such as, "Do you have any questions?"

This type of query will not likely encourage many return questions or reponses. More can be achieved by discussing specific situations or by giving specific examples.

SAMPLE LESSON PLAN

The following is a sample lesson plan for teaching basic movement in fighting.

Objective

1. To develop the student's ability to move with speed and smoothness without telegraphing his intent to the opponent.

2. To develop the student's ability to start and stop movement, to switch direction with ease and grace, and to evade counterattacks.

Content/Instruction

1. Step with the foot closest to the direction of travel first, adjusting the width of your stance with your rear foot in order to maintain a consistent distance between your feet.

2. Stay on the balls of your feet for speed, agility and balance.

3. Move forward, backward, left and right, while adding strikes and kicks to your movement.

4. Incorporate pivot-steps to evade counterattacks.

Common Errors

1. Loss of focus and telegraphing intent to the opponent.

2. Poor balance, particularly when switching direction.

3. Poor adjustment of rear foot, causing a narrow, wide or unbalanced stance.

4. Poor timing when striking or evading counterattacks.

Completion Standards

The lesson is complete when the student has achieved reasonable proficiency in moving and evading counterattacks without telegraphing his intent to the opponent.

 SCENARIO 31

Your instructor has taught half of the lesson, when she suddenly forgets what to teach next. Students are looking at her and waiting. What should your instructor do to save face?

1. Turn and look for the lesson plan somebody should have written.

2. Walk out the door and say, "I'll be back in a minute."

3. Laugh and say, "I just forgot what I was gonna teach!"

4. Improvise.

 ★★★★★

Stalling or going blank in the middle of a lesson may be an embarrassing moment for the professional instructor. To avoid this pitfall, your instructor can decide on a prompt she can give herself to serve as a lesson reminder. The prompt can be as simple as taking three minutes to stretch, or it can be more complex, such as an extra credit technique that she has thought about beforehand and can teach at the spur of the moment. However, my experience is that few students disrespect an instructor who stumbles on occasion.

TEACHING A LESSON, NOT AN HOUR

Lessons should not be put together haphazardly or according to "what sounds good." In order to be effective, the instruction must have meaning and be useful for the particular group of students being taught. For example, a beginner might need to approach the material differently than a black belt. How the student intends to use the material should also be considered. Learning for competition differs from learning for self-defense, and learning for law enforcement differs from attending an ongoing class for the entire family. Instruction should not be overly simple, nor should it be overly complicated. When your instructor knows something about your background, he can gear the lesson accordingly. Your instructor can also look back at and draw from his own learning experiences. Or he can interview you to find out what your goals are. If you feel that your instructor is "lost" or is teaching irrelevant material, you can help by offering him information about your background, goals and desires.

Lessons should be planned so that your instructor teaches a lesson and not an hour. However, she should be able to cover the subject in the allotted time. If a lesson is to last for an hour, it should be planned so that the material can be taught in an hour. If it takes a few minutes longer, then so be it; at least it had a beginning, middle and end. I have found that students appreciate complete lessons. The material taught must also be thought through and presented in a logical sequence. Trying to learn 20 concepts or techniques in the same lesson is too much information for the student to digest, and makes the lesson seem confusing and disorganized. If the lesson needs to be split in the middle, your instructor should pick up next time where she left off, but may need to conduct a short review of the lesson. Too little material, on the other hand, results in boredom, impatience and inefficiency.

But what if your instructor finishes the lesson much too early? When planning the lesson, a thoughtful instructor asks himself:

1. Can I cover the material in an hour (the standard class time)?

2. Do I need to break the material down into two or three classes? If so, where is the logical dividing point?

3. If I cover the material in 30 minutes, what will I do for the rest of the lesson?

Your instructor should have a back-up plan if things don't work out quite as planned. As an instructor, I have found that I seldom run out of material to teach. Questions, unexpected situations, techniques or concepts that I want to elaborate on tend to pop up during the lesson, and it is far easier to go over the allotted time than to finish early. However, as a student you can think about the techniques beforehand that you wish to work on. If the instructor does run out of material to teach, you can then take charge of your training and ask him to help you with your specific points of interest.

THE ESSENTIAL TASK

Each new lesson should build on the previous one. New material being introduced should relate to the old material from the previous lesson. A lesson plan is therefore not an entity in itself, but rather a building block for the entire course. A lesson plan should spend some time reviewing material from the previous lesson. There might also be subjects for discussion or further training objectives that surface once the lesson has started. The instructional objectives should be broken down into smaller tasks; the instructor should identify the *essential task* of the lesson. This may be a technique or a concept. For example:

1. When learning forms for a tournament, you must know something about your competition so that you can focus on how to win.

2. You must know what moves tend to score high with the judges. For example, if aerial maneuvers score high, you shouldn't be learning traditional forms.

The essential task can also be concept-oriented:

1. When learning self-defense techniques, disarming your opponent could be a concept.

2. The exact means by which you achieve the disarming technique are irrelevant. Examine a variety of situations and techniques.

Next you must identify the steps required to achieve the objective. When learning forms:

1. The first steps might be to determine how limber and acrobatic you are, and to learn a definition of the aerial techniques that are to be performed. You might then learn these techniques one at a time until you have mastered them.

2. If you are practicing musical forms, you must find some music that you like and start choreographing.

When learning weapons disarming techniques:

1. The first step might be to determine whether the attacker is holding a knife, club or gun.

2. If a variety of disarming techniques are taught, you might start by focusing on the knife attack and identifying different types of knife attacks, such as stabbing and slashing.

3. Since the essential task is disarming your opponent, you would not be learning complicated joint locking techniques at this point. Instead, identify ways to get to a superior position from where you can proceed with a disarming technique. For example, you might have determined that you can restrict your opponent's mobility best from the ground, so you learn a takedown first.

The essential task might be to progress from white belt to black belt, and your school might have specific techniques listed as the requirements. You must now focus on these specific techniques in their logical sequence and know what standards you will be measured against. It is also a good idea to set a deadline. You should be given a goal: to test for your yellow belt two months from now, for example, and in order to do that you must learn one new technique every week. Now that you know the steps required to reach the goal, you can determine how often you should attend class to learn these new techniques. For example, it might be appropriate to attend class three times a week: once to learn the mechanics of the technique, and twice to practice it. Again, the task is broken down into smaller, more manageable parts.

When your instructor evaluates you later, part of the purpose of the evaluation is to determine whether you can reasonably achieve your goals within the timeframe and standards that have been set. If you achieved the goal early, your instructor may want to cut the time or make the requirements stricter for future goals. If you did not achieve the goal, then he must identify why. Perhaps the moves weren't taught in a logical sequence, perhaps he gave you too much information too fast, or perhaps you hadn't developed the athletic ability needed to do the techniques. Your instructor must now make adjustments to his lesson plan, so that he can make it more efficient for future students. Few instructors go to this length when teaching and much time is therefore wasted.

Is wasting time such a bad thing? I think it is, but unfortunately it is often the norm. I have had instructors who asked, "What would you like to work on today?" Each lesson should not be an entity in itself, but a prerequisite for the next lesson. Your instructor must therefore know what lesson be will cover next. I believe that instructors often forget that they exist primarily for the students. Instructors often go along in the same rut every day, without giving much thought to the student's progression.

THE LOGICAL LESSON

When teaching the logical lesson, your instructor relates techniques taught at the beginning of the lesson to those taught later in the lesson. Learning several different techniques may be confusing to you. For example, if you learn the front kick, a knife disarming technique not involving kicks, and a grappling move, you have learned

If the essential task is a takedown, the exact means by which you accomplish this is less important than the end result: to take your opponent to the ground.

three distinctly different techniques. A better way is to learn just one technique — the front kick — and explore its many different uses. In the next lesson, you can build on the front kick by learning how a punch can be combined with the front kick, for example, or how the punch can be used to set up the front kick through a fake attack. You are now relating the new technique (the punch) to the old technique (the front kick). You will remember and appreciate the concepts more when studying related material than when learning a series of unrelated techniques.

Your instructor must also help you remember the information he has given you. If he presents the techniques in a logical order, you will be able to associate the second technique with the first technique, and the third technique with the second and first techniques. As an instructor, I usually avoid teaching punching, kicking and joint locks in the same lesson because these techniques are not closely enough related. One exception would be if I intend to specifically teach how to use punching and kicking as set-ups for the joint locking technique. If I were to teach joint locks, I might start by teaching proper falling techniques since many joint locks end with a throw or takedown. Or I might review basic balance and theory of joint locking from the ground. If I were to teach punching and kicking, I might incorporate timing and distance; I might talk about how to kick when both you and your opponent are on the ground. Once you have learned both striking and joint-locking techniques, I might teach a lesson that combines both, for example, by showing you how to lock the elbow and simultaneously execute a strike against the joint, or by showing you

how to use kicks as softening techniques to split an opponent's focus in preparation for a joint-locking technique.

Some techniques must be learned in smaller segments over a longer period of time. You can learn a throw, for example, by:

1. Starting with a circular takedown and learning how to fall safely;

2. Turning the takedown into a throw or learning throws from a kneeling position;

3. Learning how to throw an opponent when initiating the technique from a variety of angles; and

4. Learning what to do once the throw is successful, or what to do if the throw fails;

When you have learned smaller segments of a technique, they should be combined to form the whole. For example, when you have learned individual strikes and kicks, you can combine them into a self-defense technique. Your instructor can also show you how the same principles apply to many different techniques. When you have learned individual techniques, you can combine them into a martial arts form, or you can practice them as defense against multiple opponents. When you have learned a number of forms and techniques, you can compete in a tournament.

Sometimes one learning experience assists another learning experience, and sometimes it hinders it. For example, learning a front kick may help you learn a roundhouse kick, while learning a hard style of karate may hinder you when learning a soft style. If your instructor has made an effort to know your previous experiences, she can relate the new material to what you already know. If you have studied another form of martial art, your instructor can relate the "new" art to the "old" art, thereby creating a relationship that you can profit from. For example, if you have studied high school wrestling and your instructor teaches grappling, she can show you that grappling is much like wrestling while pointing out the exceptions, such as you don't lose by touching your full back to the floor. She has now stated both a similarity and a difference. In order to relate two stand-up arts, she might say that all the hand techniques in kickboxing are identical to those of boxing with the exception of the spinning back fist.

INSTRUCTION AND PRACTICE

At the beginning of the lesson, your instructor should state the objective and the steps required to achieve it. For example:

"Today we will focus on the sidekick and how to use it strategically. But first we will warm up with a couple of rounds of bag work."

Stating the objective prepares you for the lesson. When you warm up on the heavy bag, you are already thinking about the sidekick and its uses. Your instructor might want to teach or review the mechanics of the technique first, let you kick shields and bags, and finally have you spar and use the kick at least once in each round. Next, he may teach you strategy and when to use the kick; for example, as a deterrent against an advancing opponent. More complicated objectives don't need to be accomplished in one lesson. Consider these additional issues:

1. If the class has an uneven number of students, is it a good idea for your instructor to pair up with one of the students? Why or why not?

2. In what ways can you practice the techniques if you choose not to do partner drills?

3. At the end of the class, it might be a good idea if one student explains and demonstrates to the rest of the class how to use the technique. This recap summarizes the material and helps your instructor determine to what extent his teachings have made sense.

As you become more proficient, verbal instructions will mean more. "Say what you are going to say, say it, and say what you just said," is actually a pretty simple, workable, and straight forward approach. Your instructor states the objective. Then she teaches the technique. And finally she reviews it. Your instructor should not assume that the objective is obvious. For example, when learning a self-defense technique, the immediate objective may not be to kill your adversary, and even if it were, then how exactly would you achieve it? If you are learning a knife disarming technique, your objective may be to escape without getting cut rather than disarming your opponent. If your objective is to avoid getting cut, you need to learn concepts rather than specific techniques. Learn to be aware of where the knife is, or what to do if you are controlling your opponent's knife hand and he switches the knife to the other hand.

Work on bags or dummies should not be a mindless rut. Be attentive to your stance, exercise good form, and aim for precise targets.

Your objective might be to use the front kick effectively in sparring. But the objective needs to be further clarified and broken down into specific segments. What exactly is meant by "use effectively"? Try breaking down the objective as follows:

1. Must be able to use the front kick offensively as a deterrent to knock your opponent back.

2. Must be able to kick to precise targets (solar plexus, chest, chin, etc.).

3. Must be able to judge distance and kick with penetrating power.

4. Must be able to use the front kick in combination with a set-up strike.

When you have broken down the objective and listed the specific elements, you can start thinking about how to achieve these elements. What exercises must you do in order to use the technique effectively in sparring? Your instructor should make sure that the exercises he assigns you are workable. He should not use long segments of exhausting exercises followed by long segments of slow practice. If you go from jump rope to heavy bag work to continuous sparring, for example, you are doing too much exhaustive work. On the other hand, if you practice forms for the whole period, you may not have enough variation. If possible, alternate between slower and faster exercises, or start slowly, gradually build intensity, and finish with a slower cool-down segment. For example, you might start with warm-up in the basic techniques, then progress to step-by-step learning of one specific technique, and finish with bag work. At the next lesson do a brief review and engage in sparring, using the technique you have just learned. Your instructor can end with a review of the technique, comments on the sparring, and shadowboxing for a cool-down.

SCENARIO 32

Your instructor has planned and prepared a specific lesson for intermediate students, but beginner students show up for class unexpectedly. How should she deal with it?

1. Teach the lesson as planned.

2. Improvise.

3. Call for another instructor.

No matter how much planning your instructor has done, there will be times when she has to improvise. For example, some students will arrive with injuries that need special attention. Or some students will learn faster or more slowly than expected, resulting in a need to teach more or less material than initially planned. It is a good idea for your instructor to have a loose outline or notes that she can refer to occasionally. The notes help jog her memory and keep her on track. They also allow her to tailor the lesson in advance, while still giving her the leeway to change course if needed. How organized does your instructor seem? Some instructors seem organized because they have taught the same material a hundred times, but if you suddenly throw her a curve ball, how would she handle it?

OBJECTIVES AND STANDARDS

What is wrong with the following objectives?

To become the best that you can be

To become an Olympic champion

To learn how to defend yourself in a street encounter

They are too broad, too general. What does it take to be the best, or to become an Olympic champion, or to defend yourself in a street encounter? How do you get there? Without knowing the steps, the final objective is worthless. When your instructor has written down the objective, he must define exactly what you must do to get there. There is a difference between using a front kick effectively in touch sparring and using it effectively on the street. Since the final objective is not the same, the steps required to get there also vary.

A goal is not the same as an objective. A goal might be to win the world championships,

A strike to the throat must be practiced with care in the training hall. How do you know that the way you have trained for it is effective in a street situation?

but the objective lists the steps required to get there. As you can see, a goal is general, while the objective is specific regarding not only the required steps, but also the conditions under which you are expected to perform. If the objective is "to be able to do forms," what are the specific qualifications within that objective? Do you have to do the forms with speed and crispness? Exactly how precise must the moves be? Do you have to break the forms down into their component parts and explain each move? Understanding the standard is important in order to give the objective meaning.

A standard is a level of conduct that must be adhered to in order to bring a credible level of professionalism to an individual or organization. Let's say that you took second place in a tournament. Is this good or bad? We can't make that determination unless we also know how many contestants were in the tournament. If there were just two contestants, taking second place was not particularly admirable. If there were a thousand contestants, taking second place is pretty darn good. The standard therefore measures your ability in comparison to others.

When your instructor writes the objective and sets the standard, she must be as precise as possible and use words that are concrete. What is wrong with the following objective?

To know how to put together combinations of kicks and use them effectively in sparring.

What is the standard? How do you evaluate "to know"? What is meant by "use effectively"? It is better to state:

To explain which kicks naturally go together and why, to demonstrate the best times to use these kicks, to identify situations where these kicks might fail, and to solve the problem of a failed kick.

Your instructor should avoid using vague descriptions or anything that can be interpreted in more than one way. Use this test to determine whether the instructional objectives are specific enough: In general, if your instructor uses words such as "list," "name" or "demonstrate," the objectives are specific. If he uses words such as "to know" or "to understand," the objectives are too vague. To what desgree must you understand something in order to know it?

Your instructor should also state the conditions under which you must perform. For example, do you have to ward off your opponent successfully with the front kick every time distance decreases between you and your opponent in a three-minute round? Or will you score higher if you use the front kick selectively and only when the time and distance are ideal? The conditions are important because you won't perform equally well in all environments. If the objectives and conditions are "to spar three two-minute rounds in front of an audience of 100 people," but the audience makes you nervous . . . you must still perform in order to pass the test, because these are the conditions. In other words, you can't do the sparring in the privacy of your own home. Conditions and standards in the martial arts can be either physical or mental.

Setting a standard is important for future evaluations. If your instructor doesn't know what the standard is, then how can she decide whether you have passed or failed? What evidence of learning can you provide for having met the standard? A good way to evaluate how you measure up to the standard is to explain, demonstrate, identify, and solve.

What is wrong with the following completion standard?

> *At the end of the lesson, the student should be able to throw five different kicks very quickly.*

First, the statement is too vague, because we don't know what those five different kicks are. Second, "very quickly" means different things to different people.

How can you make the following statement more concrete?

> *The student should be able to strike with speed and acceleration.*

It would be better to say:

> *The student should avoid falling into his opponent's rhythm; he should demonstrate a varied pace.*

If your opponent throws his punches with a speed of two strikes per second, you must throw yours with a speed of three strikes per second in order to achieve broken rhythm. Acceleration means that the last strike is faster than the first strike, regardless of how many strikes are in your combination. If you throw just two strikes, then the second strike will be faster than the first. If you throw five strikes, the second strike will be faster than the first but slower than the third, with the fifth strike being the fastest of them all.

To sum up, objectives are helpful both to you and your instructor. Once the objectives have been clearly stated, your instructor knows how to prepare for the lesson. She must break bigger objectives into smaller, more manageable parts. This breakdown keeps her organized and helps her decide exactly what exercises will help you reach your goals. You will also know exactly what is expected of you.

I told one of my kickboxing students that in order for her to pass the first-level test, she must run a mile in 12 minutes. She knew that unless she trained appropriately for the event, she should not even consider applying for the test. As a student, the requirements to prepare for my black belt test were clearly stated and I had about three months to perfect them. This enabled me to set a training schedule that slowly but steadily led me toward my goal. When I took the test I felt confident that I would pass it.

The objective should state:

1. What you should be able to do;

2. To which level you should perform; and

3. Under what conditions you should perform.

When the objectives and standards have been stated, they form a type of contract between you and your instructor. Both of you can now be held accountable for your respective parts. Your instructor must prepare the lessons accordingly; you must practice and perform. Neither you nor your instructor can say, "What shall we work on today?" In addition, you can't use the excuse that you didn't know that this was a requirement.

Likewise, your instructor can't test you on material that is not covered by the objectives. When the objectives and standards have been stated, much of the apprehension that normally goes along with testing is eliminated. You can now focus on learning, rather than on wondering whether or not you are ready to test.

REVIEWING THE LESSON

At the end of the instructional period, your instructor should sum up or take you through a quick exercise that helps you see the gist of the lesson. For example, if the lesson focused on the mechanics of the spinning back kick, your instructor might ask you to do spinning back kicks across the room once, followed by five kicks on the heavy bag, followed by five kicks on a partner. At the beginning of the next lesson, he might ask a few questions about the spinning back kick, particularly if he intends to build further on the technique. This recap helps you focus your attention on the lesson at hand.

Your instructor should be careful not to let too much time pass between reviews, because it is difficult to remember or associate what you learned a long time ago with what you learn today. Your instructor should demonstrate the relationship between yesterday's techniques and those of tomorrow. If she fails to do so, make an effort to paraphrase the relationship to yourself. You can do this after class during your drive home.

When a new technique fails to build on the previous technique, the previous technique loses much of its meaning. Your instructor should constantly remind you of the objectives, the techniques you learned earlier in the lessonor yesterday or last week, and the significance of that technique or concept. He should reemphasize the most important points at the end of the lesson, so that you can think about them when you leave. He should then reintroduce and build upon those points in the next lesson.

11
Critique and Evaluation

WHAT IS A CRITIQUE?

It has been said that criticism is okay as long as it is constructive. I think this statement is a contradiction. To the student who is serious about her performance, criticism hurts no matter how constructive. However, critique is not the same as criticism, although many people use the two words interchangeably. When your instructor criticizes, he finds faults. Criticism is therefore always negative. When your instructor critiques, on the other hand, he assesses your skill; he faces the facts without personal biases and includes both the good and the bad. A critique includes not only what went wrong and what you need to work on, but also what went right and how to use that to strengthen your techniques. When you understand the difference, you will more readily accept the critique.

A thorough evaluation of your performance helps your instructor identify your strengths and weaknesses, and locate areas where you need additional training. Your instructor should check on your progress regularly in order to build a trusting relationship. When I was 10 years old, I was assigned to write about a person who differed from others in some significant way. I sat at the kitchen table all day, unable to come up with a good story. When my mother came home from work at 10:00 p.m., I was desperate. I had never failed to turn in a homework assignment on time. My mother sat down with me and helped me create a great story about my Grandpa. The next day I impatiently waited for the teacher to collect the assignments, but she never did. The other students had failed to complete their stories and the teacher simply said, "Okay, then we will skip this assignment." She never even asked to see my work. More than 30 years have passed, and despite the many other good traits of this teacher, I have a hard time respecting her. An instructor should always check progress and follow through to gain respect and build a trusting relationship.

– INSTRUCTOR TIP –

In order for an assignment to be productive, you must check on your student's progress and give him feedback.

– STUDENT TIP –

If you have an adverse reaction to a critique, make sure that you understand exactly what your instructor is critiquing. Try to use the critique to build your natural strengths.

WHAT A VALID CRITIQUE SHOULD COVER

In order for a critique to be valid, it must include some information that is useful to you. I often hear instructors say, "Good job!"

without also telling us exactly what was good and how to use that knowledge to further our skill. When your instructor compliments you, your confidence increases and you feel good. But the praise has little value without an accompanying explanation. What does your instructor mean when she compliments you? Does she compliment everybody because it has become a habit to do so?

Let's say that you are doing a martial arts form in front of the class. When you finish, your instructor says, "Okay, who is next?" What's wrong with this statement? If she doesn't offer a specific comment, the statement has little value.

Bad: That was very good!

Better: You maintained good focus on your imaginary opponent through the whole set.

If the performance was less than acceptable, your instructor should tell you so without making you feel inferior. The critique should focus on what you can do to improve, rather than on what you did wrong.

Bad: You need to fix your stance. It's way off!

Better: Bend your knees to achieve a more stable stance and create a threatening impression.

In the sense discussed above, verbal comments might mean more than a trophy or a belt. After all, trophies and belts are awarded to many students of different skill levels within their particular rank. Two students may achieve the same color belt, but this does not necessarily (very seldom, ac-

tually) mean that they are equally skilled. When you receive concrete comments about your performance, the critique applies to you in particular. When you learn how your performance differs, the critique takes on a specific meaning and makes you feel unique.

Depending on individual student characteristics, your instructor may vary his method of critiquing. If he knows that you are sensitive to receiving a critique, he might soften the evaluation while still getting the message across; for example, by talking about how to achieve your goals rather than discussing the traits that you need to eliminate. Some students go out of their way to perform to the instructor's satisfaction and are quite self-conscious about discipline and critiquing.

 SCENARIO 33

You are an aggressive student who rushes forward in sparring and takes some good blows in the process. How should your instructor critique your performance?

1. When you rush in like that, you get hit all the time. Your defense really sucks!

2. You need to work on your control and poise.

3. Slow down a little and look at what's going on around you.

4. Fighting is about strategy, not just about who can throw the most punches.

5. You need to work on your defense and forget about offense.

★★★★★

It might be a good idea to start by discussing your strengths. Strong offense is a desirable quality in the martial arts. It is just not good if you end up taking too many of your opponent's strikes as a result of your offense. Rather than trying to eliminate your strength (your aggressiveness), a better way is to strengthen your defense so that it can work in harmony with your offense. For example, your instructor might say something like this:

Your offense and endurance are phenomenal. Now you need to find a way to take advantage of your opponent and prevent his strikes from landing. Try this: Wait for your opponent to throw the first strike. When he does, allow your defensive move to trigger your offense. The moment you block your opponent's strike, you also know that there is an opening in his defense and that he is vulnerable. You can now explode with that 10-punch combination that you throw so well.

This type of critique normally has a positive impact, because it builds on your natural talents rather than trying to eliminate or change them. It tells you how to use your talents to be a better martial artist. After receiving the critique, do some exercises with a partner so that you can comment on and refine the concepts.

A critique should be considered a step in the learning process. It is meant to facilitate learning and is therefore positive in nature. Back in my teens, when I was learning to fly sailplanes, one of the instructors told a student that he was "galloping like a horse" on landing. This student was so embarrassed about his performance that he

couldn't focus on how to correct it. It would have been better to explain that if the airspeed is slightly high on landing the sailplane hasn't stopped flying yet, which makes a smooth landing, difficult. The corrective action should be to reduce the airspeed gradually as you are nearing the ground.

A critique should provide you with direction and guidance, and ensure that your personal feelings are respected. If the critique's purpose (to improve your performance) is not fulfilled, it should be left out of the learning process.

A critique should be fair and presented with competence. If your instructor tells you that you have lousy feet when trying to improve your kicks, the critique is likely to do more damage than good. Likewise, if she tells you that you have made an error without providing an explanation, she will not help you much. You cannot act on the critique unless

When critiquing power, precision and general knowledge, your instructor can ask you to demonstrate your techniques on a martial arts dummy.

you specifically know what the critique entails. At the end of the critique, there should be no doubt as to what you did well or poorly, and you should have received suggestions for how to improve. What is wrong with the following statement?

You did reasonably well, but you know, sometimes these things just take time.

If your instructor simply tells you that "you didn't measure up," or that "you did great, but you're not quite there," he hasn't done much to give you a meaningful critique. The critique should be precise and list exactly what you did well or poorly, so that you know how to correct the problem.

Evaluation and critique help both you and your instructor determine *what* and *how* well you have learned. When your instructor evaluates your knowledge, she might ask questions that require a specific answer, generally *what* or *when* types of questions. She should not ask questions that you can answer with a "yes" or "no," since these types of questions invite guessing and are not true measures of what you have learned. Open-ended questions (*why* or *how*) require you to elaborate on the answer and are better for evaluating your knowledge. However, open-ended questions may have more than one correct answer. Your instructor must therefore listen to what you are really saying and determine if your answer has merit.

Evaluation and critique are more effective if done progressively throughout training, rather than at the end of a long instructional period. If your instructor evaluates you once at the end of a three-month period, the evaluation will not be objective or specific

enough to be helpful. Corrections are also more productive if they are given often, before you develop bad habits that are difficult to break. When your instructor offers a critique immediately after you complete an exercise, he demonstrates interest in your progress. A critique may be as simple as a few suggestions during practice. Or it can be more extensive, such as a complete "talk" after a belt promotion. Critiques can be given in private or in public in front of the whole class. Whatever method the instructor chooses, it should benefit the student.

The critique is meant to assist you in learning the material, and should not be a form of punishment. Remember, a valid critique includes the good along with the bad. If your instructor can't find anything good or bad to say, she shouldn't make something up. In high school, I had an instructor who refused to give an A, because "nobody is perfect," and because "if I give you an A now, you will be devastated when you get a C or D in college." But if you haven't made any errors, you deserve an A. However, this raises another interesting issue: Should your instructor grade on the curve? My opinion is that she should not grade on the curve. Since grading on the curve measures your performance in relation to your peers, it is not an objective grade. Your particular peer group may perform worse or better than the group from the previous year. I believe that it is better to grade according to a set standard that has been stated up front.

In the martial arts, a letter grade generally has less meaning than practical suggestions. And a grade has no meaning at all unless you clearly understand the standards that you are being graded against. Since the martial arts aren't regulated, no one standard applies across the board for all styles. It is pretty much up to your instructor or particular school to decide when you should be promoted to a higher rank. In order for a critique to help you, your instructor must display the following qualities:

1. He must be sincere.

2. He must be interested.

3. He must be knowledgeable.

4. He must be competent.

5. He must act with authority and not allow himself to get into a situation where he needs to defend the critique given.

– INSTRUCTOR TIP –

Teach with integrity. How much respect would you have for a police officer who wrote you a speeding ticket but broke the speed limit himself when off duty?

– STUDENT TIP –

A valid critique should contain concrete descriptions and examples. The critique should also be given regularly before performances pile up. If your instructor critiques you only a few times a year or after a belt promotion, ask for specific suggestions each time he has watched your performance.

CONDUCTING AND INTERPRETING THE CRITIQUE

Your instructor can conduct the critique in several ways. For example, she can critique by holding a group discussion, allowing students to critique each other. As an instructor, I use this method when critiquing forms practice. First I let the student demonstrate the form in front of the group. Then I solicit comments from the group. If using this method, however, your instructor must prevent it from turning into a free-for-all talk session. The objective is not for your peers to say bad things about you. Your instructor should lead the discussion with specific questions. For example, rather than saying, "Name one bad thing about the performance," she might ask, "What can the student do to appear more confident in his performance?" Your instructor may also specify beforehand what standards your peers are to use when critiquing you. For example, she might explain that one way to appear confident in forms practice is by maintaining eye contact with your imaginary opponent. When your peers evaluate you, they must consider this criterion. Still another method is to ask your peers to name only the good things about your performance, or to name only those things that need improvement. However, students should not be allowed to mention *everything* they can think of, because this would dilute what is really important. For example:

He knew the techniques, he was fast, he made eye contact, he varied his speed, his stances were deep, he was balanced...

How would you critique a peer who is not performing well? Perhaps he was slow and hesitant. You can still bring out the positive aspects in his performance and give him something to think about for future training. For example:

Bill's form wasn't as intense as Joe's. But since Bill has worked on this form only for a few days, it is unreasonable to require perfect performance. The fact that Bill took the time to do the moves correctly demonstrates that he gave each technique a lot of thought.

Although the critique should include both the good and the bad, praise is more likely to reinforce learning. You can also reinforce your own learning by telling others what you did well, and why. However, if your instructor praises you just because he is in the habit of handing out praise, the praise will eventually get stale and lose its meaning. Praise should be something that you strive for and look forward to; not something that everybody gets all the time.

If the instructor uses the group method of critiquing, the criteria for the critique should be clearly stated. For example, you may be asked to critique another student on how well he maintains eye contact with an imaginary opponent.

When your instructor asks you to critique your own performance, she should ensure that you understand the guidelines for the critique. Rather than asking how well you did, she should present leading questions that help you recognize what went well, what needs attention, and what measures you should take to improve. Also consider how objective your self-evaluation is. If your self-critique is only negative, you are either trying to be humble or you are lacking confidence, and neither is appropriate. As an instructor, I have found that students tend to be overly critical about their performance and name just about every error they can think of. They also tend to leave out the good things. If this is happening with you, make a point to name one thing that you did well.

 SCENARIO 34

Your instructor asks you to critique your own performance in sparring. You tell him, "My sidekick is good, but my hands suck." How should he respond?

1. Your hands don't suck. I think you're doing quite well.

2. Yes, we need to work more on your hand techniques.

3. Your sidekick is fair, but you need to work more on your timing.

4. Since you have good reach with the side-kick, use it more often.

★★★★★

Remember that a critique that is not specific has little value. What exactly do you mean by "good" and "suck"? Your instructor should ask you to name at least one element that you did well and one element that you need to work on. He could also ask you to describe a specific situation where you used a good sidekick and where your hand techniques were less than admirable.

Videotaping your performance may prove beneficial after you have learned the basics and gained some experience. Some background knowledge is necessary in order to know what to look for when observing yourself on tape. I videotaped a sparring session with one of my students recently. After we were done, I gave her the tape and told her to go home and write down two things that she did well, and two things that she needed to work on. The next week when I checked on the assignment, she told me how difficult it had been to limit the "bad" list to only two items, because she had noticed so many things that she needed to work on. I gave her a new homework assignment: To view the tape again, but instead of looking at her own technique, to look at my technique and write down two things that I needed to work on. Remember, I was her instructor; I was not supposed to make mistakes. But the point is that if you look hard enough, you can find mistakes in the techniques of any master. This exercise was intended to show her how to be realistic about her progress.

In order for a critique to be valid, it must specify the corrective action. If your instructor tells you that your second kick wasn't as good as your first kick, the critique has little meaning. It would be better to say, "Which kick was better, the first or the second? Do you know why?" When the reason has been identified, your instructor should capitalize on it until you can consistently throw a good kick. A critique that says, "Your kicks are too slow and telegraphed," might lead to frustration, unless your instructor also works with you on how to speed up the kicks or hide them within a set-up move. What's wrong with the following critique?

Okay, good!

Praise that you don't understand or can't capitalize on has little meaning. Likewise, a negative critique is of little value if your instructor simply tells you that you did poorly without also telling you how to improve. Telling you, "You have lousy hands," is not going to work any wonders. Your instructor should also avoid allowing one strength or defect to overshadow the whole performance. For example, if he tells you to improve, but you are unable to take his advice because of a permanent disability, the critique will do more harm than good. Perfect practice does not always make perfect. Not everybody can improve in all areas with practice. There are limits to human performance, and these limits are not the same for every person.

– INSTRUCTOR TIP –

Along with administering critique, evaluate your student's understanding of the technique. For example, your student might perform a technique flawlessly in the air, yet be unable to apply it in sparring or adapt it to different situations.

– STUDENT TIP –

Identifying the problem is only the first step, and may not be valuable at all unless your instructor also helps you take the next step toward solving the problem. When your instructor gives you advice on how to correct an error, make a point to paraphrase the advice in specific words that you can understand. Paraphrasing reinforces learning; you can use it to teach yourself how to correct the error.

TEN WAYS TO BENEFIT FROM A CRITIQUE

1. Most of us have an "off-day" every once in a while. Your instructor should observe and know how you perform most of the time, and base his evaluation on your common performance rather than on the performance of one particular day. How you perform in a single tournament, or on test day, may not be a true display of your skill. If you have a bad experience with a critique, look back at your martial arts career as a whole in order to prevent this one negative critique from demoralizing you.

2. Your instructor should avoid taking sides with the class. She should be clear and direct with her comments, yet avoid inviting arguments. She should not place herself in a position where she has to defend the critique. As a student, you should respect your instructor enough to listen to and accept what she says. If you believe that your instructor is wrong, start by giving her the benefit of the doubt and making an effort to follow her advice.

3. When you receive the critique, you should be left with an impression; you should have some idea of what you need to work on. Your instructor should not cover too much in the critique; it may

seem confusing. The more he covers the less value he gives each individual point. He should also avoid absolutes, such as "always" or "never." If the critique seems confusing, choose one particular part on which to focus over the next few weeks.

4. Pride facilitates learning. We tend to feel more pride when we find out in a roundabout way what we are doing well. You will no doubt feel proud when your instructor tells you directly that you did well, but if she tells your spouse instead, who then tells you, the praise will seem to have more meaning. Look for hidden clues of a positive critique that will boost your confidence; for example, a nod or a smile.

5. The critique must fit certain criteria in order to be useful. Your instructor's personal biases should not interfere with how he grades you. But being unbiased can be difficult. On belt exams, I recommend testing in front of a panel of judges in order to avoid your instructor's personal biases. Compare yourself with your peers in order to understand your placement in more objective terms.

6. The critique must be fair and applicable to the situation. If your instructor requires you to know a certain form, and then tells you that she cannot promote you because you lack knowledge of a *different* form, the critique is unfair unless she has also stated prior to the test that you needed to know both forms. Make an effort to find out the exact requirements for a belt promotion and make sure that you know your techniques well.

7. Your instructor must be certain that the comments he gives you in the critique are valid. You should not feel a need to question your instructor's knowledge, competence or authority. When I was teaching karate, the school owner walked in and observed my lesson. Later he negatively critiqued my teaching technique, which led me to question his competence. Although I felt that he was the better martial artist, I did not feel that he was the better instructor. I was therefore reluctant to accept the critique. If you give your instructor the benefit of the doubt but still feel that the critique was unfair, ignore the critique and move on.

8. You must be able to use the critique. If your instructor tells you that your spinning back kick needs improvement, she must also state how and why. The "how" and "why" evoke insight and understanding and trigger the desire to correct the technique. Being told to improve without getting help to improve is of little value. Ask your instructor for specific suggestions. When you have practiced for some time, ask her for a new evaluation.

9. The critique should be given in good taste. You should not feel resentment toward your instructor as a result of the critique. If your instructor says, "You are not very good, because . . ." understand that he really means, "The technique won't work well when done that way, because . . ." Some instructors are just poor communicators, but still mean well.

10. The critique must be specific and cover the good along with the bad. "Your forms are fine, but your sparring needs work," is not valuable because it doesn't state what is fine about your forms and what needs work in the sparring. A better comment is, "I was impressed with the precision of your forms. I can tell that you have thought a lot about how to apply the techniques. Your offense in sparring is also good, but we need to work a little on defense. Until next time, think about how to use the parry. And since your offense is so good, also think about how and what types of techniques you can use after parrying your opponent's punch." Your instructor has now given you specific things to work on, along with specific reasons. If in doubt, always ask.

SAMPLE MARTIAL ARTS EVALUATION

What the evaluation will cover: The student will be evaluated on stances, strikes, blocks, kicks, grab techniques, punch techniques, forms and sparring. The student will be graded on a scale from one to four, as follows:

One = Novice

Two = Learner

Three = Skilled

Four = Expert

The following material is a description of each area to be evaluated, and contains examples of what to look for before administering a grade.

Balance: The student will be evaluated on his ability to maintain correct posture and switch stance without falling, stumbling or telegraphing his intent to the opponent.

Novice: The student constantly stumbles and lacks all sense of direction. The student fidgets and telegraphs his intent to the opponent.

Learner: The student takes extra steps when struck, but is able to maintain balance.

Skilled: The student maintains a low center of gravity with very little overextension when striking or blocking.

Expert: The student demonstrates stable stances and is difficult to take off balance. He maintains a low center of gravity with no fidgeting or telegraphing of intents. All moves are performed with the center of gravity balanced.

Use of the nonworking hand: The student will be evaluated on his ability to use the nonworking hand as a check against low and high strikes. The student will be evaluated on his ability to use checks to cover openings and to redirect strikes.

Novice: The student does not use the nonworking hand at all, and does not appear to be aware of its existence.

Learner: The student is beginning to use the nonworking hand, but is somewhat rigid and uncoordinated in his moves.

Skilled: The student uses the nonworking hand frequently, and has the ability to change from low to high and back to low positions.

Expert: The student uses the nonworking hand fluently and in coordination with other moves. The student has the ability to use the nonworking hand as a strike.

Crispness and target accuracy: The student will be evaluated on his ability to use sharp and definite moves and communicate the techniques to an audience.

Novice: The student uses sloppy, imprecise and uncoordinated moves, and seems unaware of target accuracy.

Learner: The student displays good snap and crispness with the moves and is beginning to choose different targets.

Skilled: The student displays coordination and is able to strike most targets with speed and accuracy.

Expert: The student uses sharp and well-communicated moves and strikes all targets with speed and precision.

Attention to detail: The student will be evaluated on his accuracy and ability to strike specific targets with power. The student will be evaluated on his ability to switch stance and gain a superior position.

Novice: The student overextends his strikes and leaves targets open for counterstrikes. The student is unable to use a variety of strikes and blocks in combination.

Learner: The student has good knowledge of target areas, but is unable to strike small or precise targets.

Skilled: The student is beginning to control his opponent's moves, is able to redirect an attack, and can switch stance without telegraphing his intent.

Expert: The student converts blocks and parries into strikes with little effort. The student adjusts to his opponent's position with ease and understands the anatomy of the human body.

Fluency: The student will be evaluated on his ability to relax, to move without pausing, and to change his rate of motion at will. The student will be evaluated on his ability to group moves together while maintaining rhythm and control. The student will be evaluated on his ability to use combinations of linear and circular moves.

Novice: The student is tense and demonstrates little extension in his strikes. His moves are jerky, stiff and rigid.

Learner: The student is able to break techniques down into groups of moves, but uses only linear strikes.

Skilled: The student employs broken rhythm and begins to combine linear and circular moves.

Expert: The student remains relaxed throughout the technique. He switches between linear and circular moves with ease, and uses set-up strikes to confuse his opponent.

Focus: The student will be evaluated on his ability to maintain focus while being distracted. The student will be evaluated on his ability to use peripheral vision to detect danger.

Novice: The student frequently flinches or looks away, and misses the target when striking.

Learner: The student maintains a strong focus on his opponent, but loses concentration when distracted.

Skilled: The student maintains focus through most distractions, and can detect movement through the use of peripheral vision.

Expert: The student is in total control of the situation. He stays calm under pressure and has good mind and body coordination.

Power and control: The student will be evaluated on his ability to strike effectively with varying amounts of force.

Novice: The student is unable to control his power. He misses targets by more than six inches or strikes with excessive force.

Learner: The student displays better control with his hands than with his feet, and can generally strike within a quarter-inch of the target.

Skilled: The student uses his hands and feet in balanced combinations, and can strike with varying amounts of force within a controlled environment.

Expert: The student can execute quick and effective blows to any target in an instant, using either his hands or feet.

If your instructor is using a written form to evaluate you, ask to get a copy of the criteria well in advance so that you have time to study the standards you are being measured against.

DATE				
BALANCE				
USE OF THE NONWORKING HAND				
CRISPNESS / TARGET ACCURACY				
ATTENTION TO DETAIL				
FLUENCY				
FOCUS				
POWER / CONTROL				

12
Testing

WHEN SHOULD YOU TEST?

I have yet to hear of a martial arts school that doesn't employ some kind of test or belt promotion. Tests are important for grading your level of skill and also serve as a motivational factor. After years of hard work, you want some form of reward. After all, what do people ask when you tell them you're a martial artist? "Are you a black belt?"

Every lay person knows what a black belt symbolizes, even if he or she doesn't know the details required to get it. A test should be an indication of how far you have come; it should tell you that you have done what others have not dared to do. You should be made aware of the testing requirements well in advance.

 SCENARIO 35

You come to class sporadically, but you practice a lot at home with your brother-in-law who is a Navy SEAL. Should your instructor allow you to test?

1. Yes, because the Navy SEALs are much better than the rest of us.

2. Yes, because you display good form in class.

3. No, because the military and war are bad.

4. No, because you have not learned the required forms.

 ★★★★★

Since the Navy SEALs learn to kill in combat, they don't learn martial arts as practiced in the training hall and may therefore not be appropriate instructors for students of the martial arts. Additionally, a martial arts instructor must be able to teach and instill good judgment, not just perform. My recommendation is that your instructor should not allow you to test (and you should not ask to) if you haven't put in your time.

How do you determine when it is appropriate to test for a higher rank? When to take the test is often a judgment call that should be made on an individual basis. In general, you should have a fair understanding of the required techniques. But perfection, or even near perfection, is seldom attained or required until you have had many years of practice behind you.

 SCENARIO 36

You have been a yellow belt student for six months, while all of your peers have moved ahead. You do the same techniques over and over with little difficulty. Your instructor suggests that you test for the next level, but you tell her that you need more practice. How do you think your instructor should respond?

1. Ask if she can help you sharpen your techniques.

2. Leave you alone to practice more.

3. Push you to test.

4. Praise you for being so dedicated.

Some students are afraid of testing and want to polish their techniques indefinitely. But sometimes waiting hinders the learning process rather than helps it. Absolute perfection is almost impossible to attain, and there is a point at which your progress has peaked for the effort. When the price becomes greater than the value, we must reconsider our focus. Your instructor may now want to push you to test.

Most of us agree that a student shouldn't be awarded a higher rank unless he deserves it. On the other hand, there are situations when advancing a student a little early can help him progress, such as when he has reached a learning plateau. If you struggle with one particular phase of training without achieving significant results, mental factors such as lack of confidence and frustration could be blocking the learning process. Your instructor must now find a way to move you past this barrier, and he might choose to advance you to a higher rank even if you're not quite ready. If you

remain in one rank for a long time, it may also be because you lack focus. I remained a first-degree black belt for many years, not because I wasn't ready to advance, but because my interests did not lay in preparing for another test. If you truly don't desire to test, your instructor may feel inclined to leave you alone. However, there is another issue—liability—that must be considered. For example, if you want to learn the techniques and participate in class but you don't care about rank, when you spar with higher ranking students and get hurt, there might be a problem with insurance, depending on the agreement the school has with the insurance company. Some schools only allow students of intermediate or higher rank to spar using contact. If a student with no rank spars and gets hurt, has he violated the policy?

 SCENARIO 37

You answer a question asked by a panel of black belts. One of the judges says, *"What?! Did your instructor really tell you that?"* The pressure has suddenly shifted to your instructor. How do you think he should handle the situation?

1. Look the other way and pretend that he didn't hear.

2. Look straight into the judge's eyes and try to intimidate him.

3. Whisper that he is not your instructor.

4. Raise his hand and say, "Let me explain . . ."

These sorts of embarrassing situations normally don't occur, but it is worth thinking about. If your instructor is a professional and somebody criticizes his work, he should defend himself. However, he must make sure that he does so intelligently and courteously so that others don't question his professionalism.

– INSTRUCTOR TIP –

The student should not take unfair advantage of your professionalism. It took you many years to reach black belt and beyond. When you recommend a student for a belt promotion, that student represents you and should therefore act in a way that makes you proud to be her instructor. Don't promote students who are unwilling to put in their time.

– STUDENT TIP –

Those "remote" schools that advertise video classes and video testing make it sound as though you'll be buying your black belt through the mail. Is it possible to conduct a fair test this way? Will you get any satisfaction through a mail-in video? More importantly, consider whether you really learn usable skills this way. Proficiency in the martial arts requires real practice, preferably with a variety of students. Join a school and attend classes regularly.

HOW IS A VALID TEST CONSTRUCTED?

The testing and evaluation process requires good judgment. The test should be comprehensive enough to sample the whole area of your understanding and ability. The test should also be objective in nature. Instructors commonly rely on their own subjective judgments, using obsolete standards or overemphasizing trivial details. Some instructors attempt to appeal to parents and attract children to the school by tying the belt promotion to the student's performance in grade school, or the completion of chores at home. Aside from being questionable ethics, this method fails to demonstrate an understanding of the learning process. One thing does not necessarily lead to another. For example, some students are better athletes than they are students. If a student is an underachiever in school, doing well in the martial arts may help him find a niche and increase his confidence. Moreover, how can this policy be transferred to adults who are their own bosses and don't go to school? Is it appropriate to have two standards, one for children and one for adults? I feel that it is important to keep irrelevant activities apart. It is not necessary to become a nurse before becoming a doctor, or to become a flight attendant before becoming an airline pilot. These are distinctly different professions and should be treated as such. Likewise, doing well in grade school should not be a prerequisite for doing well in the martial arts.

Holding a fair and objective test is not as easy as it sounds. Instructors tend to grade their favored students higher, even if these students don't actually perform that well on test day. We tend to see what we want and expect to see. Also, if the instructor is too strict when judging student performance, fair grading is not possible. There should be some leeway for student differences and personality traits. Furthermore, it is almost impossible to measure *exactly* how well a student does. For example, you should not be tested on your ability to throw a punch at a speed of X miles per hour, as this would be much too specific and difficult to measure.

Test questions that allow you to demonstrate your knowledge of a principle are better than questions that nit-pick for tiny details. When I renewed my flight instructor license recently, one of the test questions concerned altitude's effect on night vision. The question asked at what altitude a pilot should start using oxygen: at 4800 feet, 5000 feet, 5125 feet, 5700 feet or 6000 feet (or words to that effect). This question stems from the concept that night vision is the first thing to deteriorate (because of lack of oxygen) when flying at high altitudes. But the *exact* altitude at which this happens is too difficult to determine and differs somewhat between individuals. This test question was therefore not objective; it was simply a test of the student's ability to memorize numbers rather than understand the concepts. When constructing a test, your instructor should make sure that she asks what is important. Doing so requires some forethought.

Your instructor must also consider how reasonable the questions are. He may need to perform some test items himself, or have a student perform them beforehand in order to determine if they are reasonable and effective. The test items should also be practical and relevant:

1. Do the techniques make sense?

2. Are the techniques effective?

In order for a test to be valid, it must be comprehensive. For example, it is not enough to test you on forms and assume that you know how to spar, or vice versa. Likewise, your ability to answer questions correctly may not be an indication of your knowledge, but rather your ability to memorize and repeat information. Your instructor should give the test a lot of thought; it should not be an exercise that she puts you through simply because it seems like the right thing to do.

Your instructor must also give himself adequate time to prepare the test, and not decide at the last minute what the test is to cover. If the test seems haphazard, you will question its importance. It is the instructor's job to construct a valid test and prepare you accordingly. Your instructor should not test your working knowledge of concepts and the techniques he hasn't taught yet. Some consideration should also be given to the individual characteristics of the students. For example, your success or failure should not be based on another student's success or failure.

Finally, you should question whether it is fair to pair up students to spar with only the "winner" passing the test. Since this one sparring session is not a true measure of the ability of either student, my opinion is that this method would be unfair. Had the "loser" sparred with someone else, the outcome would most likely have been different. A test that is based on exclusivity does not promote cooperation and team spirit in the classroom.

– INSTRUCTOR TIP –

Tests can be constructed as a physical challenge. Some tests last for several days and push the student past his or her perceived limitations. Tests can also be constructed as a mental challenge, requiring the student to explain and apply his knowledge in unrehearsed sce-

narios. Whatever method you choose, the test should be appropriate for the rank. Consider whether the difficulty of the material, or just the amount of knowledge demonstrated, should increase with each rank.

Think about this: Is it the test itself that is the "rite of passage," or have you already achieved your rank prior to testing, and the test is merely a formality? When you understand the purpose of the testing procedure, your new rank will mean more.

EVALUATING THE VALIDITY OF THE TEST

A well-conducted test is a great learning experience. The test should serve a specific purpose and not be something you do simply because it is what martial artists have been doing for ages. Rely on the following criteria to evaluate the validity of a test:

1. You should be tested only on material that has been taught. This may seem obvious, but some instructors can't resist adding yet-to-be aught concepts.

2. You should be tested only on material that is important and relevant. If your instructor hasn't taken the time to cover it in class, then why should it be important on the test?

3. The criteria that are to be met for a certain level must remain constant. A student who tests next year should be required to know the same material as a student who tests this year for that same rank (with the exception of minor changes to enhance the program).

4. Your instructor should give some thought to the length of the test. A test that is too short will seem ineffective. If you are prepared you will enjoy showing what you know. On the other hand, a test that is too long is also ineffective. Although much of martial arts training is about physical and mental endurance, a test that is too long often includes too much downtime.

5. A test should be difficult, but not so difficult that most students fail. In fact, everyone should be able to pass the test if they have trained appropriately. Grading on the curve is, in my opinion, unfair. If everybody deserves to pass the test, then everybody should pass the test.

6. You should walk away with a feeling of accomplishment. The test should propel you toward the next level. If you feel the test was a waste of time, it probably was.

7. The test should be about your ability to demonstrate your knowledge, and not about your ability to understand difficult language. Your instructor should be direct and clear with what she wants you to do. Some students may perform the wrong technique, not because they don't know how to do the right one, but because they misunderstand what the instructor is asking.

8. Your instructor should ask specific questions; you are not a mind reader. For example, if he asks, "What is the objective of the front kick?" and you respond, "To kick your opponent in the jaw and knock him out," that would be just as valid as they instructor's answer, "To prevent an

opponent from closing the distance," because the instructor's question was not specific. It would be better to ask, "Name three ways to use the front kick."

CONDUCTING THE TEST

There are many ways to conduct a test. When using the *informal approach*, the instructor has some leeway and can tailor the test to a particular student. These types of tests are different for each instructor and school. It is therefore not possible for a student of one school to know how he measures up against a student of another school. When using the *standardized approach*, the requirements are the same for everybody in your particular art, regardless of under which school or instructor you study. Standardized tests allow you to know your performance in relation to the rest of the nation (or world), and it is unlikely that you will get any "sympathy points" from your instructor. In other words, she can't pass you if you don't measure up to the standard. A standardized test requires your instructor to know exactly what the standards are, so that she can prepare you accordingly. In the martial arts, you won't see as many standardized tests as you do in academics. One reason is that the martial arts are not regulated. Although it would be nice if everybody with a black belt had attained a certain standard of expertise, no matter which school he attended or which part of the world he is from, martial arts instructors need not be certified to teach. In a chain of schools, instructor certification may be part of the program, but in general, this is not the case.

Most martial arts tests on the advanced level contain some oral testing and some written testing, generally in the form of a written essay. If your instructor assigns you a written portion, he should give it sufficient thought and ensure that it is appropriate for the material you have studied. The essay should not be a test of your spelling, grammar or ability to express yourself in writing. We leave this to the English classes. Rather, it should be a test of your ability to research and gain specific insight into a subject that relates to the martial arts. The essay should contain material that is useful to you, and preferably, to other students and instructors of the fighting arts. At this level, you should have enough background that you can find, within your own training experiences, the information needed to complete the assignment. You can also visit other schools and martial artists and ask them to provide you with the information. When I tested for my black belt in kickboxing, I wrote an essay about fear.

When taking the test, you should be measured against clearly stated objectives. Some schools use pretests designed to determine the student's readiness. In my opinion, the pretest is not really necessary, at least not in its entirety. Your instructor should know you well enough to also know when you are ready to test. This is not to say that a good review a week or more before the test is a bad idea.

– INSTRUCTOR TIP –

Assign advanced students extracurricular activities as part of their exam. For example, ask an advanced student to spend six months researching a specific topic, such as knife offense and defense, or methods to increase the power in his strikes.

Your instructor may specify what she wants you to study, or she may have a list of subjects to choose from. This type of exercise requires you to go outside of your own school and talk to people who have knowledge in these specific areas. When you do indepth research, you must think through every issue, which usually results in insight and permanent retention. If your instructor doesn't give you a specific assignment when you reach the higher levels, take it upon yourself to engage in research on a subject that interests you.

TESTING CRITERIA

What criteria should your instructor use when evaluating you for a belt promotion? Is it physical strength— how many push-ups you can do or how fast you can run a mile? Is it how many wins you have acquired in sparring or competition? Is it how well you have memorized your forms or how smoothly you perform the techniques? Is it how accurately you answer questions on oral and written examinations? Is it how athletic (flexible) you are, or how well you perform stunning feats (board breaking, flying kicks, etc.)? Is it how you carry yourself, and whether you appear confident?

At first, we agree that a test that is objective is more valid than a test that is subjective (up to the instructor's opinion). The test should be the same for everybody, right? However, a test that is purely objective presents certain problems, because the martial arts should fit just about anybody with a serious interest. If the requirements are too rigid, they will exclude a large number of the population. For example, will children, the weak and sickly, the disabled and the elderly, be able to pass such a test? *Should* they be able to pass such a test? On the other hand, if the standards fit just about anybody, the "tougher" students may feel cheated and feel that they are not benefiting from the test.

Should the test include a physical requirement? Some schools require you to run a certain distance and perform a certain number of pull-ups, push-ups, or sit-ups, etc. Since strength and endurance are important attributes in the martial arts, I, personally, am in favor of a physical requirement. However, this requirement must be somewhat tailored to the student's individual capabilities. Is it fair to require 15 pull-ups of everybody? An ex-Navy SEAL would laugh and quit. A slightly overweight 45-year-old housewife with no athletic background may never pass such a requirement and would quit without even trying. So how do you define the criteria? Should the requirements be set according to the strongest student, the weakest student or the instructor's ability? Or should there be a different requirement for everybody? I have a male student who can pump out 50 push-ups with me on his back, and who doesn't have an ounce of fat on his body. I have a female student who couldn't do one push-up when she started training two years ago, but who can do 15 good ones now. If I required 50 push-ups for the test, it may still seem too easy for the male student, yet be completely unattainable for the female student.

The instructor should be careful about establishing requirements based solely on gender or age. Some women can outdo men in push-ups and would like to be presented with the opportunity. It would therefore be wrong to require 30 push-ups of men and 15 of women. It might be better to use a requirement that relies on time rather than reps. For example, do push-ups for one minute, or run for ten minutes regardless of pace, or run a set distance regardless of pace. Or perhaps your instructor can give you a choice between a two-mile run in 20 minutes, or 10 minutes of continuous jump rope followed by three rounds of heavy bag work. There are countless variations.

I suggest that, unless a technique is taught as a life-saving measure, your instructor should allow some leeway for individual characteristics. Not everybody has the same ability to develop the same physique. For example, some students may have bad knees and be unable to jump rope. But both older and younger students should still be able to excel in the martial arts. Denying a student advancement because he has a physical injury or limitation would be equivalent to denying a student advancement because he only has one arm, and a left-right combination is required for the next level. After all, we are training because we want to, and not because we have been chosen as the cream of the crop.

So the question is: How can a person with a physical limitation compensate for the deficiency? If this person encountered a real-life threat on the street, she must be able to defend herself, right? Some people's limitations aren't as obvious as a missing arm, but they are still very real. I do not believe that those with physical disabilities should be given favors; only substitute exercises that they can do, and that are of equal value. A test should present a challenge and should give you a sense of accomplishment. You won't feel this if there is a double standard.

SCENARIO 38

The ability to apply a choke is a requirement for a test. You know the moves but consistently fail to make your peer students submit. Should your instructor pass you? Why or why not?

1. Yes, because he doesn't teach students to hurt their partners.

2. Yes, because there are too many variables in a real situation, and you demonstrate good knowledge of the move.

If a testing requirement is to demonstrate an ability to break out of a headlock, how much force is appropriate to use? What if your partner decides not to cooperate?

154

3. No, because if your opponent doesn't submit, the technique has failed.

4. No, because you are not aggressive enough.

★★★★★

Since a choke may be a life-saving measure, if you can't apply it properly it will not help you in a real-life scenario. In my opinion, making a partner submit should be a requirement. *The conditions under which your opponent must submit may vary and should be clearly stated.* What if a testing requirement is target accuracy, and you consistently fail to hit the target? These are criteria that are absolutely necessary for successful fighting. Physical strength is also absolutely necessary, but the exact number of push-ups is less relevant.

– INSTRUCTOR TIP –

If a student has a physical limitation that prevents him from doing certain exercises, find a substitute exercise that accomplishes the same thing and is equivalent in physical difficulty. For example, if a test requires "frog hops" (hopping low squats that burn like hell in the quadriceps) and a student has bad knees, you may want to substitute for another quad exercise such as stair climbing.

– STUDENT TIP –

If the test has a physical requirement, inform your instructor well in advance of the test of any injuries or physical limitations that you may have, so that you can agree on a substitute exercise.

TAKING THE TEST

Tests may not be the center of life for martial arts students, but just like death, they are inevitable. Most of us approach the testing situation with some apprehension, and some of us have severe anxiety before taking one. Some instructors claim this is good, because you build confidence by facing and overcoming your fear. But if you test in front of a panel of judges, it is in your instructor's interest that you pass the test. Your instructor should teach you how to take the test successfully. When you appear confident you can normally get away with more errors than if you lack confidence. Much of martial arts training is about how you present yourself. Displaying confidence is important when facing your opponent in competition and on the street against a real assailant.

 ## SCENARIO 39

On test day, you forget a move in one of the forms. Should you pass the test? Why or why not?

1. Yes, because you did all other techniques flawlessly.

2. Yes, because your instructor has seen you do this form to perfection before.

3. Yes, but only if you do it correctly the second time.

4. Yes, if you do some "extra credit" techniques.

5. No, because you didn't meet the requirements.

6. No, because a test should be challenging and give you a feeling of accomplishment.

★★★★★

A belt promotion should be challenging, and you should only pass if you perform. Allowing you to pass when you don't deserve to is unfair to those who have dedicated themselves to the study of the martial arts. It also devalues the rank you are testing for. Nervousness at testing time is a different matter, however. How well does your instructor know you? Your instructor should keep your past accomplishments in mind when determining how much you have learned. If you fail to perform on test day, your instructor should identify the cause. Did you forget a move because you had failed to practice it, or did you forget because you were nervous? How you handle the fact that you forgot the move is also an indication of your knowledge. For example, if you freeze, shake your head and start over, it may be an indication that you are so focused on each individual move of the technique that you don't understand the variations that lie beyond "perfect" technique. If you adjust to your mistake and keep going, either by making up a move or by skipping the move entirely, it may be an indication that you have learned enough to make adjustments without conscious thought, which is something you would benefit from in an actual fight. However, making up a new move may also be an indication that you are a con artist hoping that your instructor didn't notice your mistake.

Some students don't test as well as others. This is not necessarily an indication that a student lacks knowledge. It is therefore important that your instructor recognizes who you are and what you have accomplished. For example, is it fair to promote a student who tested well, but who only comes to class occasionally? Is it fair to fail a really dedicated student whose skill is well known, but who was nervous on test day?

If you are simply nervous, your instructor may try to ease your mind with a different exercise and come back to the move you missed later. Students who are nervous often perform well once they get past their initial anxiety. When one of my students was ready for her first belt promotion and I told her to assume a left fighting stance, she was so nervous that she forgot which foot was left and right. Your instructor should prompt you whenever needed.

A point should be made about "extra credit." Should students who don't know their required material receive extra credit for displaying knowledge in other techniques? My opinion is that extra credit should not be part of a test. If your instructor has stated the requirements beforehand, there should be no excuse for you not to know your material. And if you do know your material, you may feel unfairly treated if another student who does extra credit techniques is told that he is "the best." Your instructor should state clearly what is to be included in the test and stick to it.

SCENARIO 40

You fail a test in front of a panel of black belts. How should your instructor handle the situation?

1. Pat you on the back and say, "You were really close, but not quite there."

2. Tell you that had he sat on the panel, you would have passed the test.

3. Tell the judges that their judgment sucks.

4. Tell you that failing will make you stronger.

5. Thank everybody for a job well done.

An unbiased panel of judges would keep your instructor's personal feelings from interfering. If your instructor recommends you for the test and you fail, either your instructor's judgment of your skill is lacking or you failed to perform for other reasons. But it is unlikely that a student who truly knows his material will fail.

– INSTRUCTOR TIP –

If a student fails a test in front of a panel of judges and you agree with the judgment, you can point out what the student did well and provide her with additional instruction in the areas where she was lacking. If you feel the judgment was unfair, you may want to talk to the judges later, if not to reverse the decision, then at least to learn why they judged the way they did.

– STUDENT TIP –

Should you be judged on your performance on test day, or should you be judged on your overall martial arts knowledge? Some flexibility should be permitted, as you may not perform to the exact same standard every day. It helps if you know exactly what the panel will be looking for, so that you can prepare for the test accordingly.

POST-TEST DEBRIEFING

At the conclusion of the test, a debriefing that emphasizes the important points is appropriate. A debriefing allows you to discuss any issues you may have questions about. The debriefing should be positive in nature and serve as a catalyst to motivate you for further learning. Your instructor should congratulate you on your achievements, but should also make it clear that a test is not an end but a stepping-stone toward greater learning.

If a testing requirement is to demonstrate an ability to break out of a headlock, how much force is appropriate to use? What if your partner decides not to cooperate?

THE VALUE OF THE BLACK BELT

Can a once-earned rank be taken from you? For example, should you have to prove that you are worthy of your rank once a year? I don't know of any school that downgrades a student who has already earned a rank, but what if you are no longer able to do some of the requirements for the once-achieved rank? What if the style has evolved and new elements and techniques have been added? Should the black belts of yesteryear have to learn these modifications in order to keep their rank? Personally, I am against this idea as it makes the awarding of rank too subjective. An instructor could simply come up with new techniques overnight, and those who had once earned their black belts would be black belts no more.

Many years ago, I wasn't the least bit interested in the actual belt. I only cared about the skill. In fact, I wouldn't have minded wearing a white belt and letting others believe that I was a white belt while I performed at the black belt level and beyond. This doesn't work. Getting your black belt is absolute necessary if you want to continue growing. For example, how would it look if I wrote martial arts books, and the About the Author section said "Martina Sprague holds a brown belt in . . ." There would be no credibility, no matter how much I really knew. You can't teach others with any success if you don't have a black belt. Yes, the under-belts would listen to you, but they would rather learn from somebody else and would do so at the first opportunity, no matter how skilled you are, how much effort you put forth, or how good an instructor you are.

If faced with an actual encounter, having a black belt is likely to affect you mentally by making you more confident, even if your actual knowledge isn't any better than when you were a brown belt. Sometimes the best course of action your instructor can take is to upgrade you to black belt even if you are not quite there yet. Raising our skill level in our own and other people's minds often helps our physical body follow. Overloading a bit can help a student overcome learning plateaus or a lack of confidence.

My opinion is that a student should be tested for black belt when she is ready, regardless of whether she wants to test, cares about the belt, has paid her dues, is on good terms with the school, or whatever else the case may be.

Part Three
Human Behavior

13
Effective Communication

THE LECTURE

Although the martial arts are mainly practical in nature, there must be a way to deliver the information. Some lecturing is therefore necessary. Your instructor must know how to present the material with conviction and enthusiasm. She can deliver the lecture by speaking from an outline or by speaking more spontaneously. Both methods have advantages and drawbacks. While an outline organizes the material, relying too much on notes prevents the instructor from adapting to the students' reactions. Speaking without notes, on the other hand, makes her more likely to get sidetracked, forget what to say next, or appear unprepared. Your instructor can deliver the lecture part of the lesson as:

1. A briefing. This method gives you an idea of what is to come, but without a lot of elaboration at this point.

2. A guided discussion. This method allows you to participate, either by answering questions and elaborating on the answers, or by contrasting different ideas and techniques.

3. A longer introduction. This method lends itself to a classroom course taught before the practical portion, as might be the case, in a rape prevention seminar.

Regardless of which method your instructor uses, the lecture must make sense and the material be presented in a logical sequence. One way is by starting with the past (the technique you worked on last week) and going to the present (a new concept that builds on last week's technique), or by going from the simple to the complex. Your instructor should not get too technical with a beginning class. If you are attending a seminar, he may give you an outline that you can refer to and use to refresh your memory after the seminar is over.

The lecture part of the lesson gives you a choice of being an active or passive student. Since learning is an active process, retention is better if you interact with your instructor. Your instructor should plan classroom activities that support the lecture. If she uses visual aids, she should pause between demonstrations and combine speech with performance. She can also provide examples, comparisons or statistics that reinforce the material. Anecdotes or personal experiences are helpful. For example, the statistics for knife attacks have more meaning if you get to meet and talk with a victim of a knife attack than if your instructor simply reads off some numbers from a list.

WHAT IS EFFECTIVE COMMUNICATION?

Since a big part of communication consists of talking, your instructor must know how to convey the message verbally. Prior to teaching my first martial arts lesson, I had a nightmare in which I had to teach in a dojo (training hall) that was 200 yards long and held 400 students, and that I had to make my voice carry all the way to the back of the hall. The *kiais* I had been shouting for years prior to teaching helped make my voice carry. I suppose this can be called a "fringe benefit" of the martial arts.

When trying to learn new material, few things are more irritating than an instructor who mumbles. Mumbling is either the result of speaking too softly or of not pronouncing the words fully. Your instructor should therefore make sure that he directs the speech toward the students, and that he is not just thinking out loud. Other irritants are:

1. Looking down or away; and

2. Seeming preoccupied or using long pauses between sentences.

Pausing, when used sensibly, serve toemphasize important points. But long pauses tend to slow the speech and turn it into a boring drag.

So just how much should your instructor talk? When I took my flight instructor test, the examiner told me, "I already know that you can fly the airplane. Now I want to hear you teach it." If your instructor talks too little, you may feel as though she is wasting your time because she is not really teach-ing. As an instructor, I often worry that my students will get bored if I don't set a good instructional pace. But if your instructor talks too much, it may interfere with your attempts to do the techniques.

Communication must be passionate to be effective. Your instructor should clearly demonstrate that he believes in the message he is communicating. My supervisor at my day job once held a 20-minute briefing that, in hindsight, was actually a 20-minute one-man show. The dynamics of his delivery left no doubt that he believed strongly in his message, and after the lecture I wanted to applaud him. But as I allowed the experience to settle, I discovered that what had kept me so captivated was not the message itself, but his conviction in the message. After analyzing it, there were few things in his lecture that I actually agreed with.

As a listener, don't jump on the bandwagon without first analyzing what the speaker is saying. I have met many martial artists who worship their instructor and take her words for face value. It is better to gather all the facts first and then be your own judge. However, some students are overly critical of what the instructor is teaching and always take the opposite stand. I had one student who, as soon as I had taught him a new technique, asked, "Is there value there?" He frequently stated that he was no "Jim Jones follower." This student became somewhat difficult to teach, and I don't see how he could benefit much from the information I gave him. As a receiver, you must be willing to receive the message. Good communication cannot take place if you are suspicious of everything your instructor teaches. Your instructor should be sensible and avoid using extremes, but she should also require you to give her a chance.

A lesson has the greatest impact if both the speaker and the listener interact with each other. The reason that active listeners learn more than passive listeners is that passive listeners have already decided beforehand what they want to hear and can therefore not listen to what is really being said. Passive listeners sometimes wait for an opportunity to sidetrack the discussion. Or they don't hear what is being said at all and will therefore lack retention. Active listeners, on the other hand, ask intelligent questions rather than try to find something to argue about. Active listeners paraphrase the information to increase their understanding of the subject. They create harmony and, therefore, a better learning environment for everybody.

If you are a passive listener or if you like to argue your position, you might have some conflicts to resolve. Conflicts are not necessarily bad, but they become so when they are about personal issues and *who* is right, rather than *what* is right. If you get caught up in an argument, make sure it is the issue that is argued and not the person. A conflict that is handled appropriately can increase your confidence and critical thinking skills.

– INSTRUCTOR TIP –

Most of us like to be talkers rather than listeners because it gives us more attention. But keep in mind that talking is not synonymous with good communication. Speaking may simply be the result of your desire to hear the sound of your own voice. A good rule of thumb is to talk between techniques, and to observe or listen to what students have to say while they are trying the techniques.

– STUDENT TIP –

Good communication means good listening skills. Do the technique a few times, then pause and allow your instructor to make corrections. If you perform the technique in slow motion, your instructor can make corrections simultaneously. If you are sparring or working the heavy bag, you might wait for a natural pause in the action before turning to your instructor for corrections or advice.

POINTS TO CONSIDER

Too often our words don't match our actions. We say one thing and do another. An in-

If a peer student portrays a cocky or offensive attitude, or consistently takes the opposite stand in a discussion, try to sidetrack the argument by changing subjects.

structor who cannot say what he intends to say is confusing to listen to. If he teaches a technique a certain way one week and changes the technique the next week so that you can no longer identify with it, you will likely get frustrated. Sending mixed messages is detrimental to effective communication. For example, if your instructor evokes excitement about a belt promotion, but then changes the date of the promotion or pretends that he didn't set a date to begin with, you will begin to lose faith in your instructor.

Use the following list of questions to determine your instructor's communicative abilities. Then evaluate your own communication skills using the same list.

1. Does your instructor listen to everybody in the group, or just to those he likes or those who "squeal" the loudest?

2. Does he ask you to clarify questions he doesn't understand so he can provide you with the correct answer?

3. Does he know the needs and interests of each student, or is he more concerned with himself and wants to be the one who knows it all?

4. Does he let students finish speaking without interrupting, or does he "put words in your mouth"?

5. Is he honest and able to present the facts, or does he push you to accept his values?

6. Does he show openly what he thinks, or does he use abstract and sophisticated words?

7. Does it appear as though he has thought about what he wants to say before he says it?

– INSTRUCTOR TIP –

Since words seldom carry the exact same meaning from the speaker to the listener, you must eliminate abstractions and use words that narrow the image created in your students' minds. Say exactly what you mean to say, and then make your actions match your words.

– STUDENT TIP –

We often don't communicate; we take turns to talk. But half of communication is about listening and making an effort to understand the other person's perceptions. If your instructor uses confusing words or communicates in a way that gives you more than one possible solution to a problem, ask your instructor to clarify what she means.

CLARITY OF COMMUNICATION

There are many knowledgeable instructors who are extremely boring because they don't know how to present the material. And there are others who have their students in awe but are really not teaching much. Neither will develop a knowledgeable student, but the latter is at least likely to keep the dropout rate down until the student discovers that she is not learning much. The point is that your instructor must be both knowledgeable and charismatic. If he has both traits, you will listen and retain. If he is knowledgeable but doesn't know how to transfer the knowledge, it won't matter how much he knows, you will remain unchallenged.

One of my instructors used to say, "There are three reasons . . ." I thought this method worked well, because it allowed him to define exactly what I was to learned. It also eliminated abstractions. Instructors often fail to clearly explain what they mean. What makes sense to the instructor may not make sense to the students. My kickboxing instructor once told me to "get on top of your opponent's shoulders and keep working his body." When the statement was clarified, I understood that he meant for me to stay close to my opponent and strike his body, not literally climb up and sit on his shoulders!

My Aikido instructor would tell us to "extend ki." Even if you have a vague idea of what *ki* is, what is meant by *extend*? Is it something physical, like extending your arms? Or is it something mental, like extending your mind somehow? If it is mental, then what technique should you apply, and how are you supposed to know when you are doing it correctly? If your instructor uses these abstract forms of communication, she should clearly demonstrate what she means. If she says, "You will feel when you're doing it right," she has done little to enhance learning.

I thought you might be interested to know that ki or ch'i is described in the ancient Chinese military classic, Sun-Tzu's *Art of War*, which is China's oldest and most profound military treatise and was written around the sixth century B.C. Contrary to modern Western explanations of ch'i as a somewhat mystical life force, Sun-Tzu removes all mysticism from the word by describing it as fighting spirit derived from the will or intention to enter battle. How do you

achieve it? When you are well-trained, fed, clothed and properly equipped, you have established the foundation for "extending ki (or ch'i)." In essence, it means that you define your military or battle objective, assess the situation to determine if your goal is within reach, and make proper preparations in training, equipment and logistics. When this has been done, you can proceed into battle with confidence. When you have confidence, you can display proper spirit. Clear and simple, eh?

Whenever possible, your instructor should use concrete images that you are familiar with and can relate to. What is wrong with the following statement?

The behavior I witnessed in class yesterday is inappropriate.

What exactly does the behavior refer to? What is meant by inappropriate? If you were absent the day before, you will not know what he means. And even if you were present, you may still not know what he means. How about this:

Yesterday, Bill got angry with Jill for an accidental groin kick and gave her a black eye. This is not how you behave in here. When something goes wrong, I want you to take time out and let your sparring partner know. Then, if there is still a problem, let me know and I will handle it.

When describing a technique or behavior, your instructor should avoid using abstract or subjective words. Subjective means something that is up to a person's opinion, something that creates one truth for you and another for me. For example:

The test will be very difficult.

The statement is subjective because what is difficult for one person may be easy for another. Furthermore, what does very mean? In comparison to what? How about this:

The test will be the most difficult thing you have ever done.

Perhaps the instructor is a little more specific by classifying very as the most difficult. However, since she doesn't know what you have experienced in your lifetime, how can she construct a test that is more difficult than anything else you have ever done? In addition, even if she did know what your prior experiences were, how can she hold all students to the same standard? All students haven't experienced the same things, have they? How about this:

You should strive to be the best you can be.

How do you know what the best is? Let's say that you think you are the best you can be, and you still lose to every fighter you spar with. Does this mean you are a winner anyway, because you are the best you can be? It is better to find out exactly what you need to do in order to beat the competition (if that is your goal), and then train with that objective in mind. When I went to airline travel school, our instructor said that when we were hired with an airline and put through training, we could expect it to be very difficult. How difficult?

No one saw me for three weeks. That's how difficult. We had two tests a day, every day for three weeks, and if you scored less than 80 percent on any of the tests, you no longer had a job.

I had one instructor who always added, "you know what I mean," at the end of every sentence. But students were not given the opportunity to say whether or not they really knew what he meant.

 SCENARIO 41

Your instructor tells you that your technique is "generally good." What does he mean?

1. You are average.

2. You are good enough to pass the next belt promotion.

3. He doesn't have any specific corrections for you right now.

4. You know the moves, but you are sloppy.

Being told that your technique is "generally good" may seem like a compliment, initially. But if you analyze the words, generally means not particularly. If you make the substitution, how does it sound?

Your technique is not particularly good.

Now you don't have a reason to be so happy. On my blue belt test in karate, I was told that I was "the most outstanding student," which of course made me feel quite proud. However after giving it some thought, most outstanding was in relation to other students who were testing on that day. If I happened to be in with a particularly bad group of students, *outstanding* would not necessarily be that great. The remark would have been more valuable if the judges had told me that I was well into the next level, and why.

You must be able to drive home a point with clarity and ease. You must know how to adjust to the situation as problems arise. Avoid rap sessions that are void of structure.

When your instructor evaluates you, insist that she tells you exactly *what you did well and why, and* exactly *what you need to work on and why.*

THE ART OF ASKING QUESTIONS

Your instructor might ask questions in order to evaluate your understanding of techniques and concepts. Asking questions interspersed with explanations of techniques and concepts also helps him break up the monotony of a lecture and gives him an indication of the effectiveness of the lesson. What is wrong with the following question?

Do you understand?

Questions that can be answered with a "yes" or "no" should be avoided, since such questions give you a 50 percent chance of guessing the answer and therefore don't provide evidence that you understand the subject. Good questions require you to analyze the problem and arrive at a conclusion. An effective question includes specific elements:

1. It asks what is essential. I had a biology teacher who taught the essentials of but asked test questions involving material that we had barely touched upon, material that nobody could remember and that didn't emphasize the main points. As a result, few students passed the test.

2. It is stated in the everyday language you are used to. You shouldn't have to guess what your instructor is thinking. A good question allows for only one correct answer.

Visual aids can be used if they help make the question clearer. In martial arts, a visual aid can be a demonstration of a technique prior to asking a question. For example, in a grappling situation, the instructor might ask, "Which fighter is more stable: the one with the high center of gravity, or the one with the low center of gravity? Why?" If you don't understand the term center of gravity, you will not be able to answer the question even if you know the correct answer. This type of question is therefore not a true test of your knowledge. A demonstration, however, can clarify and make the question valid. If your instructor demonstrates high and low centers of gravity prior to asking the question, any confusing terms can be resolved to allow you to answer the question. Generally you can form an effective question by asking what, where, how and why.

Bad: "Is the knee a valid target for the sidekick?"

Bad: "Do people pass out within 10 seconds of a properly applied choke?"

Better: "Why is the knee a valid target for the sidekick?"

Better: "Name a valid target for the sidekick."

Better: "Why do people pass out within 10 seconds of a properly applied choke?"

Asking what, where, how and why eliminates the tendency to guess the correct answer. In the above case, it also brings about a discussion of human anatomy and function, the correct way to kick or apply the choke, the possibility of a successful outcome, the risk of sustaining an injury, etc. Your instructor can prepare pertinent questions in advance and place them in the lesson plan. Not all questions in the lesson plan need to be asked; they can also serve to prompt the instructor on what to teach next.

A good question has only one answer and is called an objective question. The opposite of objective is subjective, which means "up to a person's opinion." Objective questions carry authority, and objective answers can be applied in reality.

TIPS FOR ASKING QUESTIONS

Asking questions is not just your instructor's responsibility. You, the student, can learn a lot by asking appropriate questions. The same rules apply. If you ask a question that allows your instructor to answer with a simple "yes" or "no," you will not learn as much as if you ask a question that allows her to elaborate or give you a specific answer.

1. When you ask a question, listen with the intent to explore the answer. Your instructor should allow you to elaborate beyond her answer. Listen both to what is said and to what is implied.

2. If your instructor seems puzzled by your question, ask the question again but in a slightly different way.

Good: "Why do we pass out within 10 seconds of a properly applied choke?"

Good: "Show me how to apply the choke properly. What is it that you are choking, air or blood?"

Your instructor might show you how an improperly applied choke allows your opponent more time to struggle and break the hold. He might also show you how you could get banged around if the choke isn't applied properly. Or he might show you how clinging to your opponent's back and wrapping your legs around his waist could prevent him from defeating the choke. Your instructor might also demonstrate how your opponent might defend against the choke, for example, by pressing his chin down and defeating your tries to restrict the blood supply to his brain.

3. Questions should be challenging or they will serve little mental purpose. They should also be applicable to what you are learning in this particular lesson. Ask questions that are concise so that there is no confusion as to what you are asking. Ask only one question at a time.

Bad: "Should you chamber the leg prior to throwing the roundhouse kick, and if so, why is it important and what are the targets?"

Better: "Why is it important to chamber the leg prior to throwing the roundhouse kick?"

4. Present "what if" questions, such as "What if I am in a tournament and I screw up in the middle of a form?" or "What if a judge doesn't see a point I score in sparring?" You can also ask yourself these types of questions to pre-

pare for a test or tournament. When you run through potentially bothersome scenarios before they happen, you are, in essence, helping yourself at a time when your instructor can't be there for you. This mental exercise will later develop into the ability to make sound decisions.

TIPS FOR ANSWERING QUESTIONS

Answering questions might seem easy as long as you know the answer. However, there is an art here as well.

1. Make sure you fully understand what your instructor is asking. Even if you have already heard the answer several times, you should not respond to the question mechanically. Give the question some thought and try to provide the rest of the class with new information. Remember, others are learning from your answers. After you have answered the question, look for a response in your instructor. She should acknowledge or elaborate on your answer.

2. Answers often trigger new ideas, tempting you to ask further questions. Depending on your background and experiences, elaboration may or may not be a good idea. Sometimes it is unwise to introduce a more complex concept. If you are curious but your instructor feels that more information would complicate the situation, she might tell you that the question is good and that she will work on spin-offs in a later lesson.

3. If you are having problems with answering a question, try asking yourself another question that starts with a *why* or a

how along the same lines. This method may lead you in the right direction and trigger a response. You can apply this technique on any test where you have some time to think about the answer. If you can derive the answer from your own elaboration, you will remember the material more easily and may learn something in the process. You will, in a sense, be teaching yourself.

4. If your instructor asks a question that can be answered with a simple "yes" or "no," try to resist the temptation to give such a simple answer. Giving a more thorough answer ensures that you actually answer what the instructor is asking.

5. It has been said that there are no dumb questions. Well aside from the fact that this phrase is trite, there are, in fact, dumb questions. But when your instructor asks one, try not to let it show. If you see an opportunity to provide slightly more information than what your instructor is asking for, or if you see a way to clarify for other students what your instructor did not express so eloquently, by all means do it, but do it with good taste. The question-and-answer session is supposed to be a learning experience and not an attempt to ridicule your instructor or another student in class.

QUESTIONS A GOOD INSTRUCTOR AVOIDS

Certain questions have no learning value and should be avoided. These include:

1. Questions that are too open, such as "Do you have any questions?" A shy student

may not speak up, even if he has questions.

2. Questions that are too complex or require you to solve a "puzzle." The purpose of asking questions is not to determine whether you can figure out what your instructor is thinking.

3. Questions that have a catch. This is not a test of who is smarter.

4. Questions that cover everything, such as "What should you do to increase your chances of success in a tournament?" These types of questions are too broad and allow for the possibility of a vast number of answers. It is better to ask about one specific thing that pertains to the situation.

5. Questions that give you a choice of "this" or "that." These kinds of questions are often not valid because they force you to identify one answer as the correct one, even if both answers are incorrect. For example, a peer student who finds your attitude irritating might ask: "Are you dumb or arrogant?" Technically he has presented you with a choice of "this" or "that." However, the true answer to the question is, "No, I am neither dumb nor arrogant. I am educated and am trying to help you."

14

Psychological Factors of Learning

PHYSICAL AND MENTAL STRESSES

Learning is enhanced when you are physically and mentally comfortable. But since the martial arts are about combat, there are many times when you won't be perfectly comfortable. You succeed more easily when you commit yourself to learning also about the limitations of combat, including your own personal limitations, and become confident that you can deal with physical and mental stresses. Learning to deal with stress is practiced best after you have familiarized yourself with the training regimen. In other words, you should not be made uncomfortable on your first day.

Everybody feels stress to some degree. Positive stresses help us meet challenges. Negative stresses can make us feel overloaded and sick. The level and type of stress we feel vary greatly among individuals. Some of us feel stress when going to a competition or a belt promotion. Others feel stress just by coming to class. A certain amount of stress is good for you, because it prevents complacency. But if the stress interferes with your well-being to the point that you are getting sick, it will also interfere with your ability to learn and might cause you to drop the class. When you get overly stressed, when you are unable to cope with the stress, you may show physical, emotional or behavioral symptoms.

Physical symptoms can range from stomach upset to shivering and muscle tenseness. This type of stress might also inhibit your ability to think clearly. For example, you might not be able to state the correct answer to a question, even if you know it. At the beginning of a belt promotion, these symptoms can be eased by doing a group warm-up to overcome tenseness and get your mind in tune with your body.

Common emotional symptoms of stress are depression and withdrawal. Behavioral symptoms may include skipping class or looking for "a way out." Rationalization is also common. You may have a number of excuses for not coming to class, such as that you were sick, had to work overtime, or simply forgot that this was class night. If you are subjected to stress, your instructor can try to motivate you by calling you at home prior to class or by helping you in private after class. But this method only works if you have the basic drive to go to class. If not, it is unfair to take advantage of your instructor's time and effort. Some stresses are caused by factors outside of the martial arts; for example, you may need time off to cope with a problem at home.

Advanced students can, and often should, be pushed from their comfort zone. Physically you can be pushed from your comfort zone by working in hot or cold temperatures (be watchful of your health and understand how your body is likely to react), working to exhaustion and engaging in contact sparring. Mentally you can be pushed into stressful situations by sparring against multiple attackers, or being critiqued while performing forms in front of your peers. If your instructor explains in advance the purpose of working outside your comfort zone, you are more likely to cooperate and learn from the experience.

As students, we also have the social need for belonging. Some ways to satisfy our social needs are by wearing a uniform, doing group exercises and *kiai* shouts, and participating in tournaments or demonstrations.

 SCENARIO 42

You are frustrated in class because you are not "getting it." What should your instructor tell you?

1. It will come.

2. Do the exercise 100 times at home, and if you still don't get it, I will help you.

3. You're doing just fine.

4. Why don't you get it?

★★★★★

Frustration in learning is a common phenomenon. You can get frustrated:

1. If you feel that you are not getting it;

2. If you are getting it but your instructor isn't giving you additional information fast enough;

3. If you have to work on a technique for a long period of time without your instructor offering advice or checking on your progress; or

4. If you feel that you are being treated unfairly.

Frustration comes from many different factors. Personally, I feel that the single most frustrating factor is when your instructor fails to respond to or take seriously your requests for help with troublesome techniques. Perhaps he might show you some little detail that is irrelevant and tell you to work on it for a week, but then he forgets about your problem and never checks back with you. When you feel frustrated with a technique or concept, start by identifying from where your frustration stems. Then ask your instructor to help you advance past the frustrating factor. When you have clarified your frustration to yourself, you can verbalize it to your instructor and get help easier.

COPING WITH ANXIETY

Sometimes we lack confidence in our ability because of preconceived ideas of who we are. For example, you might say, "I am too old," or "I am so uncoordinated," or "I am not very flexible." Even if you are stating facts, they need not prevent you from becoming a great martial artist. However, in order for your instructor's responses to these statements to be convincing, they must include specific examples. If you complain that you are too old, and your instructor says, "Oh, you'll be fine," he is not really basing his answer on anything concrete. So why should you believe him? It is better if he can tell you a true story about someone your age or older who has accomplished the same goals that you have set for yourself. For example, he might point out that George Foreman was competing and winning past the age of 50, or that Don "The Dragon" Wilson made a comeback and was winning over fighters half his age, or that your instructor himself is 20 years your senior, or that a man 80 years of age tested for his black belt last weekend.

If your complaint is lack of coordination, however, it can be overcome with training. When your instructor takes you through some simple exercises like the reverse punch or the front kick, it will generally show you that you are not as uncoordinated as you thought. On flexibility issues, keep in mind that the low kick to the legs is an extremely effective technique that doesn't need a lot of flexibility. You don't have to be flexible enough to do full splits in order to be a good fighter. Sure, some of us need to work more on coordination and flexibility than others. But most of the time, we complain because we lack self-esteem. Age and lack of flexibility do not automatically qualify you as a slow learner or poor martial artist. It is important that both you and your instructor understand the difference.

A psychological factor that tends to hinder of learning is undue concern over getting hurt. If you tense and shy away every time another student throws a technique toward you, you need to take some corrective actions. You can legitimately get hurt by punches and kicks, by falling or getting thrown, through joint lock techniques, and on equipment when striking it incorrectly. You can also get hurt when doing push-ups or other physical exercises. If you have a physical problem, like a bad wrist or knee,

Tensing or shying away as a result of undue concern over getting hit is a factor that could interfere with learning.

make sure that you tell your instructor about it, so that she can suggest extra protection or other exercises that will not aggravate the problem.

If you are afraid of falling or getting hit, your instructor must educate you on the art and build your confidence gradually. For example:

1. Fear of falling can be eased by practicing falls from a kneeling position.

2. Fear of being hit can be eased by getting used to seeing a strike coming toward you, and knowing that there will be no actual contact.

173

Your instructor should be the one working with you on these exercises, because other students may not have developed the necessary control yet. Pay attention to your physical condition. If practice sessions are too hard for your current condition, they can cause nausea or other discomfort.

 ## SCENARIO 43

You shiver and turn white with anxiety every time you get ready to spar. What should you do?

1. Ignore it, because the problem will go away once the first blows are exchanged.

2. Tell yourself to relax and have fun.

3. Explain to the others what is wrong with you.

4. Sit down and ask another student to take your place.

Get introduced gradually to new techniques, such as the forward roll, in order to overcome fear and minimize the risk of injuries.

5. Say, "I don't care if I am scared, as long as I don't puke on the carpet."

How do you handle the situation while still saving face? For your continued confidence, it is important to understand that being anxious is not equivalent to being a bad fighter. Anxiety has nothing to do with skill. Some of the world's best fighters feel queasy or shaky prior to a bout. An anxiety attack, however, may be a critical moment in your development, especially if your peers (or worse, girlfriend) are watching. I have found it best to talk about my fears before they materialize. Volunteer information about your fears to another student whom you trust, and see if you can get some feedback regarding similar feelings. If you prefer not to talk with others, at least acknowledge the fear. Say to yourself, "I am afraid, and it's okay." Be aware that fear of any kind does not need to affect your career negatively. When my mother studied to be a nurse for newborns, she fainted the first time she had to draw blood from the tiny foot of a baby only hours old. She came home in tears and told us, "Today something happened that will destroy my whole career." Her assessment of the problem was unreasonable, of course. She overcame it with some practice and worked successfully in the nursing profession for many years.

Anxiety attacks don't necessarily come during sparring. For example, some students are extremely uncomfortable performing solo in front of others. Most belt promotions that I have attended require some solo performance in front of a panel of judges. If you freeze up, get the shakes, or faint on a test, does it mean that you can never achieve a higher rank? To most people, nervousness occurs mostly in the anticipation of the performance and goes away once they start performing. Your ability to perform successfully when you are nervous or afraid generally improves with time and practice.

– INSTRUCTOR TIP –

Sometimes, a student simply needs a pep talk. To help your student's psychological state, offer support, preferably in the form of practical solutions. But don't "baby" the student. Doing so might make him feel worse rather than better.

– STUDENT TIP –

Much of the fear you feel can be eased when you understand that you are not alone. If you feel fear prior to competition, remind yourself that you are your opponent's worst enemy.

COPING WITH THE UNUSUAL

I once had a lady come in for a minicourse on self-defense. She took her shoes off but refused to remove her socks because, she said, she didn't have any toes! I didn't believe her for a second, of course, but since she was attending only a four-day course, I let her prevail. On a different occasion, a male student didn't want to take his socks off because, he said, his toes were so unusually long. Since he was in the program for the long haul, I didn't find it appropriate for him to train with his socks on. When I told him that I found long toes sexy, he gladly removed his socks.

Some of us have unusual problems that are difficult to communicate to our instructors and peers. For example, you might get claus-

trophobic from wearing the headgear. One of my students suddenly stopped in the middle of a round of sparring and started tugging at his headgear shouting, "Help me off with this, I can't breathe!" I led him to the mirror and showed him that since the headgear didn't cover his face, he could indeed breathe. I told him that I would open the door to let more air into the studio. Another student told me that he couldn't breathe while wearing his *gloves!* Some problems make sense only to the person experiencing them.

"BAD" PARENTS

If you are taking the martial arts together with your child, remember that your goals are not necessarily your child's goals. A parent in one of the classes I was teaching kept pushing his eight-year-old son to test for a stripe on his belt, but the boy wasn't ready. And more importantly, the boy knew that he wasn't ready and didn't want to test. After several requests from the father, I finally agreed to test the boy. But the boy was so tense and stressed that he froze in the middle of the required karate form and started crying. I discontinued the test and scolded myself for letting it go that far. A private test that did not allow the parents to sit in might have helped ease the child's mind, especially if the parents were the driving force and the child was afraid of displeasing them.

If you are a parent wishing to enroll your child in a martial arts class, at what age is it appropriate to do so? The answer differs depending on the circumstances. The maturity of the child plays a role, so there is no absolute minimum age. Children, just as adults, should also have a true desire to learn. It is not uncommon that it is your own desire for the martial arts that makes you enroll your child. But well-meaning parents need to understand that learning takes time, and that children are more likely to be good students if the idea to study the martial arts rests with them and not with you. If your child has shown an interest in learning the martial arts, you might start by interviewing her to determine from where her desire stems.

 ## SCENARIO 44

The classes consist mostly of children, and the head instructor needs an assistant to help him. He asks you to teach the children's class, but you are not interested in teaching children and tell the instructor so. What should he do to motivate you?

1. Tell you that you must teach in order to advance, and this is where he needs your help.

2. Tell you that children are more challenging than adults, so teaching children will make you a better instructor.

3. Ask you to teach an adult class instead.

4. Waive your dues if you agree to teach the children's class.

Many martial arts schools cater to children. When your instructor chooses his assistants, he should first and foremost consider what is best for the students. The first qualification for assisting in a children's class is that you enjoy being around children. If not, then stand by your decision and decline the request to teach.

COPING WITH SCREW-UPS

Most of us have heard that "history repeats itself." The human race often fails to learn from past experience. The good news is that a mistake is an opportune time for learning. But your instructor's reaction when you screw up can affect your outlook on the martial arts. If you screw up in public, such as in a tournament or on a test, it is particularly important that your instructor doesn't blow up, uses inappropriate language, or ridicule you. A loud, "What the hell do you think you're doing?!" does not present a professional image and is likely to embarrass you. If your behavior truly warrants your instructor's anger, it is a good idea to let emotions cool before deciding on disciplinary action. Reprimands might be handled best in private. Your instructor must still be ready to intervene to save you or a peer from a potentially dangerous or inappropriate situation.

It can be argued that if you are so sensitive that you can't handle a critique or discipline, perhaps you should seek another activity that doesn't require you to do so. However, it is your instructor's job to help you advance regardless of your personality traits, even if it means adapting her teaching style to your needs. The instructor's personal ideas of how tough a student should be are irrelevant. Her job is not to weed out the crybabies, but to improve the strength of every student.

Now that we have talked briefly about your screw-ups, it might be appropriate to ask what to do if your instructor screws up. Let's say that he explains a technique to the class, but when demonstrating it in sparring, the technique fails. How should he explain the discrepancy? When the unexpected happens, it is a good idea to talk about why and what can be done about it. Both you and your instructor should see it as an opportunity to broaden your knowledge. If your instructor demonstrates the spinning back kick and misses the target, he might want to identify why he missed, such as because he failed to make eye contact with the target. The next time he lands the kick, you will know why the kick worked.

– INSTRUCTOR TIP –

It is better to correct mistakes in the middle of an exercise than after it is over, so that you can end the lesson on a high note. If a student is negatively affected by poor performance, give him a challenge and set his sights on learning something new that can bring back the excitement of learning.

– STUDENT TIP –

If your instructor punishes the whole class with push-ups for one student's mistake and you don't enjoy this kind of discipline, let it go because you know you have autonomy and can walk out the door any time you feel like doing so.

COPING WITH CHALLENGE MATCHES

If a stranger steps into the training hall and challenges you to a fight, what will you do? Before this happens, you may want to evaluate your reasons for studying the martial arts and whether you have a need to prove your knowledge or toughness to a stranger. Next, consider the legal implications should some-

Don't feel forced to accept a challenge. If another student wants to know how "tough" you are, can you smile and walk away with confidence?

body get seriously hurt. My advice is: If somebody challenges you, ask him or her to leave or ask your instructor to handle it. If the challenge is presented as a threat, consider helping your instructor by offering to call the police.

If you are interested in a challenge just to see what you are capable of, you may want to accept it but present it as friendly competition rather than a challenge. Consider how others will view you if you accept the fight. Will you be admired or will you lose respect? Does winning or losing impact how others view you?

Fortunately, it is not common for strangers to present challenges, and my opinion is that accepting such challenges hardly ever benefits you or your instructor. But what if one of your peers challenges you to demonstrate how good you are? When I was new to teaching and was assisting with lower level belts, I often worried that a student would challenge me to demonstrate a technique on an uncooperative bigger student. How do you save face if a bigger and less-experienced student grabs your wrist, asks you to show him how to "get out of it," and the technique you have learned as the proper defense doesn't work? In a situation like that, discussing and understanding the element of surprise may help drive home a point. If the "attacker" knows in advance what the prescribed defense for the technique is, you have eliminated the element of surprise and the technique may therefore not be successful. Had it been a real situation, however, you could have relied on the element of surprise and used a softening or distracting technique first. As a student of the martial arts, understand that no technique will work 100 percent of the time. What are the dangers associated with being overconfident?

 SCENARIO 45

Your instructor is teaching karate. You are a new karate student, but you have considerable experience in grappling. You take your instructor down and try to submit her. How should she respond?

1. Enjoy the challenge.

2. Smack you hard in the face.

3. Lie still and tell you to let go.

4. Expel you from the school.

Although grappling is a great and highly effective activity, when you study karate under a karate instructor, this is the art you should practice when in class. If you approach your training with a bad attitude, you won't gain as much as if you are cooperative and come with a desire to learn. Making somebody else feel inferior does not make you superior. Although it is good to further our learning in other arts, our egos often tend to hinder rather than help. Certain order has to be kept in the training hall. Allowing students to exercise any technique or behavior they want, no matter how effective, is not conducive to the learning environment.

A student who is new to the martial arts is not necessarily new to fighting. A "bully" student may want to draw attention to himself; he may want to embarrass your instructor or other students publicly. Others may want to test themselves against the instructor's skill just to see how far they can take it. But if your instructor is too busy defending himself against a student who is trying to beat him up, he will not be a very effective instructor. Your instructor should be careful not to place himself in this position. Whenever I sense that a student wants to show his "superiority," for whatever reason, I tell him that this is a learning environment and if he wants to beat somebody up, he has to enter a full-contact or no-holds-barred competition.

SLOW AND FAST LEARNERS

A student who consistently lags behind her peers will naturally have less confidence than others. We tend to believe that the slower student is shy, frustrated, embarrassed, perspires more, or avoids confrontational drills. But the problem may also manifest itself in the opposite way. The student who is well aware of being a slow learner sometimes tries to act as if she is faster, better or more confident than the others. For example, she may brag about herself or talk others down. Although the cocky student could be a slow learner who needs a bit of cockiness in order to rise to the challenge, it should not be assumed that every student who brags is slow or lacks confidence. If a student is cocky as a result of being slow, the instructor or other students must help her find a way to build her confidence. But if she is cocky as a result of being better than the others, she may need more challenging material.

Some students seem slow initially, but suddenly have some sort of breakthrough that allows them to excel almost overnight. Persistence is often more important than natural talent. Those who win in tournaments are not necessarily the best martial artists. Rather, they win because they return time and time again, regardless of how well they do. One of my students in aviation struggled with the theoretical stuff but did really well on the actual flying. I took her all the way to her flight instructor's license, which is a test with a reputation for difficulty. On the day of the test, my student phoned me and said, "You know, I am actually excited about doing this today." She passed the test on her first try. Her persistence and attitude had overtaken her difficulties with the textbook stuff.

Sometimes, it doesn't matter how easy a task seems, you are still slow and uncoordinated.

For example, your instructor might tell you to take a step forward from your fighting stance, starting with your lead foot. You put some thought into this, and then hesitantly and off balance attempt to step forward. This kind of low coordination might be an indication that you learn better through sight than sound. Some people have trouble translating verbal instructions into actions. If your instructor had demonstrated the action instead, you might have done just fine.

There is also the other extreme type of learner who does everything well from the start. If this is you, your instructor may worry that you will get bored with the lesson, or that he will run out of material to teach you. If you are a fast learner, you should be given much opportunity to refine your skills on bags or in sparring. You might also want to explore strategy and other issues beyond simple mechanics of technique.

On occasion, a peer student might get the idea that he is the instructor and say, "Let me show you how this works." These types of students can either be helpful or be true irritants. Either way, you should not allow this student's behavior to sidetrack you. You might want to capitalize on his ideas with your instructor at the end of the lesson or privately after class. If possible, ego should not get in the way of learning. An inquisitive mind is a welcome addition to the learning environment, but if you really know more than the instructor, then why are you coming to him for information? You, your peers, and your instructor should all remember who is teaching whom.

Each student has a personality that is unique. The relationship between instructor and student can have a profound impact on how well you learn. Instruction is built on logic, but emotions, such as love, fear, frustration or anger cannot always be handled logically. A skilled instructor knows how to deal with human behavior. A knowledgeable student strives to understand the effects of emotions on learning.

– INSTRUCTOR TIP –

Slow learners might seem challenging, but how should we treat fast learners? Give your fast learners new challenges; teach them new techniques, concepts and forms. Remember, *the study of the martial arts is an individual activity, even though it is practiced together with others.*

– STUDENT TIP –

If you are an experienced martial artist taking up a new discipline, the rituals and procedures will be new to you. Although you may appear slower than others initially, it is no indication of where you will be six months or a year from now. A person's achievements must be placed in perspective over a period of time in order to have meaning.

15

The Problem Student

SOME EXAMPLES OF ATTITUDE PROBLEMS

Most students have no problem following the rules and etiquette of the training hall, or complying with the instructor. However, over the course of many years, you will experience just about every type of student among your peers, and there will be a few oddballs that you must know how to deal with. These include:

1. The student who tries to initiate an argument;

2. The student who is lazy and doesn't want to participate in normal class activities;

3. The student who complains about the tiniest bit of contact; and

4. The student who tries to take advantage of you and hits too hard.

Perhaps even more important is how to deal with your own behavior if you happen to be one of these "problem students."

Going against authority is only one of many attitude problems. It is not wrong to question authority; it is only wrong when you get cocky about it. Your instructor should discourage students from getting into arguments, especially in front of the class. She should not let students challenge her in order to prove a point. Some students argue simply because they have a need to be heard, and if they take the opposite stand they will be heard every time. I believe the class can gain much by elaborating and debating, but if you engage in this type of behavior you must also ensure that you are not taking valuable time away from the rest of the class. Another reason you might take the argumentative approach is because you become so stimulated by the material you are learning that you can't wait for your instructor to finish before commenting on it. This problem has to do with an inability to listen. Since learning is a mutual activity between teacher and student, having good listening skills is essential. Learning is about listening to what is really being said, as opposed to what you want to hear.

Still another problem is when you lack patience. For example, your instructor may be halfway through describing a technique when you start trying it on the heavy bag. This sort of behavior can be annoying to your instructor and to the rest of the class. Some students also interrupt the instructor's explanation and try to finish it for him. Let's look at a variety of problem behaviors that you are likely to encounter in yourself or in others.

The student who wants to alter every technique

Chances are this type of student has studied a different art elsewhere. She hopes that altering the technique will give her attention and create the impression that she is more knowledgeable than the rest of the class. Or she is simply excited about the material and sees a way to elaborate on it. If you are this type of student:

1. Rather than interrupting the lesson, wait until your instructor has finished teaching. Or discuss your version with others after class. You can also discuss it with your instructor when he comes around to check on your progress.

2. If your version of the technique has value, your instructor should acknowledge it. If not, he should point out why. Some techniques have value only under specific circumstances. For example, if your instructor is teaching a striking art, and you have studied throws and grappling, you might say, "If you throw your opponent to the ground now, the technique will work much better." Your instructor should acknowledge your point or elaborate on it, but not change his curriculum because of it.

3. Understand that few, if any, techniques are limited to one possible version. But in order to create stepping stones for further learning and establish guidelines for testing, your instructor must limit the material to specific techniques.

The student who thinks he knows more than the instructor

This type of student whispers or clarifies the instructions to the other students. Every time the instructor has finished an explanation, the student offers his own version. He says the same thing the instructor says, but with different words, and he acts as though the rest of the class doesn't understand the instructor's explanation. The student who thinks he knows more than the instructor will most likely be deaf to the teachings and will be unable to learn. If you are this type of student:

1. Interrupting your instructor may simply be your way of learning by paraphrasing the material to yourself. Ask if you may teach a segment of the class, while your instructor watches and evaluates. Be open to suggestions from your instructor. If you are uncomfortable doing this, it is an indication that you don't know the material as well as you thought you did.

2. Ask plenty of questions to determine how knowledgeable you really are. If you feel that your instructor corrects you in error, bring it up after class instead of arguing during class. The problem may simply be that you are misunderstanding your instructor's explanations.

The student who would rather talk than practice

This type of student is often more impressed with what she has to say about a technique than with how well she performs it. If you are this type of student:

1. Ask permission to demonstrate the technique to the rest of the class. If you haven't practiced, it will show. This exercise may therefore motivate you to break your bad habit.

2. Whenever you feel a need to stop practicing and start talking, tell yourself "no." Try to outperform the person next to you.

The student who loves telling everybody how tough he is

You may overhear this type of student talking about how he beat somebody up, or how his opponent's strikes were really weak. Those who claim to be really tough may be measuring their toughness against students who are not yet proficient in the execution of a technique, or they may be lacking confidence. If you are this type of student:

1. Find out how tough you really are by volunteering to have joint locks and other painful techniques demonstrated on you. When you are the guinea pig repeatedly, you will soon discover the truth about pain.

2. Don't "wrestle" with your instructor during such demonstrations. If your instructor wants to demonstrate a joint lock and you won't let her apply it, you are not demonstrating your toughness but rather your stubbornness.

The student who hits too hard

Some students say they don't believe in the value of light contact training. However, these students are often the first to complain if they get hit hard in return. If you are this type of student:

1. Your instructor should spar with you until you learn to control the amount of contact when sparring with other students.

2. Understand that you are in a learning environment and excessive contact is not conducive to learning.

3. If you really thrive on hard contact, seek instruction in a full-contact boxing or kickboxing gym.

The student who hits too hard may not have ill intent; she may simply not be aware that she is hurting anyone. If you are this type of student, ask yourself how you think others perceive you. For example, have you received any nonverbal cues indicate others may not want to work with you?

The student who is overly sensitive to contact

Sometimes the students who claim to be the toughies are really the crybabies. When deciding to study the martial arts, you must understand that it will be physically demanding. You can't expect to learn fighting without ever taking a fall. If you are this type of student:

1. Understand that there is a difference between being reckless and practicing with realism. If you kick the heavy bag and your foot gets a little red, it doesn't mean you sit out the next time kicking is practiced.

2. Understand the difference between a legitimate injury that shouldn't be aggravated and a little soreness due to training.

The assistant instructor who uses her position to exercise power

As a student, I found it particularly irritating when I knew that I was doing a technique correctly, but the assistant instructor tried to correct me. If you are this type of assistant instructor:

1. Make sure you understand your position and responsibilities. If the head instructor hasn't briefed you on them, ask yourself what type of assistant instructor you would like to learn from and try to emulate this model.

2. Remember that you are an assistant instructor because it helps you increase your knowledge, not because you already know more than everybody else.

The student who tells you another art is better

This type of student normally implies the opposite of what he is saying. It is not unusual to hear a student of stand-up fighting talk about how he would punch or kick a grappler before the grappler has a chance to use his moves against him. The opposite also happens: You may hear a student bragging about an art other than the one he is learning. He might have studied this art at one point. Much of this behavior may stem from insecurity, where the student wants his peers to think he knows a lot about other arts. If you are this type of student:

1. Explain to the rest of the class the specific details of another art that you have practiced. When in front of your peer group with your instructor evaluating, you may not be as eager to argue. It is far easier to say to a single person, "My other instructor does it this way" than to say it to the whole class.

2. Should you be highly proficient at what you preach, then why did you switch to another art? If you desire to gain insight into another art, then you must also apply yourself within the study of this art and stop criticizing or downgrading it.

3. Seek to study whatever art that thrills you, and learn whatever you can from whomever you can, but always remember the Golden Rule.

The student who says she is experienced in every conceivable art

"I used to take karate . . ." or "When I studied . . ." But when asked about what style she has studied, she doesn't remember the name. She doesn't even remember which rank she achieved! She says that she quit studying because her instructor moved away and she couldn't find another school, even though martial arts schools are a dime a dozen. What this student really means is that she took one or two lessons as a kid many years ago, which is not the same as "taking karate." Just because you have seen something once, it doesn't mean you have studied it. If you are this type of student:

1. Your instructor should treat you like a new student and move on.

2. Remember that the only way to legitimately claim you are a martial artist is by practicing the martial arts with consistency.

Some people like to imply they are the ones who "made you." When you become a champion, everybody likes to claim a part of your fame: "I was her instructor," or "She learned what she knows from me," or "I knocked her out in a sparring match." Solution? Set the record straight.

The student who feels that others have no business in the martial arts

This type of student may make remarks about older students or children. Or she may tell everyone that women are no good, even though she is a woman: "Most women don't

hit very hard." If you are this type of student:

1. Seek the opinion of another student who is well respected at the school. If you are wrong, be sure he will let you know.

2. Analyze why you feel the way you do. Then make an effort to compliment another student on his technique or skill.

The student who can't do a technique correctly

Some students complicate matters unnecessarily. They think a technique is *supposed* to be difficult, even when it is not. Or they lack confidence: "I am really clumsy, I am not very smart." Some students are very nervous and stiff, and can't do the moves even when they get step-by-step instruction. They say they understand but still continue to do the wrong move. Others get discouraged and feel that no matter how much they study, they will not be able to persevere in a real fight. If you are this type of student:

1. Sometimes it is a matter of giving yourself enough time to allow your body to adjust to the new environment.

2. Ask your instructor to work with you on exercises that help build your confidence and show you that you are not helpless. For example, ask that he show you how you can use your skill to help a friend.

The student who "sucks up" to the instructor

These types of students are hanging around the instructor before and after class. By the way, this is a common phenomenon in the workplace, too. You know who these people are, because they are always hanging around the supervisor's office or lighting a smoke together. Unfortunately, many instructors allow this to happen; they socialize a bit too much with their students. If you are this type of student:

1. Make an effort not to become part of this group. Leave as soon as class is over. The training hall should be a fair environment.

2. Ask for or offer assistance with a technique from a peer instead of from the instructor. Or practice your forms alone for 10 minutes after class, then leave.

The student who is in search of something spiritual

These "new age" students, as I like to call them, can't talk enough about Zen or Buddhism. They have a tendency to exaggerate their breathing, often with their eyes closed in meditation. They would rather sit and meditate than engage in physical practice. They also have a tendency to believe that the arts give them certain mystical powers, such as striking somebody from a distance without touching him, sending objects flying across the room, or reaching into an opponent's chest and grabbing his heart. They may claim to have known some master who could do this, but they can't teach it to others because it is too "deadly." Of course, these types of students are detached from reality and will probably not stay in the arts for very long, but will seek enlightenment elsewhere. If you are this type of student:

Meditation is a training aid that helps you calm yourself, gain focus, and collect your thoughts. But it is an *aid*; it is not your main form of training.

1. Hold any beliefs you want but abide by the rules of the training hall and don't disturb the rest of the class. Don't degrade any student or instructor of another art. Be aware that others might find you silly.

2. Subscribe to the leading martial arts magazine and analyze how many articles support (or deny) your beliefs.

The student who criticizes one aspect of the martial arts

"Forms practice doesn't teach you anything about fighting," or "Sparring is not the way the true martial artists defeat their opponents. True martial artists rely on inner strength." When students say they don't believe in forms practice, sparring, jump kicks, etc., they normally mean that they are

186

not very proficient at these things. Rather than admitting they need some work, it is easier to say they don't believe in these techniques. If you are this type of student:

1. Make an effort to learn an effective application from a form. After giving the technique a fair chance, if you still hold the belief that it isn't effective, consider the possibility that it might still work for somebody else.

2. Acknowledge at least one good thing about the techniques you don't believe in. If you can't do this, consider studying elsewhere. If you are not passionate about the material you are learning, your martial arts studies will be slow and difficult.

The student who is selective about what she wants to learn

Some students may want to learn sparring only, while others don't want to spar at all. Some may be interested in forms practice only, or may want to study for flexibility and health, but are not interested in techniques or testing. If you don't learn what is required for the next level, you should not be allowed to test. But there is a different problem: If you resist learning certain elements of the art, you may remain a white belt forever. If you are this type of student:

1. Understand that, although you may not want to learn every technique your instructor is teaching, it is still what you need in order to progress. When you go to college, you can't earn your degree if you don't fulfill the course requirements.

2. Adhere to the curriculum, unless your instructor is teaching privately without a belt-ranking system. Adhering to the curriculum ensures that each student who graduates has the same knowledge base.

The student who comes to class sporadically

Some students come to class only once in a while, yet they want to test with the rest of the group. Or they are gone for long periods of time but still want others to respect their skill. There is no substitute for hard and consistent practice, no matter how talented you are. If you don't make training part of your lifestyle, you are not likely to advance. If you are this type of student:

1. Understand that insight is gained over a period of time. If you desire to advance in rank, make it a habit to go to class regularly.

2. Practicing a lot in a short period of time is not necessarily better than practicing moderately all the time. Likewise, practicing very little over a long period of time is not good, either.

 SCENARIO 46

You want to share techniques you have studied elsewhere. Should your instructor let you do so? Why or why not?

1. Yes, because the more you know, the better a martial artist you are.

2. Yes, because it gives your instructor an opportunity to show you why his style is superior.

187

3. No, because it may seem confusing to mix styles.

4. No, because it might dilute your instructor's style.

My opinion is that if you want to show your peers techniques that you have learned elsewhere, and if you do so before or after class, there is no harm done. After all, your instructor is trying to turn her students into the best martial artists possible, so she should be open to the free flow of information. However, if you insist on following rituals or mechanics of techniques you have learned elsewhere, I think it would be appropriate for your instructor to speak up. For example, if your instructor teaches a medium-high stance, but you insist on keeping a very low and wide stance because that's what you have learned in another art, then you, and not your instructor, should change. If you don't want to comply, then you should seek out a school that teaches the art you want to practice.

Part Four
Learning Martial Arts Techniques

16

General Learning Concepts

A PEP TALK

The next few chapters will focus on how to analyze and extract additional information from the techniques you are learning in class. This chapter will prepare you for your continued journey, and give you a better idea of how to approach your technique training.

Learning the martial arts involves more than just learning the moves of each technique. Your instructor must consider many ideas and concepts when developing a training curriculum. For example, you must learn both physical and mental conditioning. A muscular body can withstand strikes better than a weak body, and a supple body can maintain balance when performing the more difficult techniques. A strong and supple body gives you speed and ease of movement. Cardiovascular endurance may be your most important physical attribute, but muscular endurance is important as well. You don't know in advance for how long the fight will last in a self-defense scenario. In tournament competition, too, the person with greater endurance often wins over the more skilled fighter. Mentally, you must know how to deal with fearful situations without getting stunned. Having "been there" prior to the actual encounter is great for conditioning your mind and body, even if you have only "been there" in training.

Although the martial arts are popularly thought of as self-defense, it has been said that the best defense is offense. So you must learn both offense and defense. Offense should be learned with the proper attitude. The way you carry yourself in a threatening situation may determine whether you will be a victim or a winner. Some people equate proper attitude with confidence. I call it "combat presence." When you square off to spar with your opponent, you should look as though you want to be there. Combat presence can be practiced in forms demonstrations as well by practicing with intent and making the audience feel your presence in the room. Have you ever noticed how some people manage to sneak in and out unnoticed? Have you noticed how they never say anything or draw attention to themselves? Combat presence means that you strive to let others know who and where you are. You want them to notice you; you want them to understand that they'd better not enter your space.

Learning the martial arts also involves learning specific details about your particular art, what it is used for, its history, and how it compares to or differs from other arts.

THE FIRST LESSON

As already discussed, your first impression of your instructor may determine whether or not you come back for more training. The first time you meet your instructor, you are likely to be a bit tense. Your instructor should take time to ask you some general questions that tell you he is interested in your progress. Once you bow in, the setting will be more formal. But you shouldn't fear going to your instructor with concerns or questions you may have. You might want to ask him to give you some information about himself as well. For example, ask him about his experience and the masters that he has studied under.

The first lesson should be interesting, without overemphasizing any particular task. If your instructor gives you a half-hour talk about how deadly the art is, he will probably do you a disservice. It is also important that he doesn't start with teaching techniques designed to impress or frighten you, such as a sparring session where he beats you black and blue in order to determine if you have heart. These sorts of lessons are not perceived well in today's society where martial arts schools are a dime a dozen. We tend to assume that people study the martial arts because they want to learn how to fight or defend themselves. But the fact is that many arts are traditional. The instructor intends to develop your life philosophy in addition to your self-defense skills.

The first lesson is the beginning of a journey that should lead to a good relationship with your instructor and set the course for future training. If you are new to the martial arts, much of the first lesson should be used to familiarize you with the experience. When you leave, you should be looking forward to coming back. The first lesson

should make a favorable impression by teaching you something useful, such as how to clench your fist and throw a punch correctly. The first lesson should also leave you with something to think about. You should have an idea of how the first few weeks will look, when you can expect to enter your first tournament, or how belt promotions work.

In the second lesson, you will be a bit more relaxed and more information will therefore sink in. As you become familiar with the etiquette of the training hall, you can learn the material more rapidly without having to focus on remembering rituals. You will begin to understand your mistakes and visualize the learning process. Still, it often takes up to two years before students break through the mechanical stage and find a connection between the techniques they have learned.

Many schools ask students what they hope to gain from the lessons. Consider asking your instructor about the primary aim of the school. His aim does not have to be identical to the aims of other schools, but he should be able to state it clearly.

1. Does the school have a mission statement that is short, clear and to the point?

2. What sets your school apart from other schools?

WARM-UP

Warm-up prior to workout is essential to avoid injuries and may be the first element you learn in any given lesson. How long should a warm-up last and what should it include? If the classes are short (45 minutes or less), you may want to arrive 10 minutes before start time and engage in some light stretching or shadow boxing on your own. The benefit of warming up on your own is that all class time can be used for learning. The drawback is that many students don't know how to warm up properly.

A warm-up conducted in unison and led by your instructor can serve as a great motivator. The time immediately following the warm up can be used constructively to review the last lesson or talk about what the current lesson is to cover. The time allotted to warm-up should be proportional to the lesson. The instructor should remember that students pay for instruction, not for exercises they can do by themselves on their own time.

INTRODUCING NEW TECHNIQUES

Common techniques learned in the stand-up arts include stances, blocks, strikes, kicks and evasive movement. These techniques are then combined and built upon during technique practice, forms practice and sparring. Common techniques learned in the grappling arts include takedowns and throws, joint locks, chokes and a variety of leverage moves from the ground. A simple approach when introducing a new technique is to ask *what, why* and *how*. Ideally your instructor should provide an explanation and demonstration and allow you to practice. Using the front kick as an example:

What? The front kick utilizes the ball of your foot. Unlike the roundhouse kick, which impacts the target using the instep in a semicircular motion, the front kick impacts the target in a linear motion.

Why? The front kick is an excellent deter-

rent. When your opponent tries to close distance, time the kick so that it lands as he is in the process of stepping forward. Doing so adds his momentum to the momentum of your kick, and stops his advance.

How? To throw the front kick with your lead leg, start by lifting your lead knee high and pointing it at the target. Curl your toes back and extend your lower leg from the knee.

When learning a new technique, it helps to break it down into its component parts and practice each segment separately. For example:

1. The first move when learning the front kick involves chambering the leg.

2. The second move involves extending the leg toward the target.

3. The third move involves rechambering the leg after the kick has landed.

4. The fourth move involves replanting the foot on the floor and resetting your stance.

Do the technique slowly at first to ensure that the mechanics are correct. When increasing the speed, avoid leaving out one or more steps. Are you chambering your leg fully? Are you extending your leg or are you snapping the kick back before full extension? A common tendency is to cut short the extension of the technique. For example, we throw punches, kicks and blocks utilizing only arm or leg power without proper body rotation.

Many students practice the exact same pattern of techniques to such an extent that if one reference point suddenly changes even a fraction of an inch, they are unable to land their strike on the target. This also happens if the speed of the attack suddenly changes, even if the change is slight. Consider the spinning back kick, which relies on a spin in your upper body with an initial chamber in the kicking leg. The kick is then released straight toward the target. If you practice this kick at a consistent speed but suddenly speed up the spin, you are likely to over-shoot the target. Techniques should there-fore be practiced at a variety of speeds to learn that, your mental reference point changes as the speed changes. When I was a yellow belt in karate, my instructor taught me five punch combinations. He had me do number one first, followed by number two. Next he had me do number one again. Then he grabbed my lapels and pulled me off balance, and asked me to do number two. Next he had me do number three and num-ber one in combination. The point was that

Analyze proper mechanics, such as a full leg exten-sion when kicking, when working techniques in the air.

the intensity and uncertainty of this exercise placed me under pressure to respond.

When you have learned a new technique, you should practice it on a regular basis. If you allow months to pass without practic-ing the technique, you might as well not have learned it at all. Just as you must meet your instructor halfway, he must meet you halfway. If he is unprepared, he might think of something to teach you at the last minute and thus fail to build on the technique from the previous lesson. Granted, when you have learned a hundred techniques, you can't practice every one of them every time you come to class. But you should recog-nize the similarities between techniques. A *shuto* (knife hand strike), for example, is used in many techniques and covers a great variety of situations.

DRILL WORK

In karate class, we adhered to a ritual that started with the student creed, then moved on to jumping jacks and stretches for warm-up, then the basic punches, kicks and blocks. The rate of learning is increased through fre-quency and repetition. Drill work is recom-mended even when you have passed the mechanical stage of learning. Your instruc-tor must also provide you with opportuni-ties to apply what you have learned. The workout should not become a mindless rut. For example, if you warm up by shadow boxing, also work on specific techniques or concepts during the exercise.

Many martial arts schools make the students do the techniques on command. This type of drill work ensures a lot of repetition, helps the instructor observe a large group of students at once, and instills a sense of discipline. The drawback is that it stifles student creativity. If you practice the basic techniques on command for long periods of time, and your instructor suddenly asks you to shadow box combining strikes and kicks as you see fit, most students will have difficulty performing with any kind of variation. The moves will be rehearsed and predictable. I recommend a combination of practicing on command and free sparring.

It is difficult to dispute that frequent repetition results in muscle memory, and makes techniques more natural and easy to execute. But learning through repetition involves more than simply doing the same move over and over. A friend of mine went to a studio that advertised kickboxing. Although he found the drill work very tough, he said that he didn't learn much. The workouts consisted mainly of jumping rope and beating the heavy bags, which are exercises a disciplined student can do alone. Your instructor should teach constructive lessons that lead toward a particular goal. He should make a constant effort toward progress and leave you with a feeling of accomplishment. For example:

1. He might start by introducing the technique.

2. He might then show you how the technique relates to another technique.

3. He might then have you practice the technique on bags.

4. He might end by reviewing the lesson.

In the next lesson, he might start by demonstrating the technique again and then relate it to another technique or concept. Once you have learned your basic punches, kicks and blocks, you will use these in your everyday practice without really thinking about it.

When practicing with a partner, specify who is the attacker, who is the defender and when you should switch, so that both you and your partner get equal amounts of training in both positions. Ideally your instructor should observe and comment on each group's performance at least twice throughout the exercise. His feedback will give the defender the opportunity to learn before he becomes the attacker, and vice versa. It is a good idea to switch partners often, so that you get to work with a variety of people of different sizes and skill levels. Switching partners also eliminates the possibility of ignoring a student who is seldom chosen. To ensure a good mix, you might suggest forming two lines facing each other, and every two minutes move one step to the left or right. If your instructor simply asks students to switch partners, some students will consistently choose each other.

If you practice a technique many times, you may become fatigued or get a mental block that leaves you unable to perform the technique well. This happened to me once with the jump spinning back kick. I forgot how to jump! This is a sign to take a break. A break could last anywhere from a few minutes to several days.

– INSTRUCTOR TIP –

After your students have performed a technique as a group, it is a good idea to have them perform the technique at least once independently before the end of the lesson. This exercise allows you to observe the students, note individual problems, and correct them before they grow into habit.

MOVING BEYOND ROTE

Many instructors introduce new techniques but fail to discuss the principles or concepts under which these techniques should be performed. This type of teaching results in mechanical learning (rote learning), and the techniques tend to work only when your partner is cooperating. Here are some examples of mechanical learning:

1. Always defending against a rear step-through punch and never against a quick lead punch.

2. Learning techniques on only one side of the body.

3. Too much partner cooperation.

4. Women always practicing with women, kids with kids, or students of the same size and build with each other.

To avoid mechanical learning, start by examining the stages of each technique and identifying matters of importance. For example:

1. Learn the mechanics of the front kick.

2. Expand on the technique by identifying the targets.

3. Examine how to adapt when your opponent approaches you from different angles.

4. Discuss the best time to throw the kick, and why.

5. Discuss and practice how your opponent can defend against the kick.

6. Identify the dangers associated with throwing the kick. Might it result in balance loss or target exposure?

7. Discuss how a specific part of the technique relates to the whole. For example, how does chambering the leg relate to balance, power, speed and deception?

8. Name different ways to apply the technique offensively and defensively.

All of these issues need not be learned in one lesson. Over time you will gain insight into fighting and start associating specific techniques with specific scenarios. You will begin to see opportunities for using the techniques. Learning is now taking place.

Different techniques can be further related by discerning their similarities and differences. Stating the similarities helps you relate a new technique to a previously learned one. Stating the differences helps bring new details into focus. Whether your instructor focuses on the similarities or the differences depends to a degree on the purpose of the technique. For example, he might say:

The mechanics of the spinning back kick are exactly the same as those of the sidekick upon impact with the target. The purpose of the two kicks is the same: to knock your opponent back or down. The difference is that the spinning back kick employs a spin in the upper body prior to impact. The spin allows you to gain additional power by accelerating the kick through a longer distance, without having to move your body forward for momentum.

If the purpose of the lesson is to learn about impact forces, you may want to focus on the similarities of the two kicks: Training in the sidekick helps you acquire proper impact mechanics for the spinning back kick. However, if the purpose of the lesson is to learn about strategy, you may want to focus on the differences: The spinning back kick is more time consuming to throw than the sidekick and needs a better set-up.

Your instructor should not overwhelm you with too much information. She should point out the basic concepts, let you practice and then take you to the next step. She can also offer you a challenge to think about at home. For example:

1. She might teach you one half of a form and tell you the second half is the mirror image of the first half. If you work on the form at home, you should be able to figure out the second half on your own. This exercise can be done with techniques as well.

2. She might teach a technique from a left stance and ask that you do the identical technique from a right stance. Or she might ask you to reverse the moves. For example, if the original technique is comprised of a hammer fist strike, a back knuckle strike and a shuto, reverse the order to a shuto, a back knuckle strike, and a hammer fist strike.

3. She might teach a technique empty-handed and ask you to figure out on your own how to do the same technique with a stick or a knife in your hand.

4. She might teach a stand-up technique, such as a sidekick, and ask you to figure out how to do the identical technique from a kneeling position on the ground.

Upon impact with the target, the mechanics for the sidekick and the spinning back kick are exactly the same. The only difference is in the preparatory move: the spin.

Should your instructor give you the specific details of a technique at the same time she shows you the moves? I prefer to get a reasonable amount of detail from the start. Remember, we are trying to get past the mechanical stage and onto understanding, application and finally correlation.

– INSTRUCTOR TIP –

If you are an assistant instructor, is it a good idea to teach a technique you have just learned yourself? Part of teaching involves demonstrating correct mechanics of technique. The other part involves analyzing and correcting errors, which requires a more extensive background than just teaching technique. My opinion is that you can generally teach a new technique soon after you have learned it, so long as you have also analyzed it and are prepared to answer questions the students may have.

– STUDENT TIP –

It is not necessary to memorize every detail of every move in the first lesson. But if you make an effort to pay attention to detail early in your training, techniques will come to mean more. When you get home from a lesson, try writing down everything you remember about the technique.

LEARNING ADVANCED TECHNIQUES

Before classifying a technique as beginning or advanced, take some time to analyze what it is that makes it so. Granted, some techniques are more difficult to perform than others and require greater athletic ability. But a lengthy technique comprised of the basic moves may not be any more advanced than the shorter variation. When I think of advanced techniques, I generally

If you can do a technique empty-handed, can you do it also with a weapon in your hand, using the same hand motion or striking pattern?

think of techniques that require either athletic ability or good timing to perform successfully. Take spinning and jumping techniques, for example. Since these require a great deal of coordination, speed and agility, I normally don't teach them until the student has a good grasp of the fundamentals. But as far as usage goes, these techniques are not really more advanced than the front kick or the roundhouse kick. The simplest techniques are often the most effective precisely because they don't require difficult maneuvering. However, to become a complete martial artist, you must understand and be able to perform the more complex techniques as well, often for no other reason than to learn about yourself and refine your body mechanics. Some students have a natural affinity for jumping and spinning, and can therefore become proficient with these techniques from the start. If you are particularly interested in flashy techniques and display good coordination, your instructor might want to teach you these techniques at an earlier stage than he normally would.

How good does your instructor need to be at performing complicated aerial maneuvers? If these techniques are part of the curriculum, he should at least be proficient enough to demonstrate the elements of the techniques with accuracy. A jump kick doesn't have to be thrown high, however, as long as correct mechanics are used. If your instructor can only throw a low jump kick, then that's what he should demonstrate. He should then have you learn the mechanics of the jump and take you through some exercises that help you achieve height with the kick. Whether or not your instructor is a believer in flashy kicks is irrelevant. He

should still be able to take his students through this stage of training, if it is to remain part of the curriculum.

Before learning jumping or spinning techniques, consider your physical condition:

1. Will you be able to do these techniques without getting hurt? For example, if you are a heavyweight, doing jumping techniques places a lot of stress on your joints.

2. Consider injuries that are in the process of healing. If you have sprained an ankle, the extra pounding and balance required for an aerial technique may not be a good idea.

3. Techniques that involve spinning can cause dizziness and nausea. When practicing spinning techniques, you may want to do some other exercise every five kicks or so, or execute the technique in both directions to counter the tendency to get dizzy.

It should not be assumed that a student who is injured, older or heavier than her peers must refrain from performing aerial maneuvers. The exact mechanics or usage of a technique is an individual matter and should be taught as such.

Our mental attitude toward a more complex technique often affects our ability to learn it. If you make a big deal out of the perceived complexity of the technique, you might think that it is more difficult than it really is. If you are a beginner and your instructor tells you, "this is a black belt technique," you will train with the attitude that the technique is far too advanced for you to master.

Your instructor should remember that his job is to help you learn, not to impress you with the difficulty of the technique.

LEARNING FORMS

When learning forms, first look at the objectives. Do you learn mainly for competition, tradition or combat skills? If you learn for competition, you must first determine what your competition is doing and how to beat them. For example, I see more musical and acrobatic forms in today's martial arts competitions and less traditional forms. Musical forms may therefore score higher than traditional forms. If you are learning combat skills, you need to identify each move in the form and question how to apply it in a real scenario. Some students complain about having to learn forms, because they don't understand the value of learning the prearranged moves. Forms should not be practiced without thought. To get excited about forms training, try the following:

1. Identify how to use one specific move in the form both offensively and defensively.

2. Add a move or two to the original technique in the form. For example, if a form involves only punches, add a kick at the end of each punch combination.

3. Can the moves in the form be used against an opponent on the ground? Experiment with performing the form from a kneeling instead of a standing position.

4. Can the moves in the form be used to defend against an armed assailant and, if not, can they be adapted without a radical change? Can the form be used against multiple attackers? How?

5. Perhaps there are joint locks or arm breaks hidden in the form that are not immediately apparent. Identify them and practice with a partner.

6. When you have learned the form in its entirety, choose one technique from the form and work on this technique only. What new details can you discover about the technique?

Be attentive to your stance. Is it rigid, or do you use body rotation when striking? How do you hold your guard (your hands)? Sometimes tradition doesn't allow us to change the form. But adding lower body rotation and holding your guard the way you would in sparring might benefit you when it is time to apply what you have learned in the form.

You may initially learn each move of the form separately. Some students find it useful to be shown a form in its entirety before learning the moves separately, in order to get a feel for the length of the form and the difficulty of the movements. This doesn't mean that you must memorize 87 moves the first time. You can also learn an entire set of techniques, and then regress and fine-tune the stances and strikes before moving ahead to the next set.

You do not need to gain absolute proficiency with a technique before moving ahead. An instructor who waits too long before introducing the next move in the form may cause boredom and frustration. But a form normally involves many moves and angles, so it is not a good idea to get too far ahead, either. Ask your instructor to offer suggestions through each sequence of moves. Is your stance solid? Are your knees properly bent? Do you have proper focus and power?

You can do many interesting things with forms. One aspect is timing. Many practitioners make their forms look good by employing different speeds in the moves. But is the timing logical? What, exactly, are you defending against? How are the moves to be applied? For example, if the form calls for a sidekick followed by a punch technique, you may want to increase the time between these two techniques slightly in order to give your imaginary opponent an opportunity to close the distance after you have deterred him with the kick.

 SCENARIO 47

The sixth-degree black belt across the street, Sensei Schmoe, says that the blocks in forms are not really blocks at all, but deadly strikes that are taught as blocks because it is too dangerous to teach them as strikes. When you question this philosophy and bring it to your current instructor's attention, how should he respond?

1. Sometimes a cigar is just a cigar.

2. There are no hidden moves in the forms. What you see is what you get.

3. Sensei Schmoe is right, but don't tell anybody since it is a secret.

4. Let me show you what Sensei Schmoe is withholding.

 ★★★★★

If you think your instructor is withholding information until you are more advanced or "worthy," you will possibly feel discontent. Your instructor should explain that forms are comprised of many moves that can be used for a variety of purposes. A strike, block or pressure point strike may all utilize essentially the same body mechanics. Which one is "intended" for the form depends on what the practitioner visualizes. If you have learned blocks, this is probably the application you will see when practicing the form. If you have learned pressure point strikes, then this is probably what you will see. Also research the ease with which the moves must be executed. Most students learn blocks early in their training and become quite proficient at blocking strikes and kicks. If you only have a split second to defend against a real threat, a technique involving gross motor skills, such as blocks, may work to your advantage over a technique involving fine motor skills, such as pressure point strikes or joint locks.

LEARNING TO SPAR

Sparring is an excellent way to learn timing, reaction and defense. Sparring allows you to explore your performance when under pressure. Some instructors won't introduce you to sparring until you have achieved one or more belt levels. The reason may be because the instructor was taught this way and is simply passing on the tradition of the art. Or it may be because she is liability-conscious and afraid that students will incur injuries before they have developed proper control. I believe sparring should be introduced early in your training in order to acclimate you to this new environment and help you realize its value. You should not view it as something mystical reserved for the advanced students.

Sparring is great for building confidence and testing your ability to apply your knowledge in real time. When you enter the ring or step onto the mat, you know in advance that you will get hit. It takes a lot of guts to step into the sparring exercise with this knowledge. Often our fears are not about the event itself, however, but about how we will be viewed by our peers or instructor particularly if we suffer a loss. Understand that you don't have to win when sparring. Your whole career and future do not depend on this one sparring session. Initially the rounds should be kept short and limited to techniques you have learned. You should experience no extreme physical or mental discomfort. The timid student should be eased into sparring, so that it becomes a natural part of his martial arts studies and not an exercise exclusive to the advanced students.

In order for sparring to be as profitable as possible, your instructor must teach it. Although it is convenient to tell students to put on their sparring gear and do round robins, this is not what good instruction is about. Sparring should not be used to escape constructive teaching. Your instructor should explain what you are to work on, and should comment on your performance afterward. She should be clear about the purpose of the sparring session and explain what you are to gain.

In many styles of martial arts, sparring doesn't resemble the art. When you are told to put your gear on and spar, the self-defense techniques you have learned suddenly go out the door. But sparring is about more than getting your gloves and duking it out. Initially you may need to be led through sparring, just like you are led through technique and forms practice. Talk beforehand about what you wish to accomplish during the sparring session. Your instructor can also have you pause in the middle of a round and discuss techniques and concepts. Since free sparring is unrehearsed, your instructor doesn't always know beforehand what specific problems will develop. It may therefore be a good idea for him to comment throughout the practice session, rather than waiting until it is over.

Your instructor should not push you into sparring with the intent to let you sink or swim. Preferably you should spar with your instructor the first few times, so that he can control the pace and let you experience how it feels to hit another person. In the first few sessions, your instructor should be careful about hitting you. For example, he might have you work only on offense, while he performs defensively. Many schools teach one-step sparring, where one student is the aggressor and the other the defender. Your instructor might teach a predetermined technique (a front kick, for example) which you must defend against with a predetermined defense (a downward block). Or he might teach one-step sparring using random techniques. For example:

1. Student A throws any technique, and student B uses any type of defense.

2. After student B has blocked the attack, he throws a counterattack. Student A now blocks and counters. The exercise starts again.

When you gain some experience, sparring will become free flowing and natural. You will discover there are many ways to defend against a particular technique. Defense can also be learned through evasive movement, such as sidestepping or bobbing and weaving.

Another way for the beginner to learn sparring is to restrict the exercise to one or two techniques, such as a lead hand strike and a lead front kick. This type of sparring is somewhat predictable and enables you to build natural defensive reflexes. Next you may stay with these same strikes while learning broken rhythm. If a fighter can use only one technique (for example, if she is hurt and has limited movement), broken rhythm can help her become less predictable. For example:

One-step sparring or light contact drills are good exercises for preparing you for free sparring.

1. First throw a lead hand strike.

2. Next throw three lead hand strikes in rapid succession.

3. Next throw one lead hand strike, wait for a two-count, and throw two more lead hand strikes.

4. Next throw lead hand strikes with broken rhythm while simultaneously circling your opponent.

When planning a sparring session, your instructor might want to ask himself the following questions:

1. Should beginning students spar the same way as advanced students? If not, how should the sparring be modified?

2. Should the same targets be legal for beginning and advanced students? What are the legal targets?

3. If you train for touch-sparring competition, will you spar differently than if you train for full contact? Why and how?

4. If you train for sport grappling, will you spar differently than if you train for self-defense against an armed opponent? Why and how?

Your instructor may also want to add certain restrictions, depending on what he is trying to achieve in a particular session: He may allow throws but not grappling, for example. In light contact sparring, be aware that a strike or kick that doesn't hurt should not be ignored. Acknowledging a strike that lands rather than ignoring it benefits both sparring partners. When you throw a strike, you need to know that your partner respects it. When you receive a strike, you need to know that it was capable of doing damage but that your partner was kind enough to use light contact.

When planning a sparring session with a new student, your instructor might want to consider the following:

1. Introduce offense first, because most people find it easier to act than react. When offense has been practiced and become familiar, introduce defense. Start in slow motion, and speed up gradually until the moves become automatic.

2. Next implement movement, broken rhythm and angled attacks. Students should be able to discern relationships between offense, defense and movement. Free sparring without any pattern or organization is unlikely to teach relationships.

3. Next introduce counterstriking and how to work with different speeds for offense and defense. This exercise naturally leads to fakes and set-ups. It is not necessary to learn how to defend against every possible scenario. Students might want to learn two or three techniques and experiment with these over time.

 ## SCENARIO 48

Your instructor notices that you make several mistakes in a three-minute round of sparring. What should she do?

1. Call a break each time she observes a mistake and point out what is wrong.

2. Ignore it, because you will most likely discover and correct the mistakes on your own.

3. Spar with you and hit you every time you make a mistake.

4. Ask if you are aware of the mistakes you are making.

5. Ignore it, because you are beyond help anyway.

★★★★★

Students should be allowed to make mistakes. Since we are often "punished" instantly when making the wrong move in free sparring, we are likely to make our own corrections. If you make the same mistake consistently, your instructor should point it out and talk about what you can do to correct it. You should then practice while the information is still fresh on your mind. If you are clearly outranked by your peers, your instructor can spar with you and give you scenarios that you can handle confidently. She can also show you strategy that has not yet been taught to the other students in order to boost your self-image. Whether today's sparring session should build on yesterday's sparring session, or whether it should be an "orphan," depends on what you wish to achieve. Either way, your instructor should let you know where she is taking you in advance. You should be looking forward to your next session.

LEARNING FULL CONTACT SPARRING

Full-contact sparring is often rougher, both physically and mentally, than touch sparring or point fighting. If full-contact sparring is part of your curriculum, some time will be spent on developing the proper attitude toward contact. You want to respect your opponent's techniques enough to develop good defensive habits, but you don't want to be tentative about using offense. Your instructor should point out that when you engage in a sparring match, you *will* get hit. Sometimes it is necessary to take a strike in order to get one in. You need to develop the kind of attitude where taking a strike doesn't affect you negatively. It can be a fine line to walk, however. You want to avoid injury while still feeling the impact of techniques. You should know beforehand that it is full contact sparring you are learning, but you don't need to knock your partner senseless. Start with contact drills or supervised medium contact sparring, until you have built a relationship with your peers where you can spar without being malicious. Don't allow egos to get in the way of learning. If you clearly outmatch your partner, be courteous and back down on the power a little.

When you have gained some experience with your peers, attend your first full-contact competition. Be aware that most students tend to fight more aggressively when under pressure to fight in front of an audience. This pressure to perform often results in fatigue and sloppiness, resulting in less power and less target accuracy. Initially when fighting full contact, I preferred to have my instructor present, particularly since I did most of my sparring with men bigger and heavier than I. But I later found that inviting others to spar when my instructor was not present allowed us to have a more productive sparring session. We could

work on strategy under full-contact rules without worrying about having to impress anybody.

 ## SCENARIO 49

Your instructor tells you to get your sparring gear, but you don't want to spar; you just want to watch. What should your instructor do?

1. Say, "Okay!" and allow you to sit out and watch.

2. Tell you that you must spar for your next test.

3. Ask if you are feeling okay.

4. Ignore it.

If you don't want to spar, should your instructor force you to spar? Should participation in competition be a requirement for promotion to a higher rank? If sparring is part of the curriculum, should you be allowed to practice forms while the other students spar and still expect to pass the test? What should your instructor do if he schedules sparring every Thursday, and you consistently miss Thursdays?

My opinion is that if sparring is part of the curriculum, then you should be required to spar, even if you don't want to. Otherwise you will go through training never feeling really complete. As a result, you may drop out all together, or you may continue training for several years while avoiding classes where sparring is taught. Later, when you find yourself in a situation where you are challenged or attacked outright, you will question the validity of the 21 years of training you spent under your instructor's watch.

Part of the study of martial arts is about confronting your fears. If your instructor wants to be remembered for her professionalism, she should teach to the same standards as a university professor. In college you can't be selective about the exercises. But it is also the instructor's job to help the timid student by introducing him to sparring in a gentler way.

– INSTRUCTOR TIP –

Avoid using a sink-or-swim type of approach to sparring. Don't throw your students head over heels into the ring. Avoid "war stories." You might think them funny, but you'll never know whom you will scare away from sparring. Many students don't reveal their feelings openly in class. They might smile and seem to enjoy the lesson even though they really can't wait to get in their car and never come back.

– STUDENT TIP –

There comes a time when you must test yourself through the tool of sparring. The exception is the student who is merely interested in the art or the exercise, and not in the self-defense application. If you are studying for the purpose of self-defense, avoid sitting out when sparring is taught.

We have now discussed general learning concepts. The next few chapters will focus on developing critical thinking skills for learning the stand-up and grappling arts. The exercises are designed to raise questions and trigger your imagination; they are not designed to answer your questions outright.

17

Exercises for the Stand-Up Arts

LEARNING STANCE

Many karate schools teach the basic punches, kicks and blocks from a neutral stance (horse stance). Some say the value of practicing the basic techniques from the horse stance is to allow you to focus fully on your techniques without confusing you with footwork. But since we hardly ever spar from the horse stance, consider whether it might be beneficial to practice the basics from a left or right fighting stance instead of a horse stance.

Practicing the basics from the stance you will use in sparring facilitates learning, because it eliminates the extra step needed to transition from your practice stance to your sparring stance. All schools have their own ideas of how to teach and maintain the tradition of the art, but here are some things you might want to consider when learning stance:

1. You will learn to protect your centerline by training from the stance you will use in sparring.

2. If you are doing the basics from a horse stance, consider using a non-rigid stance that permits rotation in your hips and body. This will help you learn correct mechanics for powerful striking from the start.

3. When practicing from the horse stance, we often bring our hands down to our hips between strikes and blocks. If using a high guard in sparring, it may also be a good idea to use a high guard when practicing the basics.

4. Identify the value of the stance and explore the difference between a stable and an unstable one. How can you maintain the stance when moving? How can you switch stance and direction with ease?

Most of the time, you will probably train and fight from either a left or right stance (left or right foot forward). Some arts emphasize placing your stronger side forward, particularly if you rely on speed or touch sparring to score a point. The full contact arts tend to emphasize placing your stronger side to the rear, so that your rear hand has sufficient distance to build momentum for powerful striking. You will also see fighters who switch stance often and attempt to develop equal proficiency with both sides. Your stance is valuable because of the speed, power and strategy it gives you. The primary reason for learning stance is to develop balance and movement, without which you cannot throw or defend against powerful strikes and kicks.

An unstable stance neutralizes the power in an otherwise impressive strike.

Exercise 1—Mechanics

- When assuming your stance, take a moment to check your balance. You determine the correctness of your stance partly through feel, and partly through learning about correct distance and positioning of your feet and upper body. Can you take a step forward, back, or to the side with ease and efficiency? If not, how can you adjust your stance to facilitate ease of movement?

- Can you shift your bodyweight to your lead or rear leg without feeling awkward? What would be a reason for wanting to shift your bodyweight? If you had to assume your fighting stance with your eyes closed, could you do so comfortably? What are the benefits of practicing your stance through feel?

- The position of your feet is important, but what about the position of your hands? If your school recommends a specific hand position, can you identify the reason for it? What are the benefits and drawbacks of the recommended hand position? When assuming your stance, do you automatically place your hands in the proper position or do you need to think about it first? When are you the most likely to get caught off guard with your hands in a position that your opponent can take advantage of? Identify a situation when this could happen and determine what you can do to remedy the error.

- Explore the stability of your stance. How high or low should it be for maximum stability? How wide or narrow should it be? What are the benefits and drawbacks of each position? At what point do you have to make a trade-off, such as stability for mobility? If you lose your balance—for example, if your opponent pushes you or you throw a complicated spinning kick—how can you move to regain a solid stance that also benefits you in sparring? If you are an advocate of the low stance, when might you find yourself in a stance that is too low? Or is lower always better? Why?

- The martial artist needs to be flexible both in body and mind. Can you think of some situations when it is okay to use a stance that deviates from the one you have learned? If you deviate from your fundamental stance, are you aware of it and do you have a specific reason for doing so? How can you use a less solid stance without jeopardizing your balance or safety? When facing your opponent, pay attention to how comfortable he is in his stance, and whether you can disrupt his balance or take advantage of a stance that is less than ideal.

Exercise 2—Imminent Threat

• When threatened by an opponent in a street scenario, is it a good idea to assume a fighting stance right away, or is it better to wait? Why? Determine how your opponent might react if you assume a threatening stance. What are the drawbacks of failing to assume your stance quickly? What are the benefits?

• When a threat is imminent, how does your body naturally respond? Does it make you more alert? Does it make you more or less likely to carry out your defense? Identify how to move to avoid getting cornered or ending up with your back to a wall. If you do end up in a bad position, what can you do to regain mobility and a good stance?

Exercise 3—Limitations of Stance

• Explore the depth and width of your stance and identify which type of stance gives you the best protection. Which targets on your body are the most important to protect through a proper stance? Why? How does your stance change in relation to the type of attack you are facing? How can you use your stance as a barrier against strikes and kicks on vital targets?

• When striking or blocking from your stance, how could you move or change your stance in order to facilitate power

and reach? What types of strikes or kicks are most limited by your stance? Why? How can you be flexible with your stance without jeopardizing your safety? What are alternative ways to protect vital targets when switching your stance is impractical?

Exercise 4—Targets

• When engaged in sparring, pay attention to how well you maintain your stance. When is it necessary to deviate from your stance in order to serve a greater purpose? Name some situations when you were unable to maintain your stance and your opponent took advantage of you. Name some situations when you deviated from your stance by choice, and how it benefited you.

• What are the advantages and drawbacks of exposing one side to your opponent? Discuss the possibility of switching stance. What targets do you expose through the process of switching stance? How can you protect these targets?

Exercise 5—Switching Stance

• How can you switch stance without jeopardizing your balance or exposing vital targets? Is it easier to switch your stance while moving forward or backward? Why? Which is safer? What are the drawbacks of switching stance while moving back? If your opponent maintains a defensive stance that protects most of his vital areas, how can you exploit his stance and still penetrate a tight guard?

• How can you take advantage of the need to switch stance? Explore whether it is practical to throw a strike or kick simultaneous to switching your stance. Which strike or kick would you throw? Why?

• How can you conceal the fact that you are switching your stance? If you were to distract your opponent's focus away from your legs, how would you do it? Spar and pay attention to when and how your opponent switches his stance. How does it affect your ability to execute offense and defense?

LEARNING MOVEMENT AND POSITIONING

Ensure that you have good stability in order to avoid losing balance when moving.

Generally you achieve stability by not crossing your legs. There are exceptions, such as when running from a confrontation or when executing certain kicks (crossover sidekick, for example). A great benefit of movement is the ability to achieve a position of superiority that limits your opponent's movement. Movement should be smooth (to avoid telegraphing your intent) and efficient and executed in such a way that you can switch direction with ease. Good movement can help you gain an edge on a stronger opponent.

Exercise 1—Speed and Power

• When moving, pay attention to how well you maintain your stance. Do you have

Which is quicker when moving forward to throw a kick: crossing behind (top) or stepping with your feet side-by-side (bottom)? Which is safer? More stable?

a tendency to get into a wide or narrow (nearly unbalanced) stance? What can you do to remedy the situation? Which foot should you step with first, and why? What are the exceptions?

- What can you achieve by varying the speed of your movement? Name some situations when it would benefit you to move faster or more slowly. How can you take advantage of a weakness in your opponent's defense by varying the speed of your footwork?

- Experiment with how to close distance by moving diagonally toward your opponent instead of in a straight line. Does this type of movement give you superior positioning? What are the benefits and drawbacks? Is it easier or more difficult to strike with power when using lateral movement? Why?

- Is it wise to throw a strike or kick simultaneous to stepping forward or back? Name some situations when it might be beneficial to conceal your movement by getting your opponent to focus on offense. Explore the dangers associated with striking simultaneous to stepping.

Exercise 2—Momentum

- How can you use movement to your advantage when your opponent grabs your wrist and pulls? Going with the motion of your opponent's force allows you to use momentum against him. How can you redirect his force through the use of circular movement? Experiment with stepping laterally or in a circular motion in the direction of the pull. What would be a good follow-up strike or kick? Are

you ever at risk of losing balance? What can you do about it?

- Stepping back can help us avoid an attack. Is it also possible to avoid an attack by stepping forward? Identify strikes that work best from long range. Explore how to stifle the power in these strikes by moving forward and jamming them.

- Name three situations, other than to avoid an attack, when it would benefit you to step back. One example would be to create distance and lure your opponent to come forward and into your strike. Give more examples.

Exercise 3—Distance

- Most of us have a natural and invisible circle of safety that we don't want others to invade. If your opponent steps toward you, you have a natural tendency to step back. When would it benefit you to defeat this tendency and allow your opponent into your personal space? How would you train yourself to feel comfortable fighting at close range?

- Name five techniques you can use if you end up uncomfortably close to your opponent. Experiment with using distractions to gain an opportunity to flee. What types of distractions would you use, and what types of follow-up techniques can help you?

Exercise 4—Centerline

- Some of the best targets are located along your opponent's centerline. Name these targets. How would you move so as to gain free access to his centerline? What are the dangers of working along your opponent's centerline?

•· Experiment with approaching your opponent from the side rather than the front. How would you position yourself in order to attack centerline targets without jeopardizing your own safety? Name some ways in which you can gain superiority by relying on the element of surprise.

• How would you use multiple strikes to break your opponent's focus and create a weakness in his defense? Are you still at danger of being struck or grabbed? How can you guard against his offense? When is it beneficial to pause briefly between strikes?

LEARNING CLOSED- AND OPEN-FIST STRIKES

You can strike a variety of targets with either your lead or rear hand. Your lead hand is generally faster than your rear hand because of its proximity to your opponent, and can be used as a set-up or to score a quick point. Your rear hand has the ability to develop power through a longer distance. Strikes can also be with a closed or open fist. The body mechanics for different types of strikes remain largely the same.

Open-fist strikes include palm strikes, forearm strikes and shutos (knife-edge strikes). Palm strikes and forearm strikes are often used as softening blows or to take an opponent off balance in preparation for a takedown or throw. Open-fist strikes can also be used as distracting slaps to soft tissue areas, including the ears. Shutos generally aim for specific and small targets that are not easily reached with a regular punch.

Palm strikes generally cover a larger surface area than closed-fist strikes or shutos, and can be further broken down into soft- and hard-palm strikes. The soft-palm strike utilizes the entire area of the hand and fingers, and the hard palm strike utilizes the smaller heel of the palm. Soft palm strikes are generally used to send a shock wave through the target. Hard-palm strikes are generally used to break or dislocate joints, and are commonly utilized against the elbows, chin and nose.

Exercise 1—Power

• Observe how pivoting your foot, hip and body places weight behind the strike. How does it increase your power? Examine the position of your elbow in relation to your body. If you bring your elbow away from your body, at what point does power loss occur?

• When would it benefit you to throw a quick lead-hand strike without a pivot? Give some examples. Identify why power is sacrificed if a strike does not impact the target from a straight line. What can you do to ensure straightness when striking?

• Experiment with accelerating the lead hand strike in conjunction with many small steps forward. What strategic advantages can you gain from pressing the attack? How can you avoid sacrificing power for speed?

Exercise 2—Hand Position

• What are the benefits and drawbacks of bringing your hand back to a position other than the point of origin after you

When would you use a closed-fist (left) versus an open-fist (right) strike? Why? What are the factors that help determine your decision?

have landed the strike? How can you use your hand position during the returning motion of the strike to your advantage, for example, as a block, strike or grab?

- Identify ways to defend against a flurry of strikes. How can you take advantage of your opponent's lack of energy conservation? Identify ways to counter his attack while using your nonstriking hand to cover your openings.

Exercise 3—Soft-Palm Strike

- Experiment with leaving an open-fist strike in contact with the target momentarily. How does the energy transfer from the strike to the target? If the strike results in a push, you are relying on momentum more than on kinetic energy.

In what types of situations would this benefit you?

- The soft palm strike is more than a slap, and can do significant damage when thrown to the temples or body. If thrown to the body, can it shock your opponent into submission? Experiment with throwing the soft-palm strike in a relaxed manner. Allow your arm and wrist to act as a whip. How can you place your bodyweight behind the strike?

Exercise 4—Targets

- Practice soft-palm strikes to a variety of targets on the body and head (practice on a bag or dummy when striking the head). Practice palm strikes in combinations to high and low targets. Look for ways to use the double palm strike as a defense against a grab (front choke, bear hug, lapel grab, etc.).

• Discuss the possibility of throwing both palm strikes simultaneously, such as to your opponent's ears. What response is this likely to create? How can you follow up when your opponent reacts to the strike?

Exercise 5—Hard-Palm Strike

• Practice the hard-palm strike on a focus mitt, impacting with the heel of your palm. The strike can be short and snappy as when attempting to break a joint, or maintain a longer time of impact as when attempting to push your opponent off balance.

• Identify exactly which part of your opponent's arm to impact when attempting to break his elbow. Experiment with manipulating your opponent's balance by pushing the heel of your palm against his chin.

• Discuss ways to use the hard-palm strike against an opponent on the ground. What are the best targets for pinning an opponent to the floor or wall? Discuss why the neck is inherently weak and how to immobilize your opponent's body by pinning his head.

Exercise 6—Knife Edge Strike

• Identify targets for the shuto and ridge hand strikes. Explain the difference between a shuto and a ridge hand (the shuto impact with the outside knife edge of the hand; the ridge hand with the inside knife edge or thumb side) and dem-

onstrate correct hand position to avoid injury.

• Experiment with minute changes in hand position. How do they affect your strength and power? Experiment with using body momentum to increase power.

LEARNING ELBOW STRIKES

The elbow is a small and hard bone that is very useful for striking. Because of the elbow's proximity to the body, it is primarily a short-range weapon. There are different types of elbow strikes: those that travel horizontally across the target, those that travel diagonally up or down, and those that travel vertically up or down. There are also the back elbow and spinning back-elbow strike.

Exercise 1—Power

• Experiment with increasing the power of the elbow strike by taking a short step for momentum. How can you avoid overextending your center of gravity when impacting with the elbow strike? Practice the horizontal elbow strike on the heavy bag with and without a step for momentum.

• Increase the power of the elbow strike by striking straight on; avoid sliding the elbow against the target. Experiment with the use of momentum through alternating elbow strikes.

Exercise 2—Targets

• Practice the upward and downward elbow strikes on focus mitts held by a part-

strikes on mitts held by a partner. How can you make the combination fluent from one elbow strike to the other without sacrificing body mechanics?

- Experiment with adjusting for proper distance and compensating for your opponent's movement. Identify your opponent's reaction to an elbow strike thrown to the body. When would you choose to throw this strike to the body rather than to the head?

LEARNING PARRIES, BLOCKS AND DEFENSIVE MOVEMENT

Learning proper blocks involves more than learning the mechanical movement of the technique. For example, many styles of karate use the parry to redirect the path of a strike. But instructors sometimes fail to tell students which part of the hand or arm to use when parrying. Although such details may seem insignificant, failing to teach them may result in bruising of the small bones in the hand and a reluctance to use the parry again. Regardless of a person's size or strength, the ulna (the bone on the outside of the wrist) and most other bones in the hand are not strong enough to withstand the impact of a good blow. When you parry or block, the force against your hand or arm is the same as the force with which your opponent throws his strike. Newton's third law of motion states, "For every action, there is an equal and opposite reaction." To avoid injury when blocking, use a part of your body that is stronger than your opponent's striking weapon. Use the fleshy part of your arm rather than your hand or wrist. Try a parry or forearm block at an upward angle,

How would you combine several elbow strikes without losing momentum?

ner. Experiment with striking through the target by dropping your weight or springing from your knees like you would with an uppercut.

- Identify targets for the upward and downward elbow strike. Many schools teach the downward elbow strike to the back of the neck. For variation, grab your opponent's hair and bend back his upper body. Throw the downward elbow to the front of his throat.

Exercise 3—Combinations

- Put together combinations of horizontal, upward, downward and spinning elbow impacting with the muscle in your arm rather than with the bone.

When learning techniques intended to separate your opponent's arms (for example, when he reaches out to push you), try using the sides of your forearms rather than the back of your hands. Using the back of your hands can cause your wrists to bend upon impact and weaken the block. The study of defense also involves the use of head and upper body movement to avoid a strike and to leave your hands free for counterstriking.

Sidestepping an attack is a form of defensive movement, which can be practiced alone initially by learning to jump sideways from foot to foot.

Exercise 1—Forearm Blocks

- Practice the upward, downward, inward and outward forearm blocks from a stationary position. Keep your arms close to the centerline of your body until it is time to block the strike or kick. How does the position of your block prevent you from exposing vital targets to your opponent?

- Pay attention to the part of your opponent's arm you impact when blocking. When blocking to the inside of your opponent's arm, an impact below the elbow is better than above the elbow because it limits the mobility of his arm. When blocking to the outside of his arm, the opposite is true.

- Experiment with combining two or more forearm blocks. For example, throw an upward forearm block with your right arm. As your hand is returning to the guard position, throw an outward forearm block with your left arm. What types of attacks would these blocks defend against?

Exercise 2—Angled Attacks

- Practice the four basic forearm blocks in the air. Step forward or back with each block. Experiment with different angles when blocking, such as defending against overhead attacks or attacks from the side. How should you position your feet for greatest stability?

- Identify attacks that require forward or backward movement when blocking. For example, blocking an overhead stabbing attack might be done by stepping forward to intercept the attack (that is, if the attack can't be avoided entirely) and impacting your opponent's arm rather than the weapon. What are the drawbacks of stepping forward? In a straight kick attack (front kick, side kick), it may be better to move back and allow the kick to miss rather than trying to jam it. Why?

Exercise 3—Follow-Ups

• Pair up with a partner and practice the upward forearm block against an overhead strike, and the downward forearm block against a kneeing attack. Experiment with proper follow-up techniques. Can you block and follow with a trapping technique? Can you block and follow with a kicking technique?

• Identify the best point of impact when blocking a kneeing attack. Note how blocking a knee with your arms leaves your head exposed. Experiment with using your free hand as a check or simultaneous counterstrike.

LEARNING BASIC KICKS

When learning kicks, start by identifying when the kick would be used (to fend off an attacker who is closing distance, for example). Watch for proper foot positioning. Use the correct part of your foot both when impacting and when kicking the air. When learning the front kick, align your foot with your ankle and curl your toes back. You can practice foot alignment by imagining that you are walking in high-heeled shoes. Get up on the balls of your feet until your instep is aligned with your shinbone. When learning the roundhouse kick, tuck your toes

Proper mechanics for the side kick or flying side kick can be practiced while lying on your side on the floor.

tightly under with your instep like a springboard. (That is, unless you learn the roundhouse kick with the ball of the foot, in which case your toes should be curled back.) When learning the side kick, curl your toes back and extend the heel of your foot toward the target. Correct foot positioning for the side kick can also be practiced lying on your side on the floor. This training exercise allows you to work on body mechanics without having to concentrate on maintaining balance. Note that many martial arts also teach the knife-edge side kick.

Exercise 1—Targets and Follow-Ups

• If you lower your hands as a counterweight to balance when kicking, how does it affect your ability to protect your head? Experiment with different hand positions when kicking and note the benefits and drawbacks of each.

• Identify targets for the front kick and determine your opponent's expected reaction. If the kick pushes him back, what kinds of follow-up techniques will you use? If the kick makes him bend forward, how can you take advantage of the situation? What benefits can be gained by kicking an opponent who is on the defensive, such as when he is blocking or stepping back?

Exercise 2—Distance

• What benefits in distance and reach do you gain by throwing alternating kicks? When closing distance with a kick, how do you prevent your opponent from taking advantage of your advance? What techniques can he use against you?

• Some kicks can be combined better than others. These include kicks thrown with alternating legs, or kicks that follow the same direction. Identify kicks that you can throw naturally in combinations of three or four.

• Experiment with keeping your opponent at bay with a kick. Which types of kicks would best lend themselves to this exercise? Why? If you land the kick and your opponent gets knocked back, what type of move would you use next?

Exercise 3—Power

• Name some situations where you would impact with the knife edge of your foot versus the heel when throwing the side kick. Which kick is quicker? More powerful? Why? Explore how to close distance with the side kick. Which is faster: stepping with your lead foot first, or stepping with your rear foot first? Why?

• When throwing multiple kicks with the same leg and planting the foot between each kick, what are the benefits and drawbacks in speed, power and balance? Name some targets and your opponent's expected reaction to a multiple kick combination.

LEARNING ADVANCED KICKS

The spinning back kick is, just like the side kick, mainly a long-range weapon that is often used as a deterrent to keep your opponent at a distance. Impact the target with the heel or bottom of your foot. Since the kick requires a spin, it takes a little longer to throw than the side kick and is easily telegraphed. Landing the spinning back kick without getting countered requires quickness and determination. Although the kick utilizes a spin in the upper body, your leg should kick in a straight line on impact. A common mistake is throwing the kick wide (looping it) and impacting the target from the side rather than straight on.

The axe kick is generally thrown high to the head, or as a set-up to take your opponent's guard down. The axe kick strikes from above, impacting the target with the heel of your foot. Targets for the axe kick are the top of the head, bridge of the nose, collarbones, arms (to take a guard down) and, if thrown low, the front of the thigh.

The outside crescent kick strikes from the side, impacting with the outside part of your foot and shin. Targets for the crescent kick are primarily the head and the arms (to take a guard down). It can also be thrown to the legs.

How can you increase the power of an axe kick thrown from the ground? Experiment on a focus mitt.

Exercise 1—Distance and Speed

- Name some ways to improve balance when throwing a spinning kick. For example, use a point of reference (a visual mark) to help you with balance and target accuracy. Explore the difference between a wide (looping) kick and a tight kick. Why is it more difficult to maintain balance and gain speed when throwing a wide kick?

- How can you adjust for a spinning back kick that overshoots or undershoots the target? Name some reasons for missing the target with a spinning kick. How can you use your opponent's movement to increase the power of your spinning kick? Can you get him to step into the kick?

Exercise 2—Power and Strategy

- Place a focus mitt or kicking shield on the floor as a target for the axe kick. Drop your weight and impact the target with the heel of your foot. Why must you bring your leg as high as possible before dropping the kick? Use the muscles in your leg in addition to gravity. Note

how distance for the axe kick can be deceiving: Your greatest reach is straight out from the pivotal point (your hip).

- Pair up with a partner and practice taking his guard down with the axe kick. How is your opponent likely to react when his guard comes down? How can you take advantage of the situation? Identify potential dangers associated with this technique (if your foot gets caught in the crook of your opponent's arm, for example), and methods to deal with them.

Exercise 3—Movement and Follow-Ups

- Practice the outside crescent kick on a focus mitt held by a partner. Learn how to step to set your hips properly for the kick. Explore how to lead with your body and determine why doing so makes the kick more powerful.

- Experiment with using a step prior to throwing the kick. Identify which foot to step with first, and why. Discuss possible follow-up techniques after you have landed the kick. What is your opponent's expected reaction?

LEARNING KICKS FROM THE GROUND

Almost every kick thrown when standing can also be thrown from the ground against an opponent who is standing or on the ground. Rather than using your supporting foot as the pivot point, use your knees. You can also kick when supported on your back or side of body.

When kicking from the ground, you may use your knees, elbows, hands or side of body for support. Pay attention to how your reach changes.

Exercise 1—Reach and Positioning

- Get down on your knees and experiment with roundhouse and side kicks from a position on the ground. Your greatest reach for the kick is horizontally from your hip. If kicking an opponent who is standing, you must be closer than you appear in order to land the kick. Note that you can kick to the head of an opponent on the ground with ease.

- Experiment with the front kick from the ground. You must now support yourself with your hands behind you instead of to the front. Start from a kneeling position, falling back on your hands and kicking your leg forward. How can you get to your feet after landing the kick? If the kick fails to stop your opponent's advance, how can he take advantage of your position?

- Shadowbox from a kneeling position on the ground. Throw front kicks, roundhouse kicks and side kicks against an imaginary opponent. Experiment with moving smoothly from one kick to the next.

Exercise 2—Timing and Momentum

- Pair up with a partner approaching you with a kicking shield. Practice timing the kick to his advance. You are inherently more vulnerable on the ground than when standing. Why?

- Explore how poor timing allows your opponent to sidestep or jam your kick. Identify targets on an opponent who is standing. How can you use a kick against an opponent who is bending over you? In what ways can he defend and counter your kick?

Exercise 3—Targets and Movement

- Pair up with a partner on the ground and work on target accuracy, taking turns to touch the target lightly with each kick. How can you use your hands as points of support? Does doing so expose your head to blows or prevent you from using your hands as weapons?

- Work on movement from a position on the ground. Discuss how to increase the distance to your opponent and how to get back to your feet. Explore how to build momentum by rolling on your side and kicking. Can you acquire reach by using your elbows for support?

LEARNING TARGET AREAS

Fighters are commonly "headhunters." Target accuracy and an ability to take varied targets is important to the successful outcome of the fight. When practicing kicks in the air, be aware of the target you are kicking and the purpose of the kick. Be precise. Rather than thinking "front kick high," think "front kick to the chin." Aim for targets that are consistent with your own height. You can visualize specific targets for your techniques by creating different scenarios and positions for your imaginary opponent. Rather than thinking "side kick high, middle, low," try "side kick to the chin, solar plexus, and knee." The more specific you are, the easier it is to visualize your aim.

Imagine kicking to precise targets also when practicing in the air. Learn precision by kicking smaller targets, such as a double-end bag.

Exercise 1—Effective Targets

- Power strikes to targets on your opponent's centerline are likely to cause serious injury or death. Identify all targets on the centerline (nose, mouth, throat, heart, solar plexus, groin, back of neck, spine, tailbone). Identify the most appropriate strikes and kicks for these targets.

- Explore how to strike your opponent's tailbone. What types of strikes would you use? How would you get in position to throw them? Explore how to attack your opponent's Achilles' tendon. When would be a good time to stomp on this target?

Exercise 2—Defense

- Identify times when you might need to defend against two strikes simultaneously. How can you do so without jeopardizing your balance or power? For example, blocking a low kick with your leg and simultaneously blocking a strike with your arm could prevent you from using the strength of your stance to absorb the force of the blows.

- Target awareness plays a crucial role when controlling distance. Experiment with distance and how your opponent reacts to specific techniques. Not all punches and kicks work equally well from all distances. Identify strikes that are more effective at close range and strikes that are more effective at long range. How can you protect an injured body part while continuing with your offense?

18

Exercises for the Grappling Arts

LEARNING JOINT-LOCK TECHNIQUES

A joint lock is any technique that goes against the natural movement of the joint. Joint locks have the capability to cause extreme pain and severe injury. If your opponent uses muscular strength to defeat the lock, train to go with the motion into another joint-lock technique rather than fighting him at his point of strength. You do this through the "handover" don't relinquish control with one hand until gaining control with the other. Many students get confused and fumble with joint locks, mainly because of a lack of knowledge and experience in how to transition from one technique to another.

Softening techniques can be used as set-ups or distractions prior to applying a joint lock. But it is often the small details of the joint lock that are overlooked and enable your opponent to escape the technique. A joint lock that is properly applied requires very little pressure to cause extreme pain or compliance. On the other hand, if the lock is just a fraction of an inch inaccurate, the technique may fail.

There are mainly two principles that enable you to control an opponent through a joint-lock technique:

1. Tightening the lock by bending and twisting the joint against its natural range of motion; and

2. Taking the opponent to an inferior position, normally to a prone position (face down on his stomach).

Your opponent cannot escape the joint lock when he experiences both intense pain and an inferior position on the ground. He is now unable to use his natural strengths, weapons or eyesight.

Joint locks are commonly practiced from the upright position with both fighters standing. However, a fight often goes to the ground. You might also be in an awkward position with your opponent behind your back. You must therefore learn to execute the joint lock from any position. Joint-lock techniques should be learned by feel. Try training blindfolded.

Many martial arts practitioners go through the motion of joint locks without actually taking them to the point of control. Failure to do so may give the practitioner a false sense of security. A good test of the effectiveness of the technique is how well it works for a smaller person against a larger noncompliant adversary. A common mistake when executing joint locks is keeping the opponent's arm at some distance from your body. The controlling technique is more effective if you maintain close contact with your opponent and use your weight against him, particularly if he is bigger than you. Joint locks against a bigger adversary also work well from the ground, because the ground helps you immobilize your opponent's body. Since the ground acts as a barrier, you must also learn to maneuver your own body into position for maximum control.

Consider your ability to escape a joint lock technique. A common problem is panicking or freezing, or trying to escape by attacking the strength of the lock, which is also your opponent's point of strength. You can escape a joint lock by attacking a point of weakness. But the ultimate escape may be staying ahead of the controlling technique,

A joint lock that takes the opponent to the ground and that is applied in both a bending and twisting motion has the greatest chance of serving as a controlling device.

or going with the pressure *before* the pressure is fully applied. In order to be successful, you must recognize the controlling technique in its infancy.

Exercise 1—Gaining Control

- In order to apply a joint lock successfully, you must understand the mechanics of the human body. Experiment with the workings of your partner's joints: arms, hands, legs and feet. Exercise extreme care.

- Explore how to transition from one joint lock to another. Eventually you should gain enough insight into joint locks to easily make a transition or hand change without giving it conscious thought. The simplest holds are often the fastest, safest, and most effective.

- When a hand change is needed, you must first have full control of your opponent. How can you use other body parts, such as your knees, feet or head, to gain such control? There is a defense and counter for every control hold. Demonstrate through some examples.

Exercise 2—Positioning

- Experiment with joint-lock techniques from a variety of positions, including standing, kneeling, prone and supine. Explore the variety of joint locks that can be applied from each position.

- Identify how to apply joint locks when approaching your opponent from different directions, including the front, rear and sides. How can you use a distraction prior to applying the lock? If your attempt to apply the joint lock fails, how can you remedy the situation?

Exercise 3—Softening Techniques

- Experiment with a variety of softening techniques used in preparation for a joint lock. Explore strikes and kicks to open areas of your opponent's body. Identify how to split her mind and body focus with a softening technique.

- Explore the dangers associated with softening strikes. Can your opponent grab your hand or foot and reverse the situation? If she does, what is your best course of action? How is your balance affected when kicking?

Exercise 4—Escapes

- Identify escapes from joint-lock techniques. When we get grabbed, we have a natural tendency to tense, which makes an escape more difficult. How can you initiate the escape before your opponent has applied full control?

- A forward roll can be used to escape certain types of joint locks. Which are they? Explore how a forward roll can give you momentum to facilitate your escape.

Exercise 5—Reversing the Hold

- Consider what to do when your opponent resists your attempt to apply a joint-lock technique. How can you use your opponent's resistance (pressure) to gain a different hold? Identify how going with the pressure creates momentum. What new opportunities does this give you?

- How can a skilled opponent reverse your joint lock and apply a controlling technique on you? Explore how grabbing your opponent's fingers give you better control than grabbing his wrist.

Exercise 6—Gross Motor Skills

- Experiment with controlling the larger joints of the body (neck, elbow, shoulder, knee, hip), rather than the smaller joints (fingers, wrist, ankle). Controlling a large joint requires less precision than controlling a small joint and might be beneficial in a high-threat or stressful situation where fine motor skills are difficult to use.

- Controlling the larger joints places you closer to your opponent. How can you use this closeness to pin or eliminate additional weapons? No fight is picture-perfect. Sometimes you have to take what you get. Explore a variety of "what-if" scenarios, where your attempt to defend against an attack is flawed.

Exercise 7—Inferior Positions

- How can you use a joint lock to unbalance your opponent? Identify inferior positions, where your opponent has the least use of his eyesight, arms, legs and mobility.

- How can you use a joint lock to place your opponent in an inferior position on the ground? Identify targets and presses (knee presses, forearm presses, palm presses) that can be used in conjunction with joint-lock techniques on the ground.

Exercise 8—Breaking Techniques

- Identify how to go beyond control and into a breaking or dislocating technique. Discuss a breaking technique's limitations. How difficult (or easy) is it to break a joint? How do you know, if you have never actually broken one?

- Discuss the difference in anatomy between a big (heavy) and a small (thin) person, and how it applies to joint locks and breaking. Explore the difference in flexibility in the joints of different people, and how it applies to the effective execution of a joint lock or breaking technique.

LEARNING TAKEDOWNS AND THROWS

A fight can be broken down into three major parts:

1. The stand-up fight

2. The takedown

3. The ground fight

A smaller person fighting a larger adversary normally has the greatest problem with the takedown phase. The takedown must therefore be dynamic and executed with the opponent in an inferior position.

When two people meet in a grappling type battle, they often lock up with their hands around each other's necks and then try a takedown or throw. Your opponent's elbow is a great leverage point which can be used whenever he locks his hands around your neck. Using the elbow as a crank can help

you break free of your opponent's hold and move him to an inferior position.

When practicing takedowns, experiment with many different techniques, such as trapping your opponent's kick instead of blocking it, or grabbing his fingers instead of striking his face.

A throw differs from a takedown because it is designed to get your opponent on the ground quickly and violently. A throw requires closeness to your opponent and a reliance on leverage. A properly executed throw will seem almost effortless.

How can you take your opponent down the moment you lock up with her?

Exercise 1—Mechanics

- Experiment with circular motion in takedowns and throws. The tighter you keep your opponent to your own body, the easier it is to use circular motion. Discuss how to shift your opponent's center of gravity and unbalance him.

- Identify times when you can use the element of surprise to initiate a takedown or throw. What is the value of using your sense of touch? Once you learn to "feel" your opponent's motion, you need not rely on sight in order to manipulate his balance.

Exercise 2—Balance Point

- Experiment with finding the point of balance for hip throws. If your position is too deep behind your opponent's hip, you will end up carrying much of his weight. If your position is not deep enough, the throw will result in a takedown. How can you find the balance point quickly in a chaotic situation?

- A properly executed throw is a combination of circular and linear motion. When you have attained correct positioning, focus on finding the fine line between circular and linear motion. Experiment with "push-pull" movement and how it affects a throw or takedown. Identify how such movement starts a circular motion intended to unbalance your adversary.

Exercise 3—Momentum

- Explore the benefits of using momentum in throws and takedowns. Demonstrate the importance of using correct technique, speed and the element of surprise. The technique should happen in one fluid motion with no hesitation between moves. How does broken synchronization of your moves affect your opponent's ability to escape or counter the attack?

- Explore the difference between wide circular motion and tight circular motion. Which type of motion results in a takedown, and which results in a throw? Explore how to proceed once you have taken your opponent to the ground. Discuss the value of knee and forearm presses. Experiment with target points.

Exercise 4—Falling

- Practice how to fall without getting hurt. Discuss how the force of falling is absorbed sequentially, or by spreading the force over a large area of your body.

- Practice how to roll on the ground from kneeling and standing positions. Identify how the force is absorbed sequentially over your arm and shoulder rather than your head.

Exercise 5—Failed Techniques

- Identify how a takedown or throw might fail. Discuss the direction of energy in a properly executed takedown or throw. Identify the difference between circular and linear motion.

- Discuss the importance of stealing your opponent's balance before attempting a takedown. How important are distractions during the set-up phase? How can you take your opponent's vision or balance prior to a throw? Discuss the importance of proper positioning and swift execution of technique.

LEARNING GRAPPLING TECHNIQUES

Grappling includes joint locks, chokes and leverage techniques. Effective grappling requires ease of movement from a position on the ground when on your back, stomach, side or knees. Avoid exposing leverage points or placing yourself in an inferior position, such as on your stomach. Many grappling situations require small moves and a considerable amount of time to execute. Don't fight against your opponent's weight

Control the threat by controlling your opponent's balance.

or strength. Grappling is a matter of superior positioning, using the element of surprise to outwit a stronger adversary.

A ground fight must be dynamic to be successful. Take advantage of every weakness in your opponent's technique. This principle also applies to defense on the ground. Your proximity to your opponent on the ground allows you to feel his intentions before they are manifested. Perform defensive techniques explosively and without hesitation.

When executing grappling techniques from a standing position, the physically weaker fighter will often lose. When you get too technical with a technique, you give up valuable time, and you give a stronger opponent the opportunity to escape or reverse the technique. The first stage of the ground fight is therefore an unbalancing technique, rather than a controlling technique.

Exercise 1—Point of Leverage

- Experiment with finding the point of leverage that allows you to turn your opponent to an inferior position. How can you use the point of leverage to defeat a larger adversary?

- Any technique aimed at unbalancing your opponent can be used in conjunction with a point of leverage. Don't fight your opponent at the point of attack, because this is where his concerted strength is focused. A good point of leverage is the elbow. Explore how to use your opponent's arm as a crank.

Exercise 2—Positioning

- The more weapons you can use simultaneously, the greater potential you have for success. Experiment with combining two moves into one and moving your opponent to an inferior position.

- Identify superior positions and discuss how they can restrict your opponent's fighting ability. Can you conserve energy by moving your opponent to the inferior position, rather than moving yourself to the superior position? Identify techniques you can use to move your opponent to an inferior position without struggling against his strength.

Exercise 3—Chokes

- Take turns applying choke holds with your partner (tap out before you pass out). Discuss how most people fight the arm that strangles them. Experiment with escaping a choke. At what point must you initiate your escape in order to be successful?

- The awkward position neede to apply a rear choke generally gives you an opportunity to apply a front choke, and vice versa. Identify techniques that can create a reaction designed to expose the arteries on the sides of your opponent's neck.

Exercise 4—Reversing the Mount

- Experiment with reversing the mount (when you are on your back and your opponent is straddling you). Explore how to take advantage of your opponent's high center of gravity; for example, by raising your hips forcefully and pushing off with one foot to unbalance him forward and to the side.

- Explore the possibility of grabbing your opponent's fingers and executing a joint lock while at the same time using unbalancing technique. How does the move split his focus? How precise must your technique be in order to be effective?

229

Part Five
Learning Real-Life Scenarios

19

Attending the Self-Defense Seminar

HOW REALISTIC SHOULD THE TRAINING BE?

Although the two are often marketed the same, there is a distinct difference between martial arts and self-defense. All martial arts are not suited for self-defense, at least not if you want short-term results. Some arts require a lifetime to master, and some are geared toward sports rather than self-defense. You must also consider the way you train. For example:

1. Do you train for point sparring or forms competition?

2. How much contact and chaos do you implement in your training?

3. What are your background, goals, and desires?

4. Have you thought about that the art you have been learning for 20 years may not be suited for self-defense in today's society?

5. When you search for an instructor to teach you self-defense, is it appropriate for her to sell you a "three-year black belt program"?

A martial art that is truly geared toward self-defense must teach techniques that are easy to learn and remember, and that can be ap-plied by weaker, slower, or disadvantaged people. If you are one of these disadvantaged people, you should still be able to defend yourself without having to outfight your opponent. But just how do you know that the techniques you are learning will work? Have you tested them in real-life scenarios or realistic simulations? You will most likely get hurt to some degree in a real encounter. A good self-defense program must therefore include how to deal with the pain of physical contact. Your instructor must help you analyze how attacks happen and how you might react. What types of attacks are the most common? How do they start? How do they escalate? In a short self-defense course, you might want to focus on learning a few select techniques that will eliminate the need to drill the basics for months.

If you study together with a wide variety of people, your instructor may have to tailor the instruction to fit each student's individual needs. For example:

1. A small person may not be able to throw a powerful strike, because he lacks the bodyweight to produce significant momentum. However, he may be able to use balance manipulation techniques more effectively, because they do not rely on physical strength to the same degree.

233

2. A properly applied joint lock is devastating and causes extreme pain. But how easy is it to apply it properly in chaotic situations? If a person with small hands tries to apply a joint lock on an assailant with large wrists, will the bigger person simply twist out of the lock before any damage is done?

It has been said that size and strength don't matter in the martial arts. My opinion is that size and strength do matter. Sure, there are certain targets that your opponent cannot

If taken by surprise and your balance is poor, for example, because your weight is to the rear, you are less likely to succeed with a prescribed defense than if you can anticipate the move and have adequate time to prepare yourself.

flex: his eyeballs, eardrums, and testicles, for example. But you must still be in a position to strike to these targets, and you will still be in danger when getting into position to do so. How likely is it for a tiny female, a disabled person, or even a strong young man to succeed against a huge street thug when taken by surprise? What about the martial artist with 15 years of training and three black belts? How likely is she to succeed in a real street encounter? The answer to this question may lie in *how* she has trained, how much she has thought about the possibility of getting attacked, and what kind of attitude she has developed.

HOW TO MEASURE OUR SKILL

When Ali fought Frazier, did people say, "Ali will be the better man tonight, because he is wearing red shorts"? Can the skill of a martial artist be judged by the color of his belt? Many people would say, "Yes, that's why we start with a white belt and end with a black belt." The color of your belt is supposed to "communicate" to the rest of the world where you stand as a martial artist. This idea may be true in a sterile environment where the rules and expectations for obtaining the belt have been clearly stated. However, I have met many "black belts" who may have been masters of their art within the confines of the training hall, but in reality knew little about fighting outside of this known environment. Likewise, I have known people who have never taken a martial arts lesson in their lives, but who I wouldn't want to meet in a dark alley. On the street we don't wear colored belts to let the rest of the world know where we stand as martial artists. On the street, there is an

A big person can rely on strength and momentum, and doesn't need a great degree of skill in order to bully a smaller person.

unspoken hierarchy of rank and skill. A high rank is, in itself, no guarantee for success.

Since the martial arts are unregulated, you will find many skill levels among our black belt population. The martial artist, student and instructor alike, must therefore examine how realistic his training has been. You must also look at which types of techniques fit your mental inclination. Simply put, what do you *like*? Which techniques have you trained in the most? Are you flexible enough to perform these techniques with balance, speed, and accuracy? Even a highly skilled individual may not want to rely on punching and kicking his opponent into submission, because his smaller build will simply not produce the momentum needed to end a fight. Also consider that a person attacking you has probably some experience with street violence already. A strike or a little

pain is not likely to stop him.

Next, consider realistic time. If you kick your opponent and it doesn't deter him, you may try to kick him again. But will he have time to move into close range and smother you before you have a chance to launch your next kick? Many of the defenses and disarming techniques taught in the martial arts are much too slow and complex for real time. When somebody intent on killing you attacks you with a knife, she is not likely to halt her attack in mid-air and let you do an upward block and some complicated joint lock. When somebody rushes you from a distance of 20 feet, you may not have the time to reach for your gun and point and shoot.

Let's say that you set up a scenario in which the "bad guy" attacks with a punch, and where you are supposed to use some sort of predetermined combination as defense. The problem with this idea is that in real life you won't know the speed of the attack or the type of follow-up technique the assailant will use. You won't know how you will react if you get hurt. In the orderliness of the training hall your only concern may be to learn how to do the technique correctly. You can use your fine motor skills effectively in the training hall where you don't experience the mental stresses of an actual encounter, but you might not gain valuable insight into a real scenario.

You must also understand your limitations. It is good to be confident in your abilities, but it is not good to be overly confident.

1. When we train in a known environment, we tend to fall into a rut; we train with the same people all the time, and we do

Can you really intercept and block an attack coming toward you with full speed from out of nowhere? Experiment with a partner to find out what it takes. Remember to wear appropriate protective gear.

of these joint lock techniques must be very precise in order to be effective. You won't know if you have reached precision with the technique unless you take it to the point of pain.

In a real-life scenario that is taken to physical contact, it is unlikely that you will escape uninjured. You must therefore address the issue of contact. Many arts employ only light contact, while others teach "full" contact. But even in full contact arts, the practitioners normally wear some sort of protection in the form of gloves or body gear. My opinion is that if you are learning self-defense, your instructor must take you to the point of pain, show you how precise a technique must be in order to be effective, and how easily it can fail. Light contact, or just tapping the target, is not going to cut it. I am a proponent of wearing safety gear, but not to overdo it. Martial arts should, in my opinion, be felt. The difficulty is in knowing how to practice contact safely in class. Obviously, you don't want to injure your practice partner. When kicking to the knee, for example, ideally you should drive the kick all the way through the target—*hard*. But you must do so on a bag or other "dead" target and not on a live partner. Accuracy is still best practiced on a live partner. But contact to sensitive targets, such as the joints and throat, must be kept to a minimum. Much of self-defense also relies on your ability to maintain your cool when under pressure. Even if you are wearing safety gear and are not getting hurt, the stress you experience may prevent you from responding to the attack appropriately.

the same techniques over and over according to specific patterns. As a result, we become complacent.

2. When we train with people that we know, we seldom use realistic force. It is therefore difficult to determine whether or not your techniques really work.

THE USE OF APPROPRIATE FORCE

When I was studying Aikido, the wristlocks my practice partners applied seldom hurt. I don't know if the techniques failed because my peers were careful not to hurt me, or because they didn't know how to apply the techniques correctly. I tend to think the latter, because a joint lock is seldom dangerous when taken to the point of pain. Many

When attending the self-defense seminar, consider these issues:

1. If you already have a martial arts background, you may still feel as though you don't know how to defend yourself in a real encounter. Part of the problem may be because your prior martial art training has not included a great deal of realistic contact training.

2. When you step into the training hall, you may already have your mind geared toward sparring, grappling, or some sort of contact training. But a real encounter is likely to be unexpected. As a result, you will be more successful in the training hall than on the street.

3. If you are completely new to the martial arts, you must be careful not to attain a false sense of confidence. For example, it is unlikely that you will be able to defend yourself successfully after a one-day seminar.

4. Your instructor must address real issues and teach techniques that are not too complex or require the use of too many fine motor skills.

 ## SCENARIO 50

You regularly defeat everybody in karate tournaments, but you still got beat up in a bar brawl last weekend. What course of action should you take?

1. Hit a little harder next time.

2. Realize that you are not as good as you thought you were.

3. Tell others that your fighting spirit is great; you just had a bad day.

4. Maintain a positive attitude and say that only the person who thinks he is beaten is.

Training for competition does not guarantee proficiency in self-defense. If you end up in a self-defense situation and try to use your competition skills, chances are you will not fare very well. What happens on the street is chaotic. If you have a long martial arts background, you will likely be more successful than your neighbor who has not trained at all, and you will likely be in better physical shape than the average person. But don't count on walking away unscathed.

– INSTRUCTOR TIP–

A loss on the street can strip a student of her faith in the art she has spent a lifetime to perfect. Throughout a student's career, continually stress that no technique is foolproof.

– STUDENT TIP–

You see an advertisement that reads, "Learn to attack, maim, and kill your opponent." What signal does it send you regarding the class? Don't become complacent. When you understand the reality of fighting, you can focus on learning and achieving what can be achieved rather than on some abstract and distant wish dream.

EMPTY HANDED OFFENSE VS. DEFENSE

We often hear of self-*defense* training, but rarely do we hear of *offense* training. The reason may be because we have been conditioned to believe that it is wrong to take the offensive stand; that we should use violence only in defense when we are truly seriously threatened. But it is my belief that if you learn only avoidance and awareness rather than physical attack, you will be short-changed. Much of self-defense is mental, but our mental capabilities are often overshadowed by what happens to us physically. Learning awareness and avoidance is not wrong, of course, but we can read ourselves to such information in books and manuals. Intellectual knowledge of what you are supposed to do is seldom as valuable as the physical experience of a confrontation. The defensive or reactive approach may only give you a few additional seconds to live.

1. The reactive approach may save you from the first punch or knife stab. But you are also likely to freeze momentarily, which will inhibit your ability to act.

A good grip communicates both physical and psychological control. When you decide to counter-attack, practice doing so with determination.

2. When an attacker rushes you, your natural tendency is to back up. But you may not know what sorts of barriers are behind you. For example, you may be faced with obstacles such as walls, fences, cars, or trash.

It can be argued that you should step to the side rather than stepping back, but doing so requires good timing. Consider training for offense instead. Hold your ground and launch a counter-attack that hopefully neutralizes your opponent's attack. The offensive stand gives you a psychological advantage where the assailant can't use intimidation to achieve the dominant position. He might be in for a surprise, because he was probably not looking for a fight. If he had thought that you would strike back, he would not have attacked you in the first place. Work on exercises that help you overcome your natural tendency to retreat to an inferior position.

When you take the active approach, you decide when and how the fight is to go down. You will at least turn some of the odds in your favor. With this principle in mind, how effective is it to learn an elbow strike, a finger rake, or a kick to the groin? If someone is really out to hurt you, one such strike may not deter him. This is another reason you should be the attacker and not the defender. If somebody wrestles you to the ground, rather than trying to push him off you, draw him closer and finish him with a choke (providing that you have the knowledge to do so). The problem your instructor faces is how to teach these concepts to students who have never been in a physical confrontation, and who are uncomfortable with physical contact or physical nearness with a stranger. An even bigger problem is how to teach it in just a day or two.

WEAPONS OFFENSE VS. DEFENSE

Consider a weapon attack: Weapons have great destructive capabilities. Some people argue that you should not carry a weapon on your person because you risk hurting yourself on the weapon, or because your opponent may take the weapon from you. They argue that it is better to learn how to defend yourself empty handed against an attacker wielding a weapon. But the problem with empty hand defense against a weapon attack is that weapons, because they have such great destructive capabilities, and because they have better range than our hands and feet, are generally difficult to intercept and defend against. One faulty move against an armed assailant may mean death. Modern weapons, such as knives and firearm, also have certain weaknesses that, if you understand them, enable you to defend yourself more effectively. You can now draw strength from the weaknesses of your opponent's weapon. But if you don't train offensively with weapons, it is unlikely that you will gain insight into the weaknesses of the weapon.

If you attend a one or two day seminar on weapon disarming techniques and you have never fired a handgun, have no idea of the many different ways to hold and attack with a knife, and don't know the strengths and weakness of each grip, you are cheating yourself out of what might be life saving knowledge. When learning disarming techniques, as long as your assailant's weapon is not in a position where it is a direct threat, you may be better off letting him keep it

initially. You may actually be limiting your assailant's effectiveness by *not* disarming him, because a person who attacks with a weapon is likely to have tunnel vision: He will think only of the weapon attack.

CREATING AND COPING WITH STRESS

A few years ago, I had the opportunity to take part in pepper spray training at the local police department. When I put in my request to participate, the officers thought I was joking. "It is worse than getting shot, and I *have* been shot!" one officer told me. "It is still not too late to back out," they said when I arrived the day of the training. Naturally, I stayed. I have a high pain threshold but I have to admit that experiencing the pepper spray was much worse than I had anticipated. My body went into shock. We did the training outside in 90-degree temperatures, and I still shivered uncontrollably for almost half an hour. I couldn't keep my eyes open for more than a second at a time, and the pain didn't even begin to let up until 25 minutes later. I went through 200 tissues as well, and thought that I was going to drown in my own snot. Was it pleasant? Absolutely not! Would I like to do it again? No thanks! Am I glad I did it? You bet!

Many techniques that seem theoretically sound fail in the real world, because the instructor has failed to teach the stress under which these techniques must be performed. Factors that cause stress include noise, disorientation, cold, fatigue, distractions, fear, and pain. Enduring this kind of rigorous training gives you insight into how you will react when under stress. You should be taught to recognize your true limitations and not panic, which can be achieved by training in chaotic situations. Much can be accomplished once you know how you will react and what options are available. In real-life scenario training, it is especially important to evaluate the curriculum beforehand. Every self-defense move is not a matter of kicking your opponent in the groin or poking him in the eyes. How workable is a kick to the groin? Since a kick to the groin seems so obvious, an assailant may expect it and be prepared to defend against it. This technique is also much too simplistic for many surprise attacks or unbalancing moves. What about the other techniques you are learning? Can you really use them when under a great deal of stress? Try to include an element of ambush in your training. Learn how to be in control of your emotions when in danger. Much of self-defense has to do with your ability to deal with the situation mentally.

If your training calls for a kick to your opponent's knee, how likely are you to pull off this technique with precision when under a great degree of stress?

When you have experienced training that is somewhat realistic, you are less likely to freeze in a real situation. I am not saying that your instructor should hurt you in training. But he should teach with a fair amount of contact and physical closeness. Women must accept the fact that they will get grabbed and wrestled to the ground by "strange" men. The training should be done under safe and controlled conditions and should be fully explained to the students beforehand. You must also consider your psychological state. For example, a program that is offered by an authority may not be appropriate for you in particular. A rape victim may not benefit from training together with the military, police, or bouncers.

When we train with "real" situations in mind, our attitude is still often too relaxed. We tend to exaggerate the moves in the training hall. Attackers don't necessarily throw wide and slow punches. They don't necessarily expose the fact that they have a knife until they are almost upon you. People in the vicinity may not seem threatening initially, but may become so later. If the "attacker" in the training hall cooperates or does not use enough force, you may get the idea that you are more skilled than you really are. However, the whole lesson does not have to be a chaotic blur, either. For example, you can learn a particular technique or concept and practice it until you have gained reasonable proficiency. Then set up some scenarios. Your instructor should explain that it is unlikely that you will perform the techniques flawlessly when under stress. She should tell you that, for now, it is important to gain an understanding of what can go wrong and to what extent you are able to protect yourself.

SCENARIO 51

You are learning how to apply a choke and tell your instructor that you have used the choke for real in bar fights, and that it only takes ten seconds for an opponent to lose consciousness. How should your instructor respond?

1. Ask you to describe and elaborate on the situation you were in.

2. Scold you for smiling when talking about your success with the choke.

3. Ask if you work as a bouncer.

4. Talk about the dangers the choke can cause the victim.

Your instructor may want to emphasize that the material you learn in class is intended to help you get out of a sticky situation. Studying self-defense does not mean that you should go out and look for situations where you can try your skill for real. If you desire to test your skill on somebody, you might want to enter a full contact or no-holds-barred tournament. Although such an event isn't real self-defense, you will still get the adrenaline rush from the stress, which can have a positive impact on your self-defense training. Don't brag about the real fights you have encountered, especially not if you have sought them out yourself. Getting into bar brawls is hardly something to be proud of. As a trained martial artist, you should know how to avoid these situations. Having tested your skill in real life scenarios gives you credibility. However,

impressing on others that you are trying to hurt them can easily damage your reputation. Your peers should see you as a role model. They should view you as someone they want to emulate.

Most people love to talk about themselves. Your instructor, too, should be careful about getting into the "Let me tell you what happened to me at the bar last week . . ." attitude. If something worthwhile really did happen, he should find a way to implement it in your training. For example, he may have seen the bouncer use a sleeper hold to render a brawler unconscious while waiting for police to show up. The scenario can be documented and learned from: How much time passed before the technique took effect? How difficult was it to apply the technique? What were the circumstances? What went wrong, or what could have gone wrong? If this happens to you next week, what would you do differently? Later, when your instructor teaches you the sleeper hold, he can

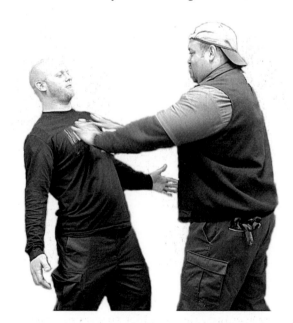

Identify how a fight is likely to start. For example, does it start with name calling, followed by a push?

draw from his experience and teach with an attitude of realism.

Training in realistic self-defense teaches a person about her limitations (perceived or otherwise). Here are some things to consider and evaluate before and after you attend a self-defense seminar:

1. Identify how a fight starts, including body language, pointing, name calling, etc.

2. How capable are you of coping with a great deal of stress? How much physical and mental training have you received?

3. If you have a weapon available, or something that can be used as a weapon, your self-defense capability depends to some extent on your ability and readiness to use the weapon.

4. What are the various types of weapons you could use or reach for in a self-defense situation? How can you use them?

5. If your assailant appears to be unarmed but suddenly pulls out a knife or a gun, how can you take the active approach?

6. Practice physical closeness with another person, for example, by carrying his weight on top of you when on the ground.

7. Consider threats that are confined to a specific area (like a room), and how to maneuver toward the door or other escape route.

20
Self-Defense Issues for Discussion

AWARENESS DRILLS

A self-defense seminar generally contains more lecture time than an ongoing martial arts class, particularly if it is geared toward a specific part of the population (women, for example). But if the instructor simply reads from a book, you might as well buy the book and sit at home and read it. The material should be introduced the way it is to be used, and not the way it is printed. An instructor who includes a scene that you can relate to, preferably from your own area or neighborhood, will get your attention more easily. For example, if a knife-wielding assailant recently attacked your neighbor in his home, you will feel a stronger urge to learn self-defense than if your instructor simply reads a list of statistics from a different part of the country. We hear about muggings every day, but few of us give it much thought . . . until it happens to one of us.

In order to understand how to avoid an attack, we must discuss the types of attacks that most often occur and how they are triggered. How can you avoid getting into the situation in the first place? If you do get into a situation, what can you do before it escalates? Divide awareness drills into segments:

1. Okay, I know I am in trouble. If I do this particular technique now, then I have a chance to get away before anybody gets hurt.

2. The attack is imminent or is already happening. What is my best course of action? Why?

A few years ago, I noticed that I was being followed on a moving sidewalk at the Orlando airport in Florida. It was late at night, and only my mother and I were in the terminal. Our follower remained a few steps behind us and slowed down his walk when we stopped momentarily. When I looked directly at the man, he turned and walked the other way against the direction of the moving sidewalk. How could we have prevented getting into this situation in the first place? How were we carrying our purses? Other luggage? Were we engaged in conversation that sidetracked our awareness? Had it turned into a robbery or other encounter, what could we have done? Where was the closest help?

1. Where is violence most likely to occur? In the home, near the home, in parking lots, with strangers or with people you know, daytime or nighttime, at places you frequent often, or at unusual places that you don't frequent often?

2. Who is your typical assailant? Male or female, what ethnic group, what age group, rich or poor, on drugs or sober?

3. Who is the typical victim? Male or female, a child, a person with a disability, young or old?

4. How should you behave? Be assertive or give in, act afraid or stay calm, scream for help or remain quiet? Why?

5. Should you report the incident even if "nothing happened"? What precautionary measures can you take to avoid getting into the same situation again?

When you sense danger, start by assessing it. Many nonverbal cues can tell you what type of attack to expect. Does the attacker seem confused or angry? What is his motive? Does he want to rob you, rape you or kill you? Is he seeking revenge? When people seek revenge, they commonly bring friends and attack as a group to ensure revenge is certain. Assess your assailant's position. Is he blocking the door that is your only escape route? What, in the immediate vicinity, can he use as a weapon against you? Might he be hiding a weapon? Does he keep his hands in his pockets or behind his back?

 SCENARIO 52

A car stops and the driver asks you for directions. How should you respond?

1. Answer any questions and help the best that you can.

2. Ignore it and keep walking.

3. Walk closer to the car so that you can hear what the driver is saying.

4. Maintain your distance.

★★★★★

Consider these issues: What if you can't hear what is being asked? What if the driver reaches for a map and asks you to show him directions? If you do go near the car and it turns out to be a bad situation, are there any escape routes available? Can the driver cut off your escape route with the car? Does it make a difference whether the person asking for directions is male or female, young or old?

When I was walking to my car at night after work, a police officer on a bicycle followed me. He told me that there had recently been a rape incident in this particular parking lot. In a situation like this, how do you know that the police officer is really a police officer, and not just somebody dressed as such? I recommend maintaining a safe dis-

If somebody unexpectedly knocks on your shoulder, how do you determine if it is a friend or a foe?

tance from any stranger. Don't let your guard down just because he is wearing a uniform. However, maintaining a safe distance does not mean that the situation warrants panic and running. Just be aware.

Surprise attacks from the rear are probably the most difficult to avoid or defend against. Since you don't know in advance that you are in a potentially dangerous situation, you can't start defending yourself until the attack is already under way, which leaves you a step behind from the start. Many other attacks can be avoided or defended against at the early stages.

1. Being aware means recognizing that danger is imminent. Who is dangerous? Maintain a safe distance from strangers who roll down their car windows and ask for information. Cross the street if you have to pass somebody suspicious on the sidewalk, or turn around and take a completely different route.

2. Maintain a safe distance from strangers when you are alone, especially if they stop to talk to you. Does it make a difference who the stranger is? Should all people be treated as equals before you know their motives, or can you use your prior experiences, education and gut feeling to determine with whom it is safe to talk?

3. If a stranger invades your personal space and forces you to back up, be aware of what is behind you. Don't back into a dead end or corner. How do you leave yourself an escape route? Next time you are out walking, look around and determine what to do should you need to defend yourself at that moment.

4. If a stranger comes toward you in a threatening manner, tell him to stop. The earlier you can see the attack coming, the better off you are. If you tell him to stop and he ignores it, what would be your next move?

 SCENARIO 53

A stranger sees you light a cigarette and asks you to give him one. What should you do?

1. Tell him to buy his own.

2. Say, "Sure!" and hold out the pack for him to take one.

3. Dig in your pocket for the lighter.

4. Say that you don't have anymore.

★★★★★

If somebody asks you for a cigarette, chances are he is just trying to get a smoke. But don't *assume* that it is safe to divert your attention. If it is dark and nobody else is nearby, it might be better to throw him the whole pack and the lighter and let him help himself. Keep your distance!

My aunt was standing outside the mall lighting a cigarette one day, when a stranger asked her for a smoke. But my aunt, rather than offering the stranger a cigarette, told him to get lost. As it turned out, the stranger wanted only a smoke and nothing else, but the offensive comment escalated the situation. He smacked my aunt across the face so that her glasses broke and she got a fat lip, and then he took off running. A little bit of common courtesy, too, can help you stay safe. Make awareness practice a habit.

1. Go to some indoor and outdoor public places and note where an assailant might hide. Behind a trash container? Behind a van or truck? Where are the blind spots?

2. Note possible escape routes. Is there a dead end? Is there only one way out? Are there other buildings with people nearby? Every time you visit a potentially dangerous area, be on the lookout for escape routes, the nearest human being, blind spots and potential weapons.

3. When you stop at a gas station at night, is it well lit? How far away are the pumps from the building? How can you pump and be aware of your surroundings at the same time? Is it a good idea to leave the doors to your car unlocked, or is it better to lock the doors while pumping? Does your decision change if you have children in the car? Why? How should you carry your money? When returning from the cashier, check your car before entering. Lock the doors once you're inside.

4. If you want to take the elevator inside a building, should you do so if a stranger wants to get in with you? How do you determine when it is safe? Does it make a difference whether it is night or day, whether the stranger is the same sex or opposite? Does the age of the stranger make a difference?

5. When faced with a threatening situation, identify weapons on your opponent or weapons in the environment that can be used to your or his advantage. Continue being aware of potential weapons both when an attack is imminent and after the attack is already under way, if possible.

6. Identify targets you could strike on a stranger you see on the sidewalk, in the parking lot or at the mall.

7. Look at a stranger for a few seconds and then try to describe him from memory. How accurate is your description? What types of things do you remember? Try to make a note of license plates or other items that may make it easier to identify the person later. Does he have any unusual qualities: long hair on a male, body piercing, odors, accents, etc.

After an attack or imminent attack is over, you need to remember things about the assailant that will help you make an accurate police report. Remembering looks, clothing, height, etc. when under stress is not easy. Advance planning can help you with this. Note the details of people you pass on the street every day. It only takes a few seconds to do so. After some practice, remembering details will become easier.

I was out walking my dog on a grass field behind a school one Sunday morning, when two pit bulls appeared from out of nowhere and started attacking my dog. The owner, who was a few hundred yards away, rushed to his car and sped toward me. When he had regained control of the dogs, he asked if I was okay and then drove off. I knew that I was okay, but I didn't know if my dog had been injured. Fortunately, I had trained myself to look for details, and was able to memorize the license plate of the car as it drove off. On my way home, I told myself over and over what the man had looked like, how he was dressed, his build, and how he wore his hair. When I got home, I wrote my observations down on a piece of paper for future reference. As it turned out, neither I nor my dog were harmed in the incident.

MENTAL PREPARATION

The martial arts are more than systems of self-defense; they are whole systems of living, with their own sets of rules and values. Most martial arts take years to master. Can a few techniques be taught to the uninitiated in a few days' time and be called self-defense? To be effective in true self-defense, you must spend a considerable amount of time on mental exercises as well. I said earlier that actual practice of physical closeness, techniques, and stress are important; however, the physical and mental aspects go hand in hand and you need to learn both. We must condition ourselves to think about and look for situations where we might need to use our self-defense skills.

Be familiar with your mental reactions to stress. If your instructor only focuses on the physical aspects of self-defense, you are not likely to respond appropriately in a real encounter. Likewise, if your instructor only focuses on theoretical knowledge, you will not know how you will react or what you are truly capable of achieving in a real encounter. A course on self-defense must therefore include both theoretical instruction and realistic practice.

Some of us find the idea of hurting another person repulsive (even in self-defense). But when placed in its proper perspective (it's either him or me), self-defense takes on a different meaning.

1. Who do you love most in the world? Is it an elderly mother or father, your spouse, a handicapped sibling, your small child, or your dog or cat? If a stranger hurt your loved one, would you not be ready to act? If you can act and protect someone you love, you should be able to do the same for yourself.

2. Is it ethical to take measures that will save you or a loved one from harm, even if it means hurting the assailant? All the knowledge in the world is of little use when you are afraid to use it. Although you don't always have to get physical—sometimes it is enough to tell a person who is trying to pick a fight that you don't like it—you should be prepared to get physical if telling him doesn't help.

3. Gaining proficiency in self-defense takes training and thought. No technique works a hundred percent of the time. A student of self-defense cannot be timid in class. If you refuse to partake in realistic practice, you will shortchange yourself and might as well save your time and hire a bodyguard.

Are tinted car windows a good or a bad idea? Will they limit your ability to see inside your car at night during the day? I work at the airport and get off work late at night. When walking to my car through the parking garage and out on the dark lot, I visualize dangers hiding in the blind spots. If my car is parked next to a truck or van, I am especially cautious. I also consider that somebody could be hiding underneath my car or the one next to it. I have my keys ready and I take a quick look inside the car before opening the door. Since I drive a hatchback and nobody ever rides in the back seat, I thought it might be a good idea to lay the seat down and make my baggage compartment bigger. But then I discovered that it was difficult to see what might be hiding back there in the dark. So I reverted back to the original position. You are less likely to get into trouble when you are prepared and have a plan. If you do get into trouble, you can act rather than freezing up.

VISUALIZATION DRILLS

Visualize not just where the threat might be hiding, but what to do if you are actually confronted. Who would hear if you

Do you know how you will react when under stress? Is it possible that you will freeze with fear, even if you are a trained martial artist?

screamed for help? What are the possibilities of escape? If you get cornered, what can you do while the assailant is closing distance? If you are driving a car and somebody pulls the door open and jumps in, what would be your course of action? Can you drive into a ditch? Bump into another car to get attention at a stoplight? The more I think about it, the more certain I am that if I were faced with an assailant wielding a weapon and telling me to get into his car, I would choose to fight even at the risk of getting stabbed or shot. What you do is your decision, but I would rather risk getting killed now than risk getting tortured first and then killed. My opinion is that assailants frequently rely on the victim's fear and inability to fight back. Of course, you wouldn't want to react the same with everybody. You must also determine how dangerous your opponent really is. If a coworker threatens you, it might be better to call for the police than to hit him. If a drunk threatens you, he may not have the balance and coordination to chase you or do any real damage.

How do you avoid panicking when a threat is imminent? If you have thought about it beforehand, you will most likely know whom to call for help. Every time you access a potentially dangerous area, know what you are getting into and be ready to act. Don't become complacent. Don't allow your conversation with a friend to dampen your awareness. Think about the "what ifs." Your hearing and eyesight should be intact. Talking on your cell phone on your way to the parking lot at night is a bad idea, because it may distract your focus away from your surroundings and may tie up your hands.

1. Visualize places that you frequent: the parking lot outside the grocery store or outside your workplace, the movie theater or the mall, the airport when you are traveling or picking up somebody. Your home is probably the most frequently visited place that is often overlooked. Mentally go through how you would assess the area before entering. Where is your money? If you have one or both hands free, how fast can you get to your keys? Might somebody be hiding in the bushes by your front door? What can you use as a weapon? There are many objects in your home that can be used as a weapon: a lamp, a paperweight or bookend, an ornament, etc. Pay attention to where they are.

2. If the assailant enters your house after you have gone to bed at night, how can you defend yourself and what are your escape routes? What can you use as a weapon? How can you get to the phone?

3. Visualize yourself getting attacked. Does the attacker approach you in a threatening manner? Does he say anything? Does he try a surprise attack? What is his motive?

4. How can you deal with the situation? What are your options? Is there more than one way you can defend yourself? This exercise helps you develop awareness and judgment, and also helps you review what to do in an actual assault. Of course, it is not likely the assault will happen exactly the way you envisioned it, which is why you need to visualize many possible scenarios.

5. What if the assailant is close enough to touch you? What if he wrestles you to the ground? What if he stabs you or cuts you with a knife? What if he forces you into his car? Visualize the assault at many different stages, so that you can recognize it and avoid it at its earliest stage.

6. Imagine the worst possible scenario: imagine yourself defeated. Then go through the drill again. What could you have done differently? Visualize yourself winning. Some instructors teach to always visualize success and not permit thoughts of defeat. But I believe that touching on the possibility of defeat arms you for success. When you understand what should not happen, you will force yourself to find a solution that can reverse the situation. Visualizing defeat may also make you angry and increase your will to fight for protection.

The beauty of visualization exercises is that you can stop an attack at any point and take your time to determine the best course of action. Visualization exercises help you discover possibilities that you may not ordinarily think of. Is the attacker reaching out to grab you? Is he reaching out to strike you? Does he have a weapon? What is his other hand doing? What are his height and build? What is his physical condition? What does he smell like? What targets does he leave open? Can you use his clothing to restrict his movement? Can you use your own clothing as defense against the attack? Visualize yourself cut or injured. Visualize yourself on the ground with the attacker on top of you. Visualize a gun pointed at your head from the rear seat in your car. What would you do?

Identify techniques you can use when coming to the rescue of another person, that are likely to end the fight in the quickest way possible.

It is also possible that at some point you will be an observer of another person trying to defend himself. If you are the only witness, how can you help him? What can you use in the environment as a weapon? How will you approach the assailant without risk of getting attacked? Can you launch a surprise attack, and what will you do if you are successful? What if the assailant diverts his attention to you? Can you solicit help from the person you were initially trying to help? How? Can you make it a two-on-one exchange where you and the other victim take up roles as attackers? If you end up seriously hurting the assailant or rendering him unconscious and there is no one near, how do you deal with the situation? Do you run

and get help? Leave him there alone? What can you use for tying his hands and feet together? Do you place him in your car? Visualizing every possible scenario and overtraining builds confidence and muscle memory.

So, you see, there are many questions you need to ask to trigger your own and other students' learning process. However, it is not enough to ask these questions without also researching the validity of what you are learning. When learning a technique intended for self-defense, find out what it really takes to use it successfully.

HOW LONG SHOULD THE CLASS BE?

Finally, how long should the self-defense seminar last? How long does an effective system of self-defense take to learn? Each system is likely to have its own set of limitations. If you are concerned with true self-defense and not martial arts, you probably ought to study from a variety of instructors, learn as much as possible from each, and then move on. If you study only one art for many years, you will be bound by that art's limitations and failures, often without realizing it. It is unlikely that one instructor can teach all aspects of fighting and all situations one might encounter. Because of the instructor's background, she is likely to favor certain techniques over others. But this does not mean that the techniques will work best for you in particular. I once heard a martial artist say that the reverse punch was the best technique for a self-defense situation. What did he base his belief on? Is it possible that he had trained in a Japanese or Korean hard style for most of his life?

When you have trained in a particular style of martial art, you are also likely to have trained with others in that particular style. Consider the fact that your training partners are normally cooperative. In my opinion, this is why Aikido techniques send people flying distances of several yards. If your opponent did not cooperate, she would be more likely to go straight down rather than 20 feet away.

– INSTRUCTOR TIP –

Not every person may be able to use every technique to the same degree of proficiency. What does it really take to unbalance an assailant, to wrestle him to the ground, and to hold him there until help arrives? These are issues you need to examine and experiment with through practice.

– STUDENT TIP –

When you seek an instructor to teach you self-defense, hopefully she will share her knowledge freely while recognizing her limitations. With your best interest in mind, she may want to send you to others who can fill in the gaps. If not, seek other instruction on your own as soon as you feel your training is stagnating.

21

Learning Self-Defense Concepts

WHAT, WHY, HOW?

In a real self-defense encounter, fine motor skills tend to go out the door along with any complex or "fancy" techniques you have learned. When attending a self-defense seminar, you must therefore focus on a few simple and highly effective techniques. Sparring, for example, is not the same as self-defense. If you can throw a good punch, you are probably more likely to throw one in a threatening situation than is a person who does not even know how to make a fist. But if it is self-defense you are learning, you are wasting time if you point spar or kickbox. I see many martial artists learning complex defenses against simple attacks. For example, if an assailant attacks you with a knife:

1. You might learn a technique that requires superior timing and precision in intercepting the attack.

2. You might learn a technique that involves striking a small pressure point on the wrist designed to make the assailant lose his grip and send the knife flying.

3. You might learn a complex maneuver that involves turning and twisting until you have acquired some sort of joint lock.

There may also be several strikes involved to many different targets. In short, the whole technique may be comprised of 20 individual moves. Not only is it time consuming to learn self-defense this way, if events don't go down as expected you will get confused somewhere in the middle of the technique. In addition, we often assume that the assailant will stand there while we complete the moves. A good approach to learning self-defense may be to learn a few highly effective techniques that instantly steal your opponent's balance or place him in an inferior position. The techniques should be easy to learn, and the average person should be able to apply them with a reasonable amount of training.

LEARNING STRIKE AND KICK CONCEPTS

Question what type of person you are likely to encounter on the street and the manner in which he might attack. Is it reasonable that you will defend against a spinning back kick or ridge hand strike, for example? Although these techniques are powerful, they only work if your opponent fights using karate. Is it reasonable that your opponent will fight using traditional karate moves on the street? Street attacks may not be "clean." Your opponent will not throw one straight punch

A strike on the street is not necessarily a clean punch. It is therefore difficult to execute a clean block, or to sidestep the strike and avoid getting hurt.

that you can sidestep or block. He will not swing at you with a knife exposed from several feet away.

How much force is needed in order to deter a person intent on hurting you? Will one good strike do the job? What should you do when you discover that this one strike failed to do damage? What type of follow-up technique will you use? How fast can your assailant cover distance? If your instructor doesn't bring these issues to your attention, you may get a false sense of security: "This was *supposed* to work!"

1. A single strike seldom stops an assailant intent on hurting you. Learn multiple strike combinations. Drill at least five strikes, then 10.

2. Relate multiple strikes to endurance. Throwing 20 strikes when under pres-

sure to perform is very tiring. If the combination fails to stop your opponent, you might not have the energy to continue. How can you economize striking?

Seasoned martial artists, too, get sloppy and imprecise with their techniques when they are overwhelmed. In a kickboxing match, for example, two fighters in seemingly superb shape and bulging muscles might be unable to do any significant damage to each other in the ring. A lengthy strike combination will tire you in seconds, especially if you don't train for quick multiple strikes with regularity. When you get tired, your defense also becomes worthless. If you were to learn just one single and highly effective strike, what type of strike would you learn? Remember that kicks are more tiring to throw than strikes, because the legs are heavier than the arms and not as precise as the hands.

You must also learn how to block an attack effectively:

1. What does it take to stop an attacker?

2. What types of full force strikes can you realistically block?

3. Exactly how stiff does your block or parry need to be in order to have the desired effect?

Experiment with blocks until you gain realistic insight. A "wimpy" block is not good enough against an opponent who swings at you with full intent. Practice with intent even when practicing with a partner. Use forearm pads to protect against injuries, then swing at your partner with considerable force and allow him to practice realistic blocking techniques.

Intellectual understanding and physical proficiency are two different things. Always think about what happens next. If you shove an attacker in the chest, you may avoid his first grab attempt. But how likely is this shove to stop him? If he is angered, how do you deal with his comeback?

LEARNING GRAB TECHNIQUE CONCEPTS

A defense against a rear bear hug calls for raising your arms and poking your opponent in the eyes, bringing your elbows down on his wrists and loosening the grip, and counter-striking with a back elbow to his chin and a shin rake and stomp to his foot. In theory, this technique makes sense. But consider this:

1. How much time is available for completing the technique? If you miss with your initial strike, what will you do next?

2. What will you do if your opponent is grabbing you so forcefully that you are unable to move? What if he is shaking you or throwing you off balance simultaneously?

3. Many martial arts teach only the technique itself, which normally consists of a variety of strikes and kicks. But is it possible to throw an accurate strike to the eyes or knee or foot of an opponent when grabbed from behind? Will the element of surprise and the adrenaline rush prevent you from responding quickly?

4. How powerful are your strikes? Since a small person is not likely to grab a bigger person, you must examine the usefulness of your techniques against

Think about the factors that lead up to a confrontation. Do you have the option of neutralizing the threat verbally rather than resorting to a fistfight?

someone who is bigger than you. Can you strike with enough force to stop a much bigger assailant?

When a friend tried to sneak up on me as a joke, I sensed the threat, and instinct from my long training took over. I swung around and struck him with a hooking punch to the temple. It wasn't until after it was over that I understood he was a friend who presented no real threat. Is it a good idea to train to the degree that you react to a perceived threat before you have evaluated the situation? Had the threat been real, would this one strike have stopped the attacker? What would my next move have been? Would I have continued with more strikes or kicks? Whether or not the attacker stops after taking the first strike may depend on his motives.

1. If he wants to snatch your purse or wallet, he might stop when the element of surprise is gone.

2. If he wants to kidnap you and no one is near, he might become more violent when

you try to defend yourself. However, I still recommend taking the active approach and defending yourself, rather than hoping that compliance will make your opponent less likely to harm you.

Let's say that your first blow is successful. It lands and stuns your opponent. But it doesn't knock him out, and it doesn't hurt him so much that he begins to fear you. What will be his next move? What will be your next move? How quickly must you react? It is interesting to consider whether a single well-placed and forceful strike is better, or if a combination of many strikes to different targets is better. In theory, many strikes to different targets have the ability to split your opponent's mind and body focus and create sensory overload, and are therefore considered effective. But how much power can you generate in your strikes in a real-life threat at very close range?

If relying on strikes to end the fight, you might have to strike your opponent before he has grabbed you. Personally, I like techniques that unbalance the assailant. For example, if he chokes me from behind, I would rather do a forward throw, using the assailant's choking arm as leverage, than striking his eyes. A throw buys you time even if it does not hurt your opponent. If he goes to the ground while you remain standing, it may even buy you a considerable amount of time. As long as your hands are free, you can defend a frontal grab by forcefully striking your opponent's chin. If your hands are tied up, your opponent's hands will most likely also be tied up. Learn to use your legs as the driving force when pushing an opponent away. If he is heavier than you, pushing with your hands against his chest may simply result in straightening your arms rather than moving back your opponent.

Consider your habits and past experiences when learning defensive moves against grabs. Carefully select the most effective techniques for the amount of time you have available.

1. Evaluate the effectiveness of each technique you learn based on how intent the attacker is. For example, if a technique employs several strikes, you may only have time for one of these strikes before the assailant grabs you.

2. Learn how to finish the fight. Don't do only one move and then pause to see what happens. Stay a step ahead of the assailant.

3. When the assailant grabs you, think: "Break free, counterstrike until he backs off, and run."

A strike or grab may be more effective than it initially appears. For example, if the assailant pulls your upper body off balance prior to applying a rear choke, your rehearsed defense may not work. Likewise, if an opponent grips you tighter than you expected, the grip will limit the use of your arms and legs. When practicing rehearsed defenses, think outside of the box. Do not stay with a technique that doesn't work.

LEARNING JOINT-LOCK CONCEPTS

How effective is a joint lock when the training partner is cooperating?

1. When training with a willing partner, take the time to analyze the effectiveness

It is appropriate to introduce the chaos of real-life scenarios after you have developed proficiency with complex techniques such as joint locks.

of the techniques and movements. Modify them to fit your particular style and build.

2. When training with a resisting partner, it is more difficult to fine-tune the techniques. Joint locks require the use of fine motor skills, so a fraction of an inch of movement in the wrong direction can mean the difference between victory and defeat.

LEARNING EVASIVE MOVEMENT CONCEPTS

Is sidestepping an attack a valuable option in a self-defense situation? How is sidestepping accomplished? Which foot should you step with first, and why? What is your immediate action after you have sidestepped the attack?

Let's say that you are facing your opponent and initiate a step to your left, stepping with

your left foot first. Why is it better to step first with the foot closest to the direction of travel? Which foot should you step with next, and in what direction? Rather than learning which foot to step with, might it be better to simply learn the concept of "getting out of the way," and letting your body handle it the best it can?

When trying to get away, evasive movement should be definite and not just enough to make the punch miss.

1. Alternating the feet as you do when running helps you cover ground faster than if you maintain a specific stance, such as in a sparring match where you normally keep the same side forward through all movement.

2. When you have sidestepped the attack, try changing the angle 90 degrees. Or position yourself so that you face your escape route. It is not necessary to continue facing your opponent after you have completed your evasive move.

3. Timing your step properly is critical. If you initiate your step too soon, the opponent can alter the attack line and still strike you. If you initiate your step too late, he may close the distance and reach out to strike or grab you.

4. When sidestepping an attack, is it a good idea to maintain a high guard? What are the drawbacks of doing so? If you lower your guard, you risk exposing vulnerable targets. But if you keep your hands high, you give your opponent the opportunity to grab your forearms or wrists.

The eyes are normally good targets, no matter how big or strong your opponent is. But don't let the idea delude you. If you are in the middle of a fight, or if your hands are tied up, attacking the eyes is easier said than done.

LEARNING TARGET AREA CONCEPTS

Good targets in a self-defense scenario might include the eyes, groin and knees. The tailbone might be a good target if you can position yourself behind your opponent, such as when coming to the rescue of another person. Attacks to an opponent on the ground might include stomps to his heel. The heel and ankle are good targets, because an opponent on the ground will try to get to his feet and a hard stomp might twist or break his ankle.

Another target often overlooked is the outside thigh area. The reason Thai boxers focus on this target is because it can cause the victim extreme pain or a dead leg.

1. If your opponent grabs you and pins your arms so that you are unable to strike him, try driving your knee into the upper portion of his thigh. The pain is likely to split his focus and force him to loosen his grip momentarily, even if it doesn't end the fight. Repeat the technique. If you miss his thigh, you may still get his groin.

2. If your arms are free, try attacking your opponent's balance by tilting his head to the rear. Place one hand underneath his chin and push his head up and back, until his upper body is arched to the rear.

LEARNING GRAPPLING CONCEPTS

If you end up in close range with your opponent, it benefits you to know how to submit him on the ground. But what if only you are on the ground? You will now be at a distinct disadvantage. A point that is often overlooked is the ability to get up from the ground if you do end up there. When learning realistic self-defense, include scenarios and exercises on how to get back to your feet quickly.

1. Do you get to your knees first before standing up, or do you use a forward roll to gain distance and momentum to get to your feet? How can you use an object in the environment to help you get up? What are the benefits and drawbacks of doing so?

2. Learn how to strike and kick while on the ground, how to grab and unbalance an opponent, and how to use him as leverage for pulling yourself back up.

Attacking your opponent's balance by tilting his upper body to the rear may help you neutralize the threat and be more precise with target areas.

3. Allow yourself to experience the energy drain of trying to get back to your feet when taken down. Go down on the ground and get back up 10 times as quickly as you can.

Grapple with a partner. As soon as he breaks free and tries to get away, immediately close the distance and take him down again. When he has no time to regroup or get to safety, when the threat is continuous, can he still stop the fight through the use of a single technique? The point is that when somebody is determined to fight you, he will continue pursuing you until either you or he collapses. There is little room for errors. You will instantly discover the futility of moves that are executed poorly.

– INSTRUCTOR TIP –

Demonstrate how quickly you can close the distance between yourself and a student, and how difficult it is to keep an attacker away with punches and kicks alone. If you are teaching a stand-up art, allow students to feel the smothering effects of a grappler at least once in their training.

– STUDENT TIP –

Be a critical thinker. Do most fights really go to the ground? Who has done the study and kept score? What were the circumstances? If you are a grappler, you will most likely support this claim; if you are a stand-up fighter, you will deny it. Do your own research. Don't take anything at face value.

LEARNING ARMED ATTACK CONCEPTS

Should a self-defense course include the use of weapons? I don't think I have ever seen "knife offense" advertised. The focus is always on "defense." If weapon training is part of a self-defense course, what types of weapons should you train with? How proficient do you need to become in order to avoid injuring yourself on the weapon?

It has been said that a weapon is only as good as the person wielding it. A weapon can't work miracles by itself, and a risk weapon users face is becoming obsessed with it. When you are wielding a weapon, you don't *have* to end the fight by using it; you can still use strikes, kicks and grabs. Although a weapon can help you succeed, it can also hinder performance. When you understand offense, you will gain deeper insights into defense. For example, if you have worked sufficiently with a handgun and have learned how to fire it, you will also understand the mechanics of the gun: when it can fire and when it can't. This bit of knowledge can be a lifesaver if confronted by a gun-wielding assailant.

When training in knife defense, how realistic is the training? How do you know whether techniques that look good and practical are really so? In a knife attack, you seldom get second chances. You will likely get cut, so embrace the thought from the start.

1. A knife is most dangerous when it is in motion. It is then capable of producing multiple cuts within seconds.

2. The movement of your opponent's knife and knife hand are difficult to time when preparing a counterattack.

3. When training to defend against a knife attack, a natural tendency is to fixate on the knife and forget there are many targets that can be attacked.

When blocking or grabbing your opponent's knife hand, remember that your free hand and feet are still available for use. The fight should not become a physical struggle over who gets the knife. The same concept applies to the person wielding the knife. If you are wielding the knife and your opponent grabs your knife hand, rather than struggling to free that hand, use your other hand or legs to attack the assailant.

Keep track of the weapon. Consider the possibility of the attacker switching hands. Many schools teach how to gain control of the hand that is holding the weapon. But what if the attacker switches the weapon to his other hand? Should you stay with the control you

have already established, or should you let go and try to control the weapon hand again? Understanding the concepts is now more important than learning the techniques. For example, keeping track of the weapon is a concept. Preventing the weapon from reaching you is a concept. Exactly how you get there is irrelevant. It is more important that the end result is safety.

1. When practicing, inform your partner of your objective before you attack him. For example, tell him, "All I want you to do for the next minute is to not give up. No matter what happens, don't give up!" This exercise teaches the mindset one needs to survive.

2. Or tell your partner, "When I threaten you, I want you to try to talk your way out of the situation. No matter what happens, don't allow me to close the distance." After completing the exercise, discuss what could have been done if the distance had closed.

At the beginning of class, identify the techniques you will be working on and the reasons you are learning those particular techniques. What are their purposes? How are the techniques to be performed? This simple pattern helps you gear your mind toward the material that is to be learned. If your instructor doesn't go into depth, paraphrase the concepts to yourself. For example:

The purpose of this technique is to unbalance an opponent who is attacking me with a knife. Instead of learning a complicated disarming technique, I will use a simpler way to eliminate the threat. First I will understand how a person's balance works. If my opponent's up-

per body is not directly above his foundation, he will be unable to maintain balance ...

Experiment with a partner in order to understand how people lose balance and how the center of gravity can be manipulated. Before you get into the details of a takedown, your instructor might want to demonstrate the technique in its entirety so you can visualize the steps that lead toward your objective. She can then divide the technique into smaller segments and let you practice each segment separately.

1. Identify how balance works and experiment with balanced and unbalanced stances.

2. Study the mechanics of the takedown. The knife or another weapon can be added to the attack once you understand balance manipulation.

3. Talk briefly about different types of knives (or other weapons), different grips, the difference between stabbing and slashing attacks, and the most vulnerable targets.

When you have had a chance to practice the techniques, you might want to discuss what can go wrong, what to do when the unexpected happens, and how to leave yourself an out—an option to escape when all else fails. The next step might be to expand on the lesson and talk about what to do when you have taken your opponent down, how to gain control of the weapon, whether or not you should use it against him, and how to use it effectively. Your focus will now shift from defense to offense. Next you might want to discuss how to react if you get injured while gaining control of the weapon.

 SCENARIO 54

You are attending a class on defense against knives and handguns. You question the validity of what your instructor is telling you. How should your instructor respond?

1. Ask you to come to the front of the room, so that she can demonstrate the techniques on you.

2. Read off some numbers from a study she has done.

3. Tell you that this is what she learned from her instructor.

4. Roll up her sleeve and show you a scar from a knife fight.

★★★★★

Many martial arts instructors teach defenses against knives or handguns. But how do they know that the techniques they teach are valid? Have they actually had to defend themselves against a knife or a gun? Unless they are police or military or former street thugs, it is unlikely they have actually experienced the effectiveness of their techniques in a real-life scenario. This lack of experience should not prompt the instructor to go out and look for trouble, however, just so he can say he has survived X number of street fights. With a lot of research and a bit of ingenuity, he can still plan an effective self-defense course. As a student, consider these issues:

1. Study with people who are qualified in the use of knives and firearms, so that you can find the strengths and weak-

nesses of the techniques you are learning. Who is qualified? Try those who carry or use weapons on a daily basis: police and military, for example.

2. Ask the instructor to invite guest speakers: law enforcement, the military, bouncers, bodyguards, rape prevention and domestic violence counselors, etc.

LEARNING UNUSUAL POSITION CONCEPTS

You are sitting down when a person approaches you in a threatening manner. Is it a good idea to stand up? What are the drawbacks of standing up? Can standing up escalate the situation? Are there other people who can be enlisted for support? Answering these questions may help you determine whether you should stand or remain sitting. Try these exercises:

1. Sit at a table and have your partner attack you. How fast can you get to your feet and escape?

2. How can a chair or an item on the table be used as a weapon?

3. How can the table be used as a barrier? Can you jump over it or run around it?

4. How can you use the table for support when throwing a kick?

5. If you are in bed when the attack happens, can you maneuver to the other side of the bed? Use the bed as a barrier? Can you use the bed sheets or pillows?

When learning defenses against attacks, learn also the underlying reasons for the attack. For example, did it escalate from a verbal confrontation to a push or a punch, to a full-out brawl, and finally to the ground? Why would you get into a verbal confrontation in the first place? Is there a way to end the confrontation before it escalates to physical contact? All attacks don't start verbally. If the assailant wants to rob you, he might attack you without any prior warning.

22

Learning Multiple-Attack Scenarios

WHY IS IT SO DIFFICULT?

You can induce stress by training in multiple-attack scenarios. But although I often witness this sort of training, I see little success even with advanced students. The so-called "two on one" type of sparring often turns into what looks like a bad joke, where the student runs from the attackers while desperately throwing some half-hearted kicks that wouldn't stop a child, until she finally ends up sandwiched between the attackers or pinned against the wall or floor. When exploring the possibilities of prevailing against multiple opponents, you will most likely find it is an exercise in futility. One punch or kick will not do enough damage to stop several people intent on hurting you. Fighting two or more attackers simultaneously is nearly impossible. We don't realize how quickly events happen, how fast an assailant can close the distance, and how little time we have available to react and do our techniques with precision and focus. If you end up on the ground, it is nearly impossible to fight more than one assailant at a time. Experiencing defeat in training puts things in perspective and allows you to focus on what you truly can do.

When fighting multiple attackers, train for:

1. **Position.** Fighting multiple opponents coming from different directions is extremely difficult. Establishing a superior

Consider for a moment the possibility of two people turning toward you with threatening looks in their eyes. What is your first thought? How would you defend yourself if necessary?

position is of utmost importance. If possible, place your closest opponent as a shield between yourself and the others. If in a room or other enclosed area, be aware of the door's location and try to position yourself near it to facilitate escape.

2. **Timing.** At no point should you allow all of your opponents to smother you at the same time. The trick is to isolate the attackers so that you only have to fight one at time. Unfortunately, it is easier

263

said than done. Try to determine which attacker you can eliminate most easily. Is it the one who is closest to you? The strongest? The one with a weapon? Keep your escape routes in mind.

3. **Target.** When you have made the decision to fight, enter the confrontation with all the determination and strength you can muster. You may benefit from initiating the fight. Making the first move allows you to take charge. Be aware of your footing. Is the ground slippery or muddy? Are you standing in two feet of snow? In general, avoid high or fancy kicks. It is better to kick low to the knees, thighs or groin.

When choosing which attacker to fight first, if possible, consider your opponents' strengths and prior experiences, as well as the level of the threat. Taking out the strongest opponent first may seem like a good strategy because it leaves you with the wimpier one, who may decide not to fight at all when his buddy is hurt. Also consider taking out the easiest opponent first. Who is the smallest? If a weapon is involved, is it better to focus on the opponent with the weapon or on his helper(s)? The one with the weapon may seem like the greatest threat and should therefore be eliminated first. Or can you take advantage of the one without the weapon by using him as a shield against the others? Think about these issues beforehand and role-play different scenarios in the training hall. There is no single correct answer to these questions; however, experimentation might give you a good idea of what to do.

Let's summarize the multiple-opponent concepts and then look at some exercises that you can explore with your instructor and other students.

TWELVE MULTIPLE-OPPONENT FIGHTING CONCEPTS

1. **Fighting multiple attackers is extremely difficult. Look for an opportunity to flee at any time during the encounter.** If the attack takes place indoors, how close is the door or the nearest help? If the attack takes place outdoors, are there others nearby who would hear a scream for help? What brought you to this situation in the first place? If you could do it over, what would you do differently? Thinking about these questions may allow you to avoid a multiple-attack scenario altogether.

2. **Establish a position of superiority.** Do not allow all of your opponents to attack you at one time (sometimes, though it is not possible to avoid this). You might succeed with this concept when fighting two opponents, but it is unlikely you will be successful fighting more than two people at the same time. If possible, use one attacker as a weapon or shield against the others by pushing him into the other attackers. Using one of the attackers as a shield does not mean you have to be so close that there is body contact. What would be a safe yet effective distance? If you push one attacker into the other attacker(s), how good must your timing be in order for the move to be effective? How hard must you push to make your first and second attacker stumble? If possible, resort to the use of a weapon that poses enough of a threat to make your opponents change their minds about fighting you.

3. **Keep your position and escape routes in mind.** If you are unable to reach your escape route immediately, how can you move in order to reach it before your attackers have closed the distance? If the attackers are aware of your escape route and they attempt to block it, what would you do next? If in an enclosed area, such as a room or hallway, strive to position yourself near the door. When the opportunity arises, feel the handle. Does the door open inward or outward? If it opens outward, can you kick it open? What type of kick would you use? If you can place the door opening between yourself and the attackers, only one person may be able to pass through at a time. How does it increase your chances to escape or counterattack? If you don't have the option of getting to the door, what would be your next best course of action? Is it possible to talk your way out of the situation? If you choose to do so, how would you start your conversation?

4. **When taken by surprise, know when it is appropriate to fight back.** What if you are talking to one opponent and a second attacker emerges and grabs you from behind? Can you use the opponent who is grabbing you as a shield by turning him toward the other attacker? Can you distance yourself from the first attacker or unbalance your opponent by pushing back against him? How easy or difficult is it to break free from the bear hug while moving back or while you or the attacker is off balance? If you manage to break free, is it possible to flee instead of counterstriking? If you flee, are your opponents following you? At what point do you determine whether to keep running or to stop and pursue

the fight? How tired are you? At what point does it become impossible to continue fighting multiple opponents? Does fleeing an attack make you feel inferior? If you are fighting one person, and he calls for help and a second attacker emerges, at some point you will have to disengage from the first attacker in order to deal with the second one. What types of strikes can you use? At what range do your kicks become ineffective? What types of kicks limit your power at close range?

5. **Avoid turning your back toward an opponent on the ground.** Avoid stepping over his body. If you must step over or near him in order to move away from the other attackers, which is better: stepping over his legs, body or head? Why? If you end up on the ground in a wrestling match with one of the attackers, it is critical to eliminate him immediately. How would you go about defeating him and getting back to your feet?

6. **If one opponent has a firearm, try to eliminate him first.** If he has any other weapon, such as a knife or a stick, try to distance yourself. The firearm differs from other weapons because it extends your opponent's reach beyond the physical reach of the weapon. An increase in distance might therefore not contribute to greater safety. The same is not true with a knife or stick, where your opponent can harm you only if he can reach you with the weapon. Experiment with your peers to find a safe distance from knife and stick attacks. How quickly can your opponent close the distance? How can he extend the reach of his weapon by switching hands? How intent is he on

using the weapon against you? Is he looking to harm you physically, or is he using the weapon primarily as a threat? Disarming an attacker may allow you to use his weapon against the others. What types of disarming techniques are effective when the threat is high and you only have a fraction of a second to act?

7. **If a weapon has fallen to the ground, do not lose sight of it.** If your opponent loses his weapon, can you find it and use it against him? When fighting multiple opponents, the accomplice(s) might pick up and use the weapon. Consider how your opponent's focus is diverted when he loses the weapon or reaches out to pick it up from the ground. Is it possible for you to counterattack or flee at this moment? If you choose to counter-attack, what type of attack would you use? Why? If you attempt to pick up a weapon from the ground, can you do so without your opponent(s) taking advantage of your lapse in focus?

8. **Use the environment to your advantage.** Parked cars can serve as obstacles between you and your opponents. Using the environment involves more than running around obstacles or finding an object that can be used as a weapon. Consider using a distraction that will turn your opponent's attention away from you. For example, look to the side and wave or shout for help to an imaginary friend. Be aware of your footing. If your footing is poor, your opponent's footing is probably also poor, and vice versa. Most objects lying about, such as a bottle or a tree branch, can be utilized as weapons. If using a natural weapon found in the environment, how would you em-

ploy it to attack or defend? Would you use the weapon in a striking fashion, or could you use it to take your opponent off balance? How?

9. **Time is of the essence.** How quickly must you react in order to handle at least two attackers successfully? Identify the types of strikes that would cause enough damage to end the fight. How precise must you be with these strikes? How will your opponent(s) react when you counterattack? How can you avoid placing yourself in additional danger when moving in to strike?

10. **When the fight is imminent, enter the confrontation with all the determination you can muster.** Initiate and stay dynamic. Consider that your opponent, if intent on hurting you, will probably attack with more than one strike and his accomplices will help him. Why is it generally better to initiate than to wait for your opponent to initiate with a move that you can defend against? Or is it? How can you take advantage of your opponent's strike or momentum to launch a counterattack? How much damage must you do in order to walk away safely?

11. **Use techniques that are likely to finish off your opponents with one or two strikes, rather than techniques designed to wear them down.** Identify strikes that you can throw with relative ease and that have a high success ratio. Keep in mind that you will probably be tired, scared and experience a high adrenaline rush. How does it affect your ability to use your strikes and kicks? Before commencing the exercise in the training hall, you may

want to tire yourself by working the heavy bag or doing push-ups until you get winded. Then have your opponents attack you.

12. **Stay in a stance that allows you to see your opponents and that gives you mobility, range of motion and power.** The stance that feels natural is generally the one that works the best, particularly if it allows you to run or move with ease. If you normally fight from a left stance, you may want to switch to a right stance if doing so prevents you from exposing your back to either of your opponents. Be aware of which targets your opponent is most likely to attack. Sometimes the events that led up to the fight can reveal your opponent's motive. Or if he has a weapon, you may be able to determine what type of attack is likely to follow. In most cases, you are probably looking for an upper body attack. Can you thwart it by doing something unorthodox, such as ducking low and attacking his legs? If you choose to do so and your opponent goes down, how does it affect your positioning and ability to fight a second or third assailant?

EXERCISES FOR FIGHTING MULTIPLE OPPONENTS

Use the following exercises to trigger your thought process regarding multiple-attack scenarios. Experiment with your peers in a controlled environment, where you can modify the situation and techniques until you have gained a fair amount of insight into what it takes to defend yourself against multiple opponents successfully. When practicing these scenarios, ask yourself, What does it take?

1. **How possible is it for a fairly skilled martial artist to defend herself successfully against multiple attackers?** Start with one opponent and identify what you can do. Then introduce a second opponent. How much do your odds of a successful defense decrease? Are you half as likely to be successful, or less than half as likely? How much do the odds decrease when defending against three attackers? What about a gang of four? Is it possible to incapacitate that many people and still get to safety? Will defeating one of the attackers convince the others to leave? If you could choose only one technique against each one of the attackers, what would you do? Why? Does the technique you chose have merit? Experiment.

2. **When are you most likely to get attacked by multiple opponents?** Discuss situations where one person is seeking revenge and brings his friends along. Role play different scenarios with your peers in order to determine whether you can talk your way out of a situation before it escalates to a physical attack. How does gang involvement increase the risks of attacks by multiple opponents? What types of weapons might be used?

3. **How should you position yourself when fighting more than one person?** Explore the difficulties of striking in different directions simultaneously. How can movement help you line up the attackers so they can only reach you one at a time? Can you maintain this position for any length of time? If not, what is your next step? Discuss the dangers of getting cornered.

4. **When surrounded by multiple attackers, which assailant would you fight first?** If you have a choice, would you fight the smallest and seemingly weakest opponent first? The one with a weapon? The biggest and most obnoxious opponent? Why? If you knew something about these people's backgrounds, how would it change your decision?

5. **What types of targets should you select?** Which types of strikes and targets would finish an opponent as quickly as possible, giving you time to deal with the next assailant? If you only have time for one strike or kick, which type would you use and to which target? If you hit an attacker in the midsection with all the power you can muster, will it deter him? If you hit him in the nose with all the power you can muster, will it deter him? How does a high threat situation affect your ability to strike with power?

6. **What types of kicks are useful for fighting multiple opponents?** How easy or difficult is it to time a kick to your opponent's advance? If you throw a kick with all the power you can muster, will it deter him? If it does, will it deter him long enough for you to escape? Explore the usefulness of the front kick, roundhouse kick, side kick, axe kick, stop kick and spinning back kick. Which is better: a linear kick (front kick, side kick), or a circular kick (roundhouse kick, hook kick). Why? Which targets would you choose to stop an opponent's advance? To hurt him? How precise must your kick be?

7. **If one of your opponents ends up on the ground, what dangers must you con-** sider regarding your positions? How can an opponent on the ground come to the assistance of the other assailants? If you have an opportunity to run but must step over the person on the ground, what dangers must you consider? Can you incapacitate the person on the ground before stepping over him? Is there enough time to do so before the other assailants will smother you?

8. **If your first opponent is empty handed, what types of techniques can you use against him?** How can you gain superior positioning against an empty-handed assailant? Is it safer to stay at long range or better to close the distance and take the fight to your opponent? If the first assailant is smaller than you, would it benefit you to close the distance, grab him and use him as a shield against the others? Can you push him into the others with enough force to stun them? If your intended defense fails, how can you adapt?

9. **What should you do if your second opponent has a gun?** Explore whether you can use the first opponent as a shield against the gun. Does using him as a shield guarantee that the second opponent won't shoot? How does adrenaline affect a person's ability to make rational decisions? At what point is it better to submit to your attacker's demands than to continue fighting?

10. **What should you do if you are in an enclosed area when attacked by multiple opponents?** Explore possible escape paths from a room. How can you position yourself to avoid getting sandwiched between the attackers and still

have the escape path available? Is it possible to take out the person standing closest to the door? If the person standing closest to the door has a weapon, is it still a good idea to take him out first? Why or why not? How does the type of weapon affect your decision? Can you use the escape path to limit the other assailants' mobility?

11. **Your first opponent is down on the ground from a kick you just threw, and a second opponent emerges. The door (the only escape path) to the room is closed. What can you do?** How can you position yourself so that you have a clear view of both attackers? How can you position yourself if the first attacker gets up from the ground? Can you take advantage of a moment of weakness in either attacker's position? Can you disrupt the second attacker's balance or momentarily disengage from him in order to handle the first attacker? Would you use strikes or kicks? How can you use balance manipulation (takedowns)?

12. **The person you are fighting calls for his friend, who emerges from around the corner. What should you do?** Explore how to avoid getting sandwiched between the two attackers. How can you keep the escape path in view at all times? If you are in a room and the door is closed, can you use the door to brace yourself for a kick? If the door is locked,

can you kick it open or push one of the attackers into it? How does a stumble or loss of balance affect your focus?

13. **When you get through the first door, you discover there is a short hallway with a second door. What should you do?** Can you use the door opening to prevent the attackers from passing through together? Can you brace yourself against the second door and throw a kick to keep the attackers away?

14. **You are in a verbal confrontation with one person, when a second person emerges and grabs you from behind. What can you do?** Explore how to increase the strength of your position. Can you place the person who is grabbing you between you and the other attacker? How can you manipulate his balance? Is it a good idea to fight the attacker at the grip? Why or why not?

15. **What can you do if the person grabbing you is really strong, and you are unable to break the grip?** Explore the possibility of hanging on to the assailant rather than trying to get away. How can you neutralize his power by staying close to him? Can you use the person who is grabbing you as a brace for a kick? How? If he is grabbing you from behind, can you disrupt his balance by pushing him back forcefully?

Part Six
Higher Learning

23

The Advanced Student

BENEFITS OF CONCEPTUAL LEARNING

Knowing *what* to do is a step toward knowing *how* to do it. You must learn proper mechanics of technique before you can learn the concepts of technique. When you understand the what and the how, the next step is learning the when and the why. Since not all techniques work equally well all the time, knowing when to use a technique is crucial. Mastering the concepts means mastering the highest stage of learning: correlation. Or as I've said previously: Give a man a fish, and he will eat for a day; teach a man to fish, and he will eat for life.

Many martial artists focus on how to perform the techniques, with minimal or no emphasis on how to make rational decisions. You learn hundreds of specific techniques without discussing or exploring how you or your potential opponent feel or react to these techniques. The ability to reason is important both to the sports-oriented competitive martial artist and to the self-defense -oriented martial artist. Understanding the human psyche, both in yourself and in your opponent, is perhaps even more important than executing a technique correctly. Techniques are predictable; the human mind is not always so.

On the last day of a law class I took in college, we were asked to evaluate the instructor. I was amazed at how few students gave the instructor a high rating. In hindsight, I feel that it was because his teaching methods were a bit unorthodox. For example, we had to go to the law library and research how to write a brief, even though the class was just an introduction to aviation law and the students didn't intend to become lawyers or legal assistants. This type of study was difficult for the students, because they had never taken a class that required them to think rather than simply learn the facts. In my opinion, the instructor who taught this class was one of a kind: highly recommended. In the martial arts, rational decision-making is an area that is often not taught but learned little by little through your own experiences.

If the circumstances are favorable, you may be able to use a memorized technique proficiently in a real-life or real-time scenario. But if you also understand the concepts behind the technique, you may be able to apply these concepts to many different techniques. Your ability to adapt to changing circumstances and your chances for success, therefore, increase. You don't have to wait until you are a black belt to learn conceptual fighting. You can learn concepts alongside the mechanics of technique, as long as you also receive experiential instruction (the opportunity to use and experience what you have learned). But concepts are easier to learn if you have already studied the martial arts for some time. When you have learned some techniques by rote (memorization), you can start elaborating on these techniques. You can talk about the purpose of the technique and the desired end result.

Technique-oriented: Learn a sweep in order to place your opponent on the ground.

Concept-oriented: Discuss center of gravity and how the body must be above the foundation in order to maintain balance.

When you understand the concept, you can begin to experiment with ways to move the center of gravity away from the balanced state. The sweep is merely one example of many.

Learning to throw a back elbow strike is technique-oriented learning; applying the back elbow strike as a way to take your opponent to the ground is concept-oriented learning.

Technique-oriented: Learn to apply the figure-four arm bar.

Concept-oriented: Learn about leverage and how to use the figure-four arm bar to shift your opponent's center of gravity away from his foundation until he goes down.

If your instructor incorporates conceptual learning early in the program, your mind will begin to adapt to this type of learning environment. Conceptual learning still relies on a structured classroom setting; your instructor must still follow a definite teaching plan, but it allows for a few more variables. When you have practiced enough conceptual scenarios, you can come up with your own techniques to fit each unique situation. No matter what happens, you will have an answer not because you have memorized a myriad of answers, but because you will see the logical correlation to your problems. This is when you will "eat for life."

Your instructor should not introduce too many concepts in the same lesson. For example, it is better to learn the front kick and then learn the uses for it, than to learn the front kick, the roundhouse kick and the side kick all in the same lesson (assuming you are new to all three kicks). If you are more advanced, you can look at similarities and differences in the uses of these three kicks, how to relate each kick to a punch, or how to throw the kicks from a standing position, a kneeling position, and from your back. When you have gained reasonable proficiency, the next step is to learn variations of the techniques, including what to do if they fail or are about to fail. For example:

1. The Jujutsu arm bar from the ground can originally be learned with both of your legs across your opponent's body. A variation of the technique employs only one leg across your opponent's body and the other leg against her rib cage.

2. A carotid choke can be learned with pressure against both sides of your opponent's neck. One variation is to apply pressure against only one side of his neck. A second variation is to use your legs instead of your arms for choking.

3. Kicks can be learned with stepping, sliding or jumping variations.

4. Punches can be learned with vertical or horizontal hand positions, while exploring the value of these different hand positions.

5. Some blocks can be learned as strike variations, such as the elbow block against the shin of your opponent's roundhouse kick.

Variations can come both in mechanics of technique and in concept or principle: mechanics when you learn jumping instead of stepping, and concept when you learn a striking block instead of a purely defensive block.

– INSTRUCTOR TIP –

When teaching conceptually, it may not always be clear whether the students truly understand the concepts. Evaluate their understanding by having them vary the techniques slightly, combine one technique with another, or apply the same principles to more than one technique.

– STUDENT TIP –

Ask plenty of "what ifs" and have your instructor show you how to use the techniques under different circumstances.

INTEGRATED LEARNING

When learning according to the integrated method, you will learn both the basic mechanics and the application of a technique at the same time. Rather than learning the technique step-by-step and gradually building upon it until you can use it in sparring, you will learn the technique and use it in sparring immediately. For example, your instructor will teach you the jab, then spar with you to allow you to discover the uses of the jab. This method is in contrast to learning the jab, and then learning it in combination with the rear cross or reverse punch, and finally practicing it on the heavy bag and in sparring. If you have never sparred before or have very little sparring experience, your instructor can limit the sparring to the most recent technique you have learned.

In some schools, students must wait several months before they are allowed to spar. In other schools, students are not allowed to hit to the head until they are brown or black belts. The integrated method allows you to use the system the way it is intended, from the very first day. You will therefore gain insight faster than your traditional counterparts. You will be taken from the rigid classroom environment on the first day and be required to perform the skills in which you have gained a theoretical knowledge. Integrated learning defies the "you must crawl before you can walk" concept. When you incorporate the newly learned technique into sparring immediately, you will have no inhibitions about sparring later.

You can also try a variation using the new technique in one round of sparring and one round of heavy bag work. When you learn by the integrated method, you should be able to throw the technique equally well in the air, on the bag or in sparring. The heavy bag is excellent for developing power and correct technique. But since the bag is rather nonthreatening, it does not teach you about defense or how slight variations in angle or distance can affect the outcome of the fight. Through the integrated method, you will understand from the beginning that just because the point of reference changes, the way the technique is executed does not, which makes the technique applicable to many different circumstances. On a broader level, the integrated method can be incorporated

When learning by the integrated method, you get to apply your knowledge on other students as soon as you have learned it. This method is likely to result in good retention, because you will discover how and why a technique works from the start.

into two different arts. For example, every time you learn a new technique, you can apply it both to stand-up and grappling arts.

Students who learn by the integrated method are likely to be more precise with their techniques from the beginning. You will also be more aware of defense and of what is going on around you. You are likely to start making corrections on your own without constant prompting from your instructor. This is not to say that your instructor or other students should take advantage of your limited knowledge. Your instructor must supervise all sparring to ensure that more advanced students don't overwhelm you with techniques that you have not yet learned. It is up to each individual instructor whether or not she wants to teach according to the integrated method. Some instructors prefer the integrated method from the beginning, while others only teach it at the advanced levels.

– INSTRUCTOR TIP –

If you teach by the integrated method and discover that a student is having problems with one particular area of learning, you might want to focus solely on that area until the problems are resolved. Likewise, if you do not teach by the integrated method and discover that a student can learn several things simultaneously without making sacrifices in the basics, then this method might be the course of action you want to take.

– STUDENT TIP –

The integrated method isn't right for everybody. If you feel it benefits you to learn techniques in greater detail before trying them on bags or in sparring, make sure you communicate your needs to your instructor.

PROGRESSIVE OVERLOAD

Progressive overload is a concept for the advanced student, or at least for the student at the intermediate level. Progressive overload means that you set goals that are consistently out of reach. The idea is to force you to attempt more than you are capable of, which, in turn, forces you to overcome your perceived limitations. But since you will never actually reach your goal when using the progressive overload concept, you must understand and be in agreement with how this concept works to avoid getting discouraged. Progressive overload should not be used with the new student. The new student is often unable to see her progress clearly because she lacks previous experiences to relate it to, and may therefore think she is consistently failing.

LEARNING FROM THE INSTRUCTOR WHO IS LESS ADVANCED THAN YOU

When you have gained some experience in the martial arts, it is possible that you will encounter an instructor who is less advanced than you. Learning from a less advanced instructor could create a problem both for you and the instructor. If your instructor sees a need to correct your technique, how can he do so without offending you? First, you must understand that to the experienced martial artist, there is not just one way of doing a technique. When your instructor teaches beginners, he must show them one specific way, so that they have something concrete to relate to and use as a foundation for continued growth. But at the advanced level, the student has already gone through many years of habit building.

Many of these habits may have been acquired because of adjustments you have made to fit your own body structure and mental inclination. You can therefore not have hard and fast rules regarding proper execution of technique. The same concept applies to students who have studied other arts for many years. Although you may be new to the particular art you are studying right now, you have formed certain habits from your previous studies. At this level, trivial details, such as how to hold the hands, how to turn the wrist, the name of a technique, etc. are difficult, or even foolish, to try to change.

At this level, your instructor's job is not to tell you how to do the technique, but rather to observe and help you learn more about what you already know. He should remember the golden rule of teaching: If it doesn't make the student better, don't teach it.

 ## SCENARIO 55

You have studied at a different school for many years, when your current instructor notices that you telegraph your reverse punch before throwing it. What should she do?

1. Tell you that she saw the punch coming "three days ago."

2. Whisper in your ear (for fear of embarrassing you in front of your peers) that you are telegraphing the strike.

3. Say, "I notice that you pull your hand back before throwing it. Is there a particular reason for this?"

4. Ignore it, because it is wrong to correct a student who is more advanced than the instructor.

★★★★★

If your instructor sees something that is wrong, she might begin by asking why you do the technique that way, in order to determine whether you are aware of how you execute it. Asking why is less confrontational than saying, "That's not how your hand should be turned when throwing the hook!" and might provide your instructor with some insight that she didn't already have.

I recently met a man from another discipline of karate who asked me if I fight from a high or low stance. I told him that I fight from a boxer's stance, which is a slightly crouched stance, not a low stance. Then I showed him. "Oh, that's really low," he said. "You'll get killed if you come to my school and spar that way. We fight up here." (Up on the balls of his feet and head held high. His art didn't allow strikes to the head). Comments like these, no matter how honest or well-meant, make you feel uneducated and ignorant.

Both you and your instructor should keep in mind that advanced students have already formed opinions based on their past experiences. Awareness of this fact may be especially important in a seminar setting where students from many different disciplines are attending. When you get to the advanced levels, be tolerant of the opinions of both your instructor and your peers. Trying to change what others have practiced successfully for years is foolish and likely to cause friction. Ten different students may hold their hands in ten slightly different positions when throwing the sidekick, for example. These differences do not necessarily warrant correction.

24

Becoming an Instructor

THE PROSPECTIVE INSTRUCTOR

When you have gained a few years' experience in your art, the natural progression is to teach it to others. As already mentioned, most martial arts instructors have no formal training and are thrown into teaching on a "sink or swim" kind of basis. But if you know how to be a good student, you can most likely also become a good instructor. What you have learned about the learning process in this book can therefore be used as a precurser to your teaching career.

I started teaching karateas an assistant instructor. This worked well, as long as I had my own little group (within the bigger group) to teach. When I had been assisting for a while, I was assigned my own class. I enjoyed teaching immensely, but found my instruction suffered whenever the school owner walked in unannounced. I didn't agree with many of his suggestions about my teaching style. Although I was not as proficient in the art as he was, I still felt that I was a higher authority on teaching than he, due to my long background as an instructor in aviation.

Remember that a new instructor is still a student and should therefore be allowed to make mistakes. It can be intimidating if the senior instructor constantly hovers over you.

It is better that he gives you time alone to gain confidence and find your talents. Teaching styles are as varied as instructors. When your instructor observes you teaching and makes suggestions, he should avoid absolutes. Teaching is not black and white; there are many nuances. Although he will favor one particular teaching style over another, he should be sensitive enough to allow your individuality to shine. It is more important to ensure that you are not leaving out any important elements of instruction than to correct your particular style.

 ## SCENARIO 56

You are being trained as a prospective instructor with the senior instructor acting as your student. Is this a good idea? Why or why not?

1. Yes, because the senior instructor can deliberately make mistakes to see whether you will catch them and correct her.

2. Yes, because this gives you teaching experience even when there are no other students to teach.

3. No, because you know that the senior instructor is not really a student, which makes her too predictable.

4. No, because it might intimidate you.

★★★★★

Since the senior instructor is more knowledgeable than you are, you may feel reluctant to teach her things she already knows. It is my experience that most new instructors do better when they are left alone and can focus fully on teaching rather than on pleasing the instructor. But if you don't practice your teaching technique on the senior instructor, and she doesn't hover over you when you are teaching, then how can she check on your progress and offer suggestions? Try this:

1. Ask for suggestions a day or two before you teach your next class, and discuss how to solve potential problems.

2. Tell the senior instructor what you have learned, or demonstrate your techniques to her and ask for feedback.

3. Get involved as a judge on a belt promotion. Doing so might reveal to the senior instructor your insights and instructional ability.

Many prospective instructors, because of their level of experience in the art, would prefer not to be critiqued on their performance in front of their students or other instructors. Seek some private time with the senior instructor, so that you can ask questions without being intimidated by what others might think. If you have a question you should have asked a long time ago when you were a beginner student, you may feel reluctant to ask it now. Your instructor can put you at ease by volunteering information. If you get easily offended or embarrassed when he corrects you, he can try

critiquing in the form of suggestions rather than corrections. A good instructor is sensitive to your feelings. If you are serious about teaching, you will catch on to his desire to help and adapt to the suggestions. Again, your instructor's job is to make you as good a student/instructor as possible. If the instruction, evaluation and critique you receive don't accomplish this, your instructor is wasting his time.

When you receive training as a new instructor, you should teach a range of students from beginners to advanced. We might be inclined to think that the new instructor should stick with beginners, but learning to teach advanced students is just as important. Obviously, if you are an intermediate student yourself, it will be a bit difficult teaching black belts. But assuming that you have earned your black belt, you should be able to teach beginner, intermediate and advanced classes. You should be encouraged to learn by asking questions of other martial artists and of yourself. You can also ask rhetorical questions that require critical thinking skills. You acquire insight and understanding by finding the answers yourself, rather than being given the answers outright. When exploring techniques, you will also learn as much from what did not work as from what did work. When you see the other side of the argument, you can identify and weed out the parts that hinder performance.

– INSTRUCTOR TIP –

Many teaching styles differ. When evaluating an advanced student's teaching abilities, avoid correcting individual styles. It is better to look for ways to capitalize on the student's passions and strengths.

When teaching and learning, it is not the means that are important (how we get there), but the end (what we have achieved). You can reach good end results by learning sound principles rather than specific techniques.

THE FEAR OF SPEAKING IN PUBLIC

According to a study by R.H. Bruskin Associates, 40.6 percent of the people questioned said they were frightened by speaking in public—more so than of anything else, including heights, insect bites, flying, sickness, and death! (Rudolph F. Verderber, *The Challenge of Effective Speaking*.)

Most people experience fear or self-consciousness to some degree when speaking to a large group of people. Most instructors feel that way, too. But once you gain some experience, you will find that most of the nervousness is in the anticipation of the speech and not in the speech itself. Once the first "blows" are exchanged, the immediacy of the situation tends to eradicate the fear. Think of it this way: If you were speaking to only one person, you wouldn't feel nearly as nervous as if you were speaking to a group of a thousand. But the fact is that each individual in a group of a thousand cannot feel the collective thoughts of everyone else in the group. So, in a sense, you are always speaking to only one person. Fear of public speaking is an *imaginary fear*. It is really no worse speaking to a crowd of a thousand than it is speaking to a single person.

When you place public speaking in perspective, there are many things you can do to lessen the fear. Perhaps the most important is adequate preparation. When you have done your research, you will know more about the subject than most of the audience. This knowledge gives you authority. The better prepared you are, the more excited you will be about the talk you are about to give, and the less likely you are to be hit by surprise questions or confusion. Being prepared puts you at ease and allows you to be yourself, which, in turn, strengthens your speech. When speaking to your students, keep the following in mind:

1. Appear confident. Remember, the arena is yours.

2. Don't stay in one spot. Moving around gives you a better view of the people you are speaking to, and also gives you authority.

3. If you are nervous, don't apologize. It is better to get to the heart of the matter right away.

4. Rather than gazing over the heads of the entire group, make eye contact with one person at a time. Doing so makes each person feel as though you are speaking to him or her directly.

5. Don't act as if you would rather be somewhere else. Avoid looking at the clock.

6. Invite participation. Ask questions or use anecdotes to drive home a point.

7. If you have handouts, wait until after class. Students have a harder time focusing on the speech if you give them material to read while you are talking.

8. Don't drag on beyond the allotted time. Quit while you still have interest.

INSTRUCTOR DEVELOPMENT PROGRAMS

The traditional method of selecting martial arts instructors is often inadequate for preparing you to teach. Traditionally students are selected based on their rank, dedication or school need. When you have been identified as a prospective instructor, you will be put to work assisting in class or teaching beginners. The fact that students are teaching students should be a point of concern. Certainly you have knowledge of technique, but that knowledge does not automatically make you a proficient instructor.

To become the best instructor for your students, remember what you have studied about the learning process. Understand that transferring knowledge to another student is not simply stating the facts. Having knowledge *about* something is not the same as imparting that knowledge to another. Now that you have learned the techniques of your particular martial art, you must also learn the techniques of good teaching.

If you decide to participate in an instructor development program, look for one that is taught by qualified instructors who have knowledge of both the martial arts and the learning process. A good program gives you the tools necessary for successful teaching and includes skill building in public speaking, understanding the roots of techniques (what makes them work and why), how to structure a curriculum and properly prepare the class, and developing motivational teaching and leadership skills. An organized program should be of a specified duration and ultimately result in a certificate of graduation from the course.

Below is a suggested curriculum for an instructor development program that can be taught in about 40 hours. When you sign up for a program, you might want to compare this list with the syllabus and make sure it coincides on most points. A good program:

1. Discusses the school's mission statement, policies and procedures;

2. Discusses martial arts liability, instructor responsibilities and prevention of lawsuits;

3. Discusses how to inform students of the inherent dangers of the sport, and teaches how to treat minor injuries;

4. Develops good communication skills, including clear and concise speaking skills and the ability to ask appropriate questions;

5. Teaches how to develop a class curriculum that is informative, motivating and varied;

6. Discusses how to teach introductory lessons to prospective students, and how to recruit students from walk-ins, visitors or people in the audience;

7. Develops the ability to identify and teach students who are faster or slower learners than the norm;

8. Discusses how to teach effective private lessons;

9. Develops the ability to solve problems that might be encountered with techniques and students; and

10. Includes written, oral and practical exercises for testing newly learned skills, and for testing understanding of the principles of teaching and learning.

When you have completed the course and have been teaching for some time, you should:

1. Demonstrate a reasonable degree of proficiency in all teaching techniques and concepts;

2. Understand how physical and mental fitness are acquired, and be prepared to design a fitness program to help students of lower rank set and achieve personal goals;

3. Study all techniques from infancy through application, and demonstrate your understanding by teaching one or more techniques to a new student;

4. Develop and use lesson plans, and be able to organize lessons and techniques logically;

5. Be able to adapt to student needs, and modify the lesson plan instantly to fit the situation and the student you are teaching; and

6. Understand human nature, and be able to communicate effectively (a course in public speaking is highly recommended).

I recommend that you teach under your original instructor's supervision until you have attained a complete understanding of your art. If you set out to open your own school immediately upon becoming an instructor, you risk transferring your art partially or incompletely to your students, without transferring adequate understanding of techniques and concepts. Doing so will dilute the art for future generations.

INSTRUCTOR EVALUATIONS

Your school might include instructor evaluations, where the senior instructor or your students evaluate you after you have been teaching for some time and before you can advance to a new level. If this is not the case, you can ask for such an evaluation. But before doing so, make sure that it is really what you want, and you are ready to take advantage of the information contained in the evaluation.

How's my driving?
Dial 1-800-...

What's wrong with the above headline? Well, it invites conflict. But even more importantly, it invites conflict from people who do not know you and are not necessarily authorities on the subject. This type of evaluation can be extremely destructive. In Chapter 11, we talked about how an evaluation of you as a martial arts student must be specific and objective in order to have value. The same is true about the evaluation you receive as an instructor. A subjective evaluation is always unfair to the person being evaluated. When you ask for an evaluation, make sure that you ask to be critiqued on specific techniques or concepts, and not on your personality or your teaching style in general. The person who evaluates you must understand the standards he is supposed to adhere to. For example, if he grades you on personality traits rather than on your instructional ability, the grade will not reflect your skill in a true or satisfying way. Competent instructors use their students' input to help them stay in tune with their students' needs and desires. Take constructive suggestions to heart and discard the rest.

TEACHING SPECIALIZED GROUPS

You are a police officer and see the following advertisement in a martial arts magazine: "New and proven martial arts system taught to law enforcement and Navy SEALs." Would you recommend this program to your department?

I have read many advertisements by martial artists claiming to teach their system of self-defense or street fighting to law enforcement and the military. What qualifies a martial artist to teach these specialized groups? I once had a Navy SEAL attend my Kenpo karate classes. He did 40 pull-ups when the rest of us did five. But I wouldn't dream of marketing myself as a "teacher of Navy SEALs." I have also had several police officers attend my classes. But just because they attend, I am not claiming to teach these specialized groups. It is unrealistic to think that police and military personnel need to learn martial arts techniques the way I teach them every day in the training hall. The Navy SEAL who attended my class did so for other reasons than learning to kill in combat.

Are martial arts and fighting the same things? Are martial arts and self-defense the same things? Think about it. Why do you practice the martial arts? All the philosophical aspects go out the door in law enforce-

ment or special forces operations. Even in self-defense, a traditional background with its philosophy and etiquette is not likely to be the most expedient way to learn how to defend oneself. A rapist won't care about how moral or ethical you are. I am not saying that the traditional martial arts don't have value. I am saying that the traditional martial arts also focus on how to live and not just on self-defense or fighting. These are issues that specialized groups aren't interested in. They don't care about forms, philosophy, history, or prearranged sparring.

Many of the techniques taught in the martial arts are not appropriate for law enforcement. For example, techniques that tie up the officer's hands for any length of time may not be appropriate. Law enforcement aims to get the suspect under control in the least

Neither a black belt martial arts instructor nor a bar brawler who is undefeated in 200 street fights is automatically qualified to teach such specialized groups as law enforcement, whose main concern is to get the suspect into handcuffs quickly.

amount of time possible, which is contrary to some types of sport grappling matches, for example, which last in excess of 30 minutes. Those who teach law enforcement consider how they are dressed and under what circumstances they operate. Fighting in tennis shoes and sweats feels differently than wearing a full uniform and a heavy belt with gun, cuffs, stick, flashlight and other miscellaneous items. Don't assume that a technique that works beautifully in the training hall will work for a cop on the street. For example, most police agencies don't rely on punching and kicking, but on joint-controlling techniques that help the officer get the suspect into handcuffs. The techniques must also be simple enough for the officer to use successfully with minimal amount of training.

Most police agencies have their own instructors, who are also cops with firsthand experience on the job. These instructors are trained in teaching arrest and control tactics and are familiar with the specific needs of law enforcement, including extensive knowledge of the use of force liability. Those not specifically trained in or familiar with police tactics might teach techniques using excessive force. As a result, the agency risks getting sued.

A black belt martial arts instructor is not automatically qualified to teach law enforcement, military personnel or other specialized groups. Anybody teaching specialized groups must be thoroughly familiar with how they operate, the specific situations they are likely to encounter, and the legal aspects of what they are allowed to do. If you desire to teach these groups but are not an insider, before offering them your services, learn as much as you can about their specific needs, what types of training they are currently doing, and what you can do to improve on it without wasting their time or teaching what is not useful to them.

Final Thoughts

Years ago you were simply a martial artist yearning to perform your art. Now that part of your training may seem almost like an afterthought. You have trained hard to perfect your skill. You have pushed your body and mind to the extreme. You have overcome weakness, gone beyond pain and emerged as a finely tuned fighter. But the end for which you have worked so long and hard is not really the end at all, but the beginning of a new journey. Now that your body and mind have achieved oneness, now that your fighting skills are honed and razor-sharp, you have acquired the perfect vehicle to rise to a new level.

Your instructor, that powerful person, was your idol, and the black belt tied around his waist spoke silently of the long road ahead. You look at the black belt around your own waist, but somehow you are not sure you know it all. And the belt itself seems of little importance now, an infinitely small step on your thousand-mile road. But there was a dream. And your passion, your stubbornness kept you going. "As far as my body will take me," you might have thought, because in your heart you knew all along that it was meant to be.

Learning how to learn has been a fascinating journey. But the real magic, as we all know, comes when you resolve to open more doors for yourself and others. When you think about the effort you have expended on your studies, you don't know if you love it or hate it. You know only that it has given you an unyielding fortitude in all aspects of life, making you wish for higher fences, more hills to climb. There is no greater feeling.